MW00800444

The Lord's Prayer

The Lord's Prayer

Alan Cairns

Ambassador International
Greenville, South Carolina • Belfast, Northern Ireland

The Lord's Prayer

Cover design & page layout by A & E Media — Paula Shepherd, Sam Laterza

ISBN 1 932307 16 8

Published by the Ambassador Group

Ambassador Emerald International
427 Wade Hampton Blvd.
Greenville, SC 29609
USA
www. emeraldhouse.com

and

Ambassador Publications Ltd.
Providence House
Ardenlee Street
Belfast BT6 8QJ
Northern Ireland
www. ambassador-productions.com

The colophon is a trademark of Ambassador

To Joan,

the best example I have of

"continuing instant in prayer."

Acknowledgments

These studies are taken from a series of messages I preached in Faith Free Presbyterian Church, Greenville, South Carolina—which will explain my repetition of certain themes and Bible texts. In preaching a prolonged series, such repetition is necessary, and I hope it will be helpful in print. My reason for retaining it is that the truths involved are certainly worth learning well.

My wife, Joan, performed the arduous task of transcribing the recorded sermons both quickly and efficiently, so enabling me to make better progress in preparing my material for print. As I finished each chapter, I then had the help of Judy Brown and Grace Farr with the editing and proof reading. These ladies were highly professional and exceptionally fast in returning the work to me complete with a list of corrections and suggested improvements.

I am in the debt of these three willing helpers, not only for their work on the text but for their unfailing encouragement that the work was worth finishing. Each of them spoke of the blessing she had received through working on the book and looked forward keenly to its publication. That kind of positive attitude was a tonic for the sometimes flagging spirits of a reluctant writer. To Joan, Judy, and Grace I express my deepest gratitude.

I should also acknowledge the encouragement I received from many in my congregation in response to the preaching of these studies. They and many who received the messages by tape, over our church radio program, or via the Internet (sermonaudio.com) have testified how much the Lord has blessed them through these studies. That kind of unsolicited testimony gives hope that the Lord who blessed His word in its audio form will bless it to a wider public in this printed form. I therefore commit the work to Him, praying that He will use it to lead many into the experience of true, effectual prayer.

Table of Contents

Prayer God Answers

"When thou prayest, thou shalt not be as the hypocrites are: for they love to pray standing in the synagogues and in the corners of the streets, that they may be seen of men. Verily I say unto you, They have their reward. But thou, when thou prayest, enter into thy closet, and when thou hast shut thy door, pray to thy Father which is in secret; and thy Father which seeth in secret shall reward thee openly. But when ye pray, use not vain repetitions, as the heathen do: for they think that they shall be heard for their much speaking. Be not ye therefore like unto them: for your Father knoweth what things ye have need of, before ye ask him." Matthew 6:5–8

Christians pray. So do hypocrites. And so do heathens. According to the Lord Jesus Christ, hypocritical and heathen praying are neither good nor acceptable to God. They are not true prayer. True prayer is the prerogative of Christians. However, it is sadly possible for a Christian to pray like a hypocrite or a heathen. That is why the Lord Jesus issued the solemn warnings recorded in Matthew 6:5–8.

We must give serious thought to the fact that a Christian may sink to the level of a hypocrite or a heathen in his praying, for it brings home to us some important—and perhaps disturbing—truths about prayer.

- First, not all prayer is good and pleasing to God.

- Second, time spent in prayer is not necessarily time well spent. More time spent in meaningless or offensive praying makes it only more meaningless and offensive to God.

- Third, our sin is the thing most likely to hinder our praying. This is clear from the illustrations the Lord Jesus Christ chose when He issued His warnings against hypocritical and heathen praying. He spoke particularly of the sin of pride. Pride may reveal itself as the desire to be seen and admired by others for our praying, or as an arrogant sense of the merit of our words and effort in prayer. In the first form, pride is the mark of the hypocrite; in the second, of the heathen.

- Fourth, our sin is so insidious that it can poison the holiest exercise in which a Christian can engage. It would follow us right into the holy of holies to rob us of fellowship with God.

In the light of all this, it is obvious that we need to learn to pray in a manner that pleases the Lord. We need to learn the art of true prayer. That is what makes Matthew 6:5–8 so important, for it sets before us the teaching of the Lord Jesus Christ on the subject. His basic point is simple and straightforward: Prayer addresses our Heavenly Father in faith that He knows the needs of His children and that He answers their honest, humble petitions. We should give our most earnest attention to this lesson and try to grasp what our Lord teaches about prayers that God answers. Few subjects are of more immediate importance to Christians than this. Once we learn and apply to our hearts what the Bible teaches about this subject, many of the problems that appear overwhelming will fall into their true perspective. This is fundamental to everything a Christian believes, feels, and does.

In stating His teaching about prayers God will answer, the Lord Jesus does three things. First, He warns us what to avoid in prayer; second, He shows us how to succeed in prayer; and finally, He assures that we will be heard if we pray as He instructs.

What to Avoid in Prayer

Avoid Praying Like Hypocrites

"When thou prayest, thou shalt not be as the hypocrites." The word *hypocrite* is a word taken from Greek drama. A hypocrite was an actor, who covered his face with a mask as he portrayed a character that was not his own. When the New Testament uses the word *hypocrite,* it does so to describe a person who makes a pretence of holiness or who hides his true character behind the mask of a lying profession. Christ commands us not to be as hypocrites in prayer because true prayer must, above all things, be *real*. We read that Elijah "prayed earnestly" (James 5:17), or to give the words their literal force, he "prayed in his prayer." That is, he really prayed. Elijah did not put on a façade of godliness to make it appear that he was praying. No, he really and truly prayed. That is something hypocrites never do. Hypocrisy and true prayer are mutually exclusive for various reasons.

Hypocrisy is always marked by the flesh. Whatever motivates a hypocrite to pray—and, like anybody else, he may pray when he is in need or in trouble or when he is in a situation in which he may feel that prayer is expected from him—the flesh is always to the fore.

Hypocrites pay too much attention to man. They want men to know that they pray. For them, it is not enough to pray; men must know that they pray and must think of them as great men of prayer.

Hypocrites glory in the reputation of saintliness rather than in being genuinely holy. They draw attention to their devotions and publicize their religious exercises. Like the scribes of Christ's day, "for a pretence [they] make long prayers" (Mark 12:40). All this is the exercise of the flesh, and the Lord Jesus exposes and condemns it.

We need to be careful at this point, however. The Saviour does not condemn all public prayer. To do so would contradict the plain teaching of Scripture. The Lord Jesus called His Father's house "a house of prayer" (Matthew 21:13). He prayed in the sight of others (Luke 3:21; 10:21; 11:1). The early church conducted public prayer meetings and the Holy Spirit visited them with notable power and blessing (Acts 4:24–31; 12:5–12). The apostle Paul told the churches of his prayers for them and spoke of the great burden he carried to the throne of grace (Colossians 2:1; Romans 15:30; Romans 9:2). There is a legitimate form of public prayer. There is a necessary communication of burden, passion, and spiritual yearning when God's people come together to worship. So public prayer cannot be what the Lord warns us against in Matthew 6. What He condemns is self-promotion, ostentation, or courting human opinion in prayer. To apply this standard to our praying is a fearful thought. This single truth condemns most of what passes for public prayer. The Lord Jesus condemns all courting of human opinion in prayer, all concern with the people who are present and with what they think about our "performance" in prayer. All praying that is calculated to make an effect on those who hear us falls under His censure. That is what hypocrites do: They pray to be seen and heard of men.

There is something else hypocrites do: They contradict with their lives what they pray with their lips. What they say piously is very different from what they really feel in their hearts.

All this is abominable to God: "Lying lips are abomination to the Lord: but they that deal truly are his delight" (Proverbs 12:22); "The sacrifice of the wicked is an abomination to the Lord: but the prayer of the upright is his delight" (Proverbs 15:8). So the Saviour warns us against praying like hypocrites.

Avoid Praying Like Heathens

"When ye pray, use not vain repetitions, as the heathen do: for they think that they shall be heard for their much speaking. Be not ye therefore like unto them" (Matthew 6:7–8).

We must not multiply empty words. "Use not vain repetitions" means simply "do not gabble or jabber" in prayer. The noun form of the verb that appears here in the Greek text was used of the orator Demosthenes by his enemies: They called him *battalos,* the gabbler. Unfortunately, the same title could be given to all too many people who imagine that they are praying. Some people gabble to make their prayers longer, but there is no virtue in praying long merely to pray long. Some people gabble in prayer by using empty promises, pretensions, and professions in an effort to make themselves sound good to God. But we must not multiply empty words in prayer. That is what the heathen do, and it has no place in Christian prayer. We must not gabble to God!

We must not sink to idle, mechanical, or trite words or forms of prayer. Mindless repetition is heathen, not Christian. It is easy for evangelical Protestants to apply this standard to the Roman Catholic use of the rosary with the repeated recitation of *Hail Marys* and *Our Fathers,* but we may be just as guilty of equally heathen practice as we mechanically say prayers that cost us little or no thought. Prayer that involves no real involvement of the heart and mind is heathen in its form, even though the words used may be full of Christian orthodoxy.

Heathens use vain repetition for a specific purpose. At times, they mindlessly recite their prayers to deliberately disengage their minds. In this way they seek to get beyond normal, rational levels of consciousness and to produce an altered state of consciousness in which they experience what they take to be spiritual elevation or revelation. The priests of Baal who confronted Elijah on Mount Carmel provide a clear example of this practice (1 Kings 18:26, 28). Mindless repetition may produce a trance-like state in which the mind becomes open to suggestion, or in which it receives spiritual impressions, visions, and such like. The feeling of spiritual euphoria, or the assurance that God is doing something great, is for many people sufficient justification of the practice. But our Lord warns us against mindless repetition even though it may produce a comforting or elated state of mind in us.

This is a very up-to-date warning. In many parts of the Christian church, this aspect of Baal worship has been introduced to Christian churches as if it were a wonderful discovery about the nature of true prayer. Some preachers have introduced the practice of almost hypnotic singing or chanting of praise or prayer. Others have adopted the practice of visualization from eastern mysticism and have even acknowledged that they learned this technique from Buddhism! Such things are heralded as powerful tools in the place of prayer. They are not. They are heathen, not Christian, and come under the Saviour's prohibition.

True prayer is not a way of altering our state of consciousness. It is objective, directed to God, not ourselves. Though it produces subjective results, we must never fall into the trap of manufacturing those subjective feelings and imagine that they prove that we have really prevailed in prayer. Any time a preacher manipulates a congregation into a receptive state of mind by the use of mind-numbing repetition, he is guilty of imposing a heathen practice on his congregation. And any time an individual Christian uses a similar technique to produce a desired state of mind, he blatantly discards the solemn instruction of Christ.[1]

How to Succeed in Prayer

Plainly, the aim of the Lord Jesus Christ is to instruct His people in the practice of true prayer: "When thou prayest" (verses 5 and 6); "when ye pray" (verse 7); "after this manner pray ye" (verse 9). It is obvious that the last thing the Lord wants is for His people to pray to no purpose. This is a searching truth. Each of us must bring his prayer life under the searchlight of Scripture and answer these questions: Is there any purpose in my praying? Any reality? Or, is it simply a matter of fulfilling a sense of duty, a way of quelling the guilt that comes from failing to pray? Such purposeless praying flies in the face of all Christ teaches us. He wants us to pray with real purpose, to pray the kind of prayers God will answer. So He shows us what kind of praying that is.

- He begins by showing us the kind of people we must be in prayer (verse 5).

- He describes the place we must cultivate in prayer (verse 6).

- He emphasizes the practice we must employ in prayer ("use," verse 7).

- Then, finally, He teaches us the petitions we must bring in prayer (verses 8–13).

---

[1]It is vital for God's people to know the difference between emotions induced by spurious religious or psychological techniques and genuine responses to the working of the Spirit of God. The Holy Spirit uses the word of God and particularly its revelation of the love of God in Christ to open our hearts and minds (see, for example, Ephesians 1:15–22, Philippians 4:4, and 1 Peter 1: 6, where the force of *wherein,* shows that the believer's joy is firmly grounded in the theological truths listed in verses 1–5). In other words, genuine Christian emotions are the product of great spiritual truth. They are never a mere surface reaction to a fleshly stimulus. People who subject themselves to fleshly emotional stimulation in the (often sincere) belief that it is spiritually beneficial will find it a fire that burns them out, leaving only the ashes of frustration or cynicism. Those who are spiritually moved by great biblical truth—not by sensual, emotional stimulation— will discover that the fire of God burns but consumes nothing except sin. It leaves them stronger, both spiritually and emotionally.

We will consider each of these in later chapters, but for the moment we will simply try to summarize the Saviour's instructions.

First, seek the communion of God, not the commendation of man. Prayer is fundamentally the communion of a child with God his heavenly Father. This communion is to be the most real thing in the world to a Christian, the fulfilment of the deepest desire of his heart. Thus the Lord Jesus commands us to make it our chief goal and not to substitute for it the commendation of men.

Second, depend in faith on the love and power of God our Father. Without this we will not be able to pray. Faith must take its stand on the glorious fact that God is our Father, the One who truly loves us. The doctrine of the love of God is perhaps the most underrated, under-preached, misunderstood doctrine of all Scripture. Some people paint it in terms of worldly, trashy sentimentality that is far removed from the holy majesty of God. Others try to limit it to fit the confines of their notions of divine sovereignty and thereby practically deny it—like the preacher who told his congregation, "I'm sure that there are some of you whom God hates. He has hated you from all eternity and He hates you still. No matter what you do or how much you desire His love He will hate you forever." Such nonsense is a travesty, not only of the Calvinistic theology it professes to represent, but of the biblical doctrine of God's love which "is greater far than tongue or pen can ever tell; it goes beyond the highest star and reaches deep where sinners dwell." Yet when we come to pray, how often do we fall for the lie that our God is hard or unwilling, always ready to whip us at the least opportunity. I know that God is majestic and holy, but the light of biblical revelation assures us that "God is love." That is what must grip our hearts when we pray: God is our Father, who loves us with an everlasting love. True prayer therefore is to depend on the goodness, willingness, and power of God to hear and answer us.

Third, speak to God openly, honestly, humbly, and from the heart. The famous words of Hebrews 4:16 elaborate on this point: "Let us therefore come boldly unto the throne of grace, that we may obtain mercy, and find grace to help in time of need." The word *boldly* means openly, freely, and frankly. It is to speak to God with confidence and assurance, yet never forgetting the glory of the One to whom we come. The Saviour clearly is commanding us to deal with our flesh and its pride and so to make our approach to God's throne. We must never forget that "God resisteth the proud, but giveth grace unto the humble" (James 4:6).

Fourth, pray simply. "Ye ask him" (verse 8) is how Christ defines this vital aspect of prayer. When we truly pray, we acknowledge our personal need and our Father's ability to meet our need. These acknowledgments will lead to the adoration of our God and the confession of our sin, but they will not allow us to stop there. They will impel us to ask the Lord to meet our need. "Ye have not, because ye ask not" (James 4:2). We have not prayed if we have not asked. Asking is the very essence of true prayer.

Fifth, pray briefly, at least as a usual practice. Nowhere is Solomon's dictum more true than in the place of prayer: "In the multitude of words there wanteth not sin" (Proverbs 10:19). We do well to take the warning of Ecclesiastes 5:2 to heart: "Be not rash with thy mouth, and let not thine heart be hasty to utter any thing before God: for God is in heaven, and thou upon earth: therefore let thy words be few." The model prayer that Christ has left for us is a very brief prayer, yet it is a powerful prayer. C. H. Spurgeon commented that it is strength, not length, that counts in prayer. Billy Bray, the Cornish miner who was a greatly used evangelist, answered an inquiry about the length of prayer by taking an ornament off the mantle and polishing it. He said, "That didn't take long. You see, if you polish it often, it never takes long to clean it." Prayer is a lot like that. C. H. Waller said that we should spend less time praying and more time meditating on what we should be praying about. Instead of stumbling into God's presence without a moment's thought or preparation—which usually leads to the gabbling of meaningless or trite words—we should take time to let God's word sink down into our hearts and formulate our thoughts to worship, to adore, to confess, and to ask. When we do this we will not waste words in prayer. That doesn't mean we try to keep our words few and to the point for the purpose of saving time, however. In fact, when we pray this way, we will probably end up spending more time with the Lord; but it will be more time listening and less time gabbling. And what we do say will be more subject to the Lord's will and guidance. So, usually, we should pray briefly—and often. Spurgeon is said to have professed that he rarely prayed for more than fifteen minutes and that he rarely went fifteen minutes without praying.

Sixth, pray in secret (verse 6). Withdraw from company and from all distractions of the world in order to concentrate intensely on the Lord and on the matters to be brought before Him. If we do not concentrate in this way, we are not praying. The mere act of entering a closet and shutting the door does not guarantee true praying. We may shut the door of the closet, but bring the world in with us. We may shut the world out in a physical sense, but yet have such a worldly mind, or a mind so worried about the things of this world, that we fail to concentrate on the Lord Himself. That secret meeting with the Lord, when we are shut off from the world and shut in with Him, is so important that nothing—not even the church prayer meeting or the family altar—can take its place. *Pray to thy Father which is in secret* is a command we must never forget. It is this life of secret prayer that God honors and blesses. The man who is diligent in the secret place is a man whom God will answer.

Seventh, aim to crucify the flesh and to glorify God. Identify the hypocritical traits and the heathen tendencies that are natural to our flesh; confess them and crucify them. And, of course, from first to last we must seek to glorify the Lord. As we shall see, this thought of glorifying God is so fundamental to the whole idea of getting alone with God that the Lord Jesus makes it the subject of the first—and foundational—petition of His model prayer.

Receiving the Reward

The Lord Jesus assures us that God will hear us when we pray in this manner. His clear message is that God hears and answers prayer (verse 6). When we pray, we come to our Father in heaven, who knows what we need, not just what we ask for. Every human parent knows that there are times when his children ask for things that he knows he must refuse. He must give what his children need rather than what they ask for. God's children may ask passionately but wrongly because of a lack of understanding or because of immaturity. At those times, the Lord looks beyond our words to meet our needs. What good father who has the resources to meet the needs of his children fails to answer their cries for help when he sees their need and knows that the time is right to meet it? As the Saviour argued, "If ye then, being evil, know how to give good gifts unto your children, how much more shall your Father which is in heaven give good things to them that ask him?" (Matthew 7:11).

Our Father "rewards" us when we pray. What is this reward? In many ways, prayer is its own reward. It brings us into fellowship with God and we cannot but be better off for that. There is no joy or pleasure in the world to compare with really meeting with God. And there are further rewards. The word *reward* tells us that our Father will *repay* us for all the time and effort that go into true prayer. The word *reward* also means that He will *give* us what we need and that He will *restore* what we have lost. This is one of the sweetest aspects of getting through to God in prayer. He restores our souls. He restores the years that the locusts have eaten (Joel 2:25). He restores the peace that we have lost through sin, the joy of our salvation that we have lost through backsliding.

These are wonderful rewards for the man who prays. But the reward of prayer goes much further. By answering our prayers, God acknowledges that we are His people, just as by praying we acknowledge that He is our God. The idea of rewards naturally causes us to think of that great day when we shall "all appear before the judgment seat of Christ; that every one may receive the things done in his body, according to that he hath done, whether it be good or bad" (2 Corinthians 5:10). We may view God's answering our prayers as an anticipation of the verdict of the Judgment Day. David certainly recognized the connection.

He equated God's refusal to answer prayer with His verdict of rejection on the Judgment Day (Psalm 28:1).

On the other hand, on that day the Father will reward His children openly. It is not too much to say that He will acknowledge them in terms like these: "You glorified me on earth, especially in the secret place, striving in prayer against sin and the flesh. You believed me and my word. You pleaded my promises. Now I openly acknowledge you and welcome you to the everlasting fruit of your praying." Is this not essentially what Isaiah was commanded to tell God's people? "Say ye to the righteous, that it shall be well with him: for they shall eat the fruit of their doings" (Isaiah 3:10). God answers prayer and crowns it with an eternal reward. No hypocrite or heathen can gain such a reward. "They have their reward," that is, the praise of foolish men in this life—the commendation that means so much to them—is the only reward they will ever have. It is temporal and illusory. But for Christians who know how to pray so that God will answer, the reward is real and eternal.

That is what makes Christ's instructions on this subject so urgently important. None of us can afford to fail to hear them. We must learn how to pray prayers God will answer.

2

Closet Praying

"When thou prayest, enter into thy closet, and when thou hast shut thy door, pray to thy Father which is in secret; and thy Father which seeth in secret shall reward thee openly." Matthew 6:6

In most people's estimation only hypocrites have a closet life. After all, isn't the closet the place hypocrites hide their skeletons, the things they don't want the public to see, so that they may appear before men to be what they know they are not before God? It is a pity that this is the only closet life many people know, for there is a very different kind of closet life—a closet life that no hypocrite ever lives. It is this kind of closet life to which the Lord Jesus Christ calls every Christian.

The Lord Jesus has warned us against two real dangers in prayer. First, there is the danger of praying like hypocrites; second, there is the danger of praying like heathens. And He gives straightforward instruction on how to avoid each. The root of hypocritical praying is the desire to be seen of men and to gain their applause. The answer to the danger of falling into such hypocrisy is to cultivate private praying (verse 6). The root of heathen praying is vain repetition as a means of working the worshipper into an ecstacy in which he imagines that God will hear him on account of his exalted feelings and because of the great time and effort he has invested in prayer. The answer to this danger is to reckon on the character of the Lord and on the relationship we have with Him (verse 8).

In this study we will consider the first of these truths: "When thou prayest, enter into thy closet, and when thou hast shut thy door, pray to thy Father which is in secret; and thy Father which seeth in secret shall reward thee openly." The heart of what the Saviour is saying is that the best means to crucify the flesh and to enter upon real communion with God is to cultivate the secret place of prayer.

The Lord Jesus takes it for granted that His people pray. To speak of a prayer-less Christian is a contradiction in terms. Christians pray. Just as we cannot live physically without breathing, we cannot live spiritually without praying. Prayer is the air a Christian breathes. The Lord Jesus does not say, "*If* you pray," but, "*When* you pray." However inconsistent a Christian feels himself to be in prayer, however defeated he feels, however impotent he feels his efforts may be, the one thing he cannot do is abandon the secret place. He cannot give up praying. A person who can live happily without prayer is one who needs to be saved. Our Lord takes it for granted that His people pray, and He establishes private prayer as an essential part of the Christian life. There is a place of public prayer in the worship of the church, and there is a place of family prayer, but neither can take the place of private prayer. The secret place where we get alone with God is an essential part of the Christian life. That is the plain message of our Saviour.

Christ further establishes that Christians may pray anywhere. The word *closet* literally means "a storeroom," or "an inner chamber," but by extension it includes any private room, indeed, any place we can get alone with God. Some churches carry a notice, "This building is open for private prayer." For many people who cannot find a quiet place to meditate and pray that is a wise and thoughtful provision. But the notion that something is lacking in prayer unless it is offered in a consecrated building is false. No "holy building" is necessary, just a place that is conducive to our withdrawal from the business of life to get alone with God. For the Lord Jesus Christ that place was sometimes a mountain retreat (Matthew 14: 23; Luke 6:12), while at other times a garden such as Gethsemane was His chosen prayer closet (John 18:1–2). For most of us, a conducive place means a *stated place*. We may pray anywhere, but it is wise to have a place to which we can go, our peculiar and particular place to meet with the Lord. It makes good sense that when we have established a suitable place that is conducive to private prayer we should use it habitually. The Lord Jesus "was wont" to go to the Mount of Olives and "ofttimes resorted" to the garden of Gethsemane to pray (John 18:2; Luke 22:39). Even in such an itinerant ministry as His, He maintained stated places to which He constantly resorted to be alone in prayer. His teaching to us to enter into our closet is a plain lesson that, if it is possible, we should have an appointed trysting place with God.

Having made these preliminary truths clear, the Saviour proceeds to give us three distinct instructions about our praying. First, "Enter into thy closet"; second, "Shut the door"; and third, "Pray to thy Father." These are actions that are essential to true communion with God.

Enter the Closet

The first lesson Christ teaches us is that to get alone with God we must get away from all that would hinder or distract us. He describes an act of deliberate withdrawal, indeed, an act of physical separation. To enter our closet is to deliberately put a distance between us and our earthly surroundings. As we have noted, the closet is any private room, any place where we can be alone with God. To be alone with God is our need and it should daily be our aim. It certainly is Christ's command. To accomplish this goal, He instructs us to remove ourselves from the surroundings that we share with others and to enter into our closet to pray.

In the closet we get away from people. People are often the greatest hindrance to our praying. They often attract our attention. That is always a temptation to our pride, for it is when we are most aware of others that we are likely to pray as the hypocrites do—more to be seen and heard of men than of God. Not only do people attract our attention, they also distract our attention, and so it is necessary for us to withdraw from human contact in order to give our minds and hearts entirely to the matter of seeking the face of God.

In the closet we get away from the world. The world is imperious in its demands on us. Its work, its wealth, its worries, and its wars all clamor for our attention. The affairs of the world twine around our thoughts like the tentacles of a great octopus and demand our attention. When we enter the closet we deliberately turn aside from all such concerns and fix our minds on our God. In His light we shall see light (Psalm 36:9). In His presence we shall be able to see the affairs of everyday life in their true perspective and be set free from their tyranny over our minds.

In the closet we get away from our other employments, however legitimate they may be. When we enter into our closet we stop the daily flow of life in order to have a specific time of communion with the Lord. We do not merely try to fit Him in for a moment or two amid the myriad claims upon our time. Martha was "cumbered about much serving" and the Lord Jesus described her as "careful and troubled about many things." In contrast He declared with approval that her sister Mary had "chosen that good part" in withdrawing from such mundane matters to take time to sit at His feet and commune with Him (Luke 10:41–42).

We can all sympathize with Martha. Many of us are so harassed by the constant demands on our time that it seems impossible to set aside time to get alone with God. Many young mothers feel as Martha did. Cleaning and cooking, caring for children who all seem to need them at the same time, and usually working on too little sleep—many of them can only dream of being able to have a daily quiet time in the secret place of prayer. It seems a luxury beyond their reach. But it is not; it is a necessity, for every Christian needs closet time with the Lord. But the difficulty is very real. A godly husband will realize that if his wife is to be that wise woman who builds her house and not the foolish who tears it down with her hands, the best thing he can do for her is to ensure that she has time to meet with God. Thus he will take the pressure off her, assume the responsibilities of the home, and give her the time to go alone to the closet to meet with God.

In the closet we set aside every distraction. What is true in life generally is especially true in the place of prayer: To "run the race" we must "lay aside every weight" (Hebrews 12:1). To exercise a ministry of prevailing prayer we must get alone with the Lord. The Scriptures give us many examples of this truth in the lives of leading prayer warriors.

- Abraham: "The men [angels] turned their faces from thence, and went toward Sodom: but *Abraham stood yet before the Lord*" (Genesis 18: 22–23).

- Moses: "Now Moses kept the flock of Jethro his father in law, the priest of Midian: and he led the flock to the backside of the desert, and came to the mountain of God, even to Horeb. And the angel of the Lord appeared unto him in a flame of fire out of the midst of a bush: and he looked, and, behold, the bush burned with fire, and the bush was not consumed. And Moses said, *I will now turn aside,* and see this great sight, why the bush is not burnt" (Exodus 3:1–3).

- Daniel: "Now when Daniel knew that the writing was signed, *he went into his house*; and his windows being open in his chamber toward Jerusalem, he kneeled upon his knees three times a day, and prayed, and gave thanks before his God, as he did aforetime.... *Therefore I was left alone,* and saw this great vision" (Daniel 6:10; 10:8).

- The Lord Jesus Christ is the greatest example of all: "Rising up a great while before day, *he went out, and departed into a solitary place, and there prayed*" (Mark 1:35).

The word of God is clear on this matter. If we are to have communion with God, we must get alone with God, laying aside every hindrance and every distraction. "Enter into thy closet."

Shut the Door

The second lesson Christ teaches us is that to get away from all that may hinder or distract us, we must give our undivided attention to the matter of prayer. He speaks of something more than mere physical withdrawal. What He calls for is a mental and emotional removal from the affairs of the world, or rather, for the removal of our thoughts and feelings to a new sphere. It is easy to remove ourselves physically from the world, only to bring the world with us in our thoughts and emotions into the place of prayer. The shut door is a token of certain things being shut out and of others being shut in.

So we must give our undivided attention to the business of prayer. "A double minded man is unstable in all his ways" (James 1:8), and nowhere is this more true than in the place of prayer. We must settle down in God's presence; He commands, "Be still, and know that I am God" (Psalm 46:10). We must take time to clear our minds of lesser things and train our thoughts on the Lord and on the business we have to do with Him in prayer. That means we must determine before the Lord that by His grace nothing will deter us from prayer. In a word, Christ teaches us that we must prepare our hearts to seek our God. The Scriptures have a lot to say about this preparation of heart.

Neglecting to prepare our hearts to seek God is sin: Rehoboam "did evil, because he prepared not his heart to seek the Lord" (2 Chronicles 12:14). Are not our churches today full of Rehoboams? Are not Christians falling all around us, doing things that are not right in the sight of God, because they have not prepared their hearts to seek the Lord?

Conversely, *preparing our hearts is a "good thing."* The Lord said to Jehoshaphat, "Nevertheless there are good things found in thee, in that thou hast taken away the groves out of the land, and hast prepared thine heart to seek God" (2 Chronicles 19:3).

The Lord honors such preparation of heart. Ezra was so great a man that, according to the Jewish rabbis, if God had not given the law through Moses, He would certainly have done so through Ezra. They viewed him as the greatest man after Moses in all Israel's history. We do not need to play the game of ranking the Old Testament saints to agree that Ezra was a mighty man of God. The secret of his spiritual greatness was that the good hand of God was upon him. We are left in no doubt as to the reason God's hand was so powerfully upon him: "for Ezra had prepared his heart to seek the law of the Lord" (Ezra 7:10). Psalm 10:17 gives us God's promise to all His people: "Lord, thou hast heard the desire of the humble: thou wilt prepare their heart, thou wilt cause thine ear to hear."

When the Lord Jesus says, "Enter into thy closet," He means that if you would have communion with God you must get away from all that would hinder or distract. When He says, "Shut thy door," he means that if you desire to get away from everything that would hinder or distract, you must give your undivided attention to the matter of prayer and prepare your heart for it.

Pray to the Father

The third lesson Christ teaches us is that to give our undivided attention to prayer we must focus on our Father with faith that He loves us and hears us. How are we to focus on God? The answer is simple, though the application of it does not come easily to us. Most Christians have to confess that their praying consists of sudden rushes into God's presence with a list of instant demands, but with little consciousness that the living, eternal God is our Father. Few seem to live and pray in the enjoyment of that "Spirit of adoption, whereby we cry, Abba, Father" (Romans 8:15). So the question of how we may overcome this weakness and learn to focus our attention on our Father in heaven is urgently important.

To focus on the Lord we must attend to His word. The word and prayer go together. We greatly err and cut ourselves off from great blessing when we divorce the reading of Scripture from prayer. Some read the Bible at one time of the day and pray at another. It is good for us to give adequate time to the reading of the word, but if our reading is to be meaningful, it should always be prayerful. Equally, our praying should arise from and be based on what we have just found in the word. C. H. Waller wisely remarks, "*Speak, Lord, for thy servant heareth* is no bad preparation for *Hear, Lord, for thy servant speaketh.*" If we desire to be able to speak to God, we must first be willing to listen to Him. Scripture is insistent about this: "Keep silence before me, O islands; and let the people renew their strength: let them come near; then let them speak" (Isaiah 41:1); "Keep thy foot when thou goest to the house of God, and be more ready to hear, than to give the sacrifice of fools: for they consider not that they do evil" (Ecclesiastes 5:1).

There is wonderful wisdom in these instructions. It is almost impossible for us to deal with all the pressures of home and business—to say nothing of the constant bombardment of our minds by the filthiness of the world—and to rush into our closet in a fit frame of mind to pray effectively. We need the sanctifying power of the word to prepare us to meet with the Lord. That word will give us great thoughts of our God. It will furnish us with examples of His dealings with His people. It will convict us of sin, it will direct us into His will, and it will set our desires in the context of His will. It will motivate and enable us to pray. Indeed, any use of Scripture that does not lead to prayer is probably an illegitimate use.

So, with our focus on the Lord, *we pray*. We pray to "our Father"; we do not talk to ourselves. Prayer is not some psychological gimmick to make us feel better about ourselves or our situation. In the New Testament, the word translated "pray" in Matthew 6:6 is used solely of calling upon God. Other words translated "pray" are used of speech to men as well as to God, but not this word. It means only one thing: calling upon God, making our petitions known to Him, or communing with Him.

We should *approach* the Lord as our God. We should always approach Him with reverence and godly fear. And we should always draw near to Him on the proper ground, or merit: "Having therefore, brethren, boldness to enter into the holiest by the blood of Jesus, by a new and living way, which he hath consecrated for us, through the veil, that is to say, his flesh;...let us draw near with a true heart in full assurance of faith" (Hebrews 10:19–20, 22).

We should *address* the Lord as our Father. We should be absolutely open and honest with Him. When the Scriptures command us to "come boldly unto the throne of grace" (Hebrews 4:16), they mean that we should speak freely and frankly, without reservation, concealment, or ambiguity when we pray. We should trust the Lord as a child trusts his father. We should receive His promises and rebukes and always be assured of His care (1 Peter 5:7).

We should *ask* in prayer—simply, plainly, and submissively—resting in the wisdom of our Father's response.

This is closet praying. It is a vital part of the Christian life. But it is not the entirety of the Christian life. God makes no monks and has therefore not called us to *live* in the closet. We must frequent it, but then we must leave it and go back into the everyday world. The Lord Jesus clearly suggests this in His promise to those who will pray in secret: "Thy Father which seeth in secret shall reward thee openly." What we do in the closet will have powerful effects outside the closet. Closet prayer is the expression of faith that what we accomplish alone with God will have more real effect on the world around us than anything else we may do. This is not the opinion of the world, or even of most people in the church. But it is the teaching of Christ: Our usefulness will always be fueled—and limited—by our prayerfulness.

Moses' face shone after he had spent time alone with God. If we want the light of glory to shine through us to a darkened world, we must also spend time with God. Only then will we glow with the likeness of Christ: "We all, with open face beholding as in a glass the glory of the Lord, are changed into the same image from glory to glory, even as by the Spirit of the Lord" (2 Corinthians 3:18).

The early Christians shook the world after they had prevailed with God in prayer (Acts 4:31, 33). This is the secret of every genuine work for God. In reading church history we are fascinated by the stirring deeds of courageous men and women, but we all too often fail to see that the secret of their actions was their diligence in closet praying. We have often marveled at Martin Luther nailing his theses to Wittenberg's church door, thundering his defiance of papal bulls and excommunications, and standing like a Colossus as he battled for gospel truth against apostasy. But what we are too prone to overlook are the hours spent alone with God, for Luther was a man of prayer, a man who felt that—especially if he had a particularly heavy schedule—he should spend three hours a day in the place of prayer. Every great work of God proceeds by the power of closet praying, because as the Lord Jesus Christ promises, our Father will reward closet praying *openly*. This word *openly* literally means, "in the manifest." The Lord *manifests* His power to and through those who take time to enter the closet, shut the door upon the world, and pray.

"When thou prayest, enter into thy closet, and when thou hast shut thy door, pray to thy Father which is in secret; and thy Father which seeth in secret shall reward thee openly" (Matthew 6:6). This is how we may slay hypocrisy in our hearts, crucify the uprisings of our flesh in the place of prayer, enjoy real communion with God, and experience the genuine working of His power.

Enter thy closet. Shut thy door. Pray to thy Father. These are our Saviour's instructions. We should all take them to heart and ask ourselves a couple of searching questions. "How is my closet life? Is the closet the place I hide my skeletons, or the place I open my soul to the Lord in honest communion?"

The God of the Secret Place and the Secret Place of God

"When thou prayest, enter into thy closet, and when thou hast shut thy door, pray to thy Father which is in secret; and thy Father which seeth in secret shall reward thee openly." Matthew 6:6

T he Lord Jesus Christ denounced all ostentation in religious exercises. He who prays, fasts, or gives to be seen of men is a hypocrite. Men may conclude that such a man is very holy and good and they may therefore lavish praise and admiration on him, but God sees through his pretence. According to the Lord Jesus, the praise of men is the only praise the hypocrite will ever receive, for he will have condemnation, not commendation, from God. What a shock on the judgment day for a man to find that even his acclaimed goodness and holiness—his whole religion—are only added nails in the coffin of his doom!

None of us should miss the lesson of our text. We must ensure that we are not lying under the condemnation of God. We must proceed beyond a religion of mere external rites to a real, inward, and saving relationship with God. In other words, we must make sure that in truth, not in vain profession, we are the children of God. Having assured ourselves that we are God's children, we must live—and pray—accordingly.

As we have seen, that means we must not pray like hypocrites or heathens. Hypocrites love to pray to be seen of men. It is not that they really love to pray. No! What they love is to be seen of men. Christians are different. They *must* pray. It is the most fundamental instinct in their souls. And they *love* to pray. Even if they struggle to have a satisfying and effective prayer life, they will confess that they have no greater joy than when they have had real communion with their heavenly Father. The closet is their throne room. There they approach the mercy seat. There they touch the King of Glory.

Thus closet praying is the key to their entire life. As it goes, so goes their whole Christian experience. Their joy, peace, and usefulness—whether in the home, church, or world—are all governed from their prayer closet. That is the *measure* of closet praying. The *reason* for this is not difficult to discover. The Lord Jesus Christ points it out very clearly: "When thou prayest, enter into thy closet, and when thou hast shut thy door, pray to thy Father which is in secret; and thy Father which seeth in secret shall reward thee openly" (Matthew 6:6). "Pray to thy Father *which is in secret*." "Thy Father … *seeth in secret*." Here is what imparts such importance to our withdrawal from the business of life and from the sight of men to meet with the Lord: God is the God of the secret place. While His power and Godhead are stamped on all creation and are plain for all to see, His *face* and *grace* are hidden from all but those who enter the secret place of His immediate presence. Hence our subject: the God of the secret place and the secret place of God.

God Dwells in the Secret Place

"Pray to thy Father which is in secret." The phrase *in secret* means "hidden." The testimony of Scripture is that "no man hath seen God at any time" (John 1:18); and God "only hath immortality, dwelling in the light which no man can approach unto; whom no man hath seen, nor can see" (1 Timothy 6:16). Even when He revealed Himself to fallen man, God hid Himself: "I answered thee in the secret place of thunder" (Psalm 81:7). The reference here is to the darkness enshrouding Mount Sinai as Jehovah spoke His law to the Israelites. In the tabernacle in the wilderness, the ark of the covenant, which denoted God's presence among His people, was situated *inside the veil* in the holy of holies, to which the people had no access. In all the revelation of God in Scripture, it is the trinitarian Jehovah who reveals Himself. Yet the Trinity is hidden from our minds and inexplicable to our reason. Not only the person but also the purpose of God, His eternal decree, is secret: "The secret things belong unto the Lord our God: but those things which are revealed belong unto us and to our children for ever" (Deuteronomy 29:29).

All this touches on what theologians term the *incomprehensibility* of God. However much God reveals Himself to us, there is always a hiddenness about Him. The reason for this is readily understandable. God is infinite and we are finite. To the finite the infinite must always remain uncomprehended and to that extent hidden. Even the angels of heaven cannot comprehend God; He remains hidden to them because they are finite creatures. The same is true of the glorified saints. Though sinless and able to enjoy a knowledge of God that far exceeds anything we may know on earth, glorified saints remain finite, and the finite cannot comprehend the infinite.

Additionally, sin hides God from fallen men. Sin put man's eyes out so that even the rays of the sun of righteousness are hidden to him. He cannot help but feel some of the warmth of those rays, but he cannot see the glory of God. That means, of course, that since all creation declares the glory of God, fallen man knows nothing aright. However many facts he learns about the universe, he is ultimately ignorant of their true meaning. He knows nothing truly because he does not know the true God, in whom all truth ultimately resides.

So, as far as fallen man is concerned, God is doubly hidden. He dwells in secret. Sinners cannot find Him. Man's religion and philosophy cannot discover Him. He has no part in the beauty, pomp, and ostentatious display of the world's leading religions. Religion may wear a mystical aspect that may impress or intimidate the minds of men, but it does not impress God, for all its pomp and pageantry. God is not found as a result of human meditation or investigation. Job 11:7 asks, "Canst thou by searching find out God? canst thou find out the Almighty unto perfection?" The answer is, No! "Touching the Almighty, we cannot find him out" (Job 37:23). "His greatness is unsearchable" (Psalm 145:3). "Thy footsteps are not known" (Psalm 77:19). As the apostle wrote, "O the depth of the riches both of the wisdom and knowledge of God! how unsearchable are his judgments, and his ways past finding out!" (Romans 11:33).

Even God's grace is beyond human discovery. Paul speaks of "the unsearchable riches of Christ" (Ephesians 3:8). So, anything we ever come to know about God must be by divine revelation, not by human investigation or intuition. And even then—that is, when He reveals Himself—He remains hidden. Job said, "Lo, these are parts of his ways: but how little a portion is heard of him? but the thunder of his power who can understand?" (Job 26:14). Thus when God makes Himself known to us, He admits us to His secret place. Ever afterwards we are on a journey of discovery. God is not a theological textbook that we may learn and master. No matter how much we come to know of Him there is always infinitely more to know. He dwells in the secret place.

God Meets with Us in the Secret Place

Our Lord Jesus Christ commanded us to pray to our Father who is in secret because, though God is hidden, He is not inaccessible. He has clearly revealed Himself to His people: "God, who at sundry times and in divers manners spake in time past unto the fathers by the prophets, hath in these last days spoken unto us by his Son" (Hebrews 1:1–2). Paul tells us that God "hath shined in our hearts, to give the light of the knowledge of the glory of God in the face of Jesus

Christ" (2 Corinthians 4:6). In Old Testament times the Lord showed His people that He was the invisible God who dwelt in unapproachable glory. The structure of the Tabernacle (Exodus 25–30) taught this truth in a most telling way. The veil closed off the way into the holiest and so emphasized the fact that sinners cannot enter the majestic presence of God. But the Tabernacle also proclaimed the gospel of a coming Saviour and by types and shadows allowed believers to draw near in spiritual worship.

With the coming of the Lord Jesus Christ the age of types and shadows passed away. Shadows gave place to substance. In Christ, God has rent the veil; the moment the Lord Jesus died, "the veil of the temple was rent in twain from the top to the bottom" (Matthew 27:51). Paul explains the significance of this: "The Holy Ghost this signifying, that the way into the holiest of all was not yet made manifest, while as the first tabernacle was yet standing" (Hebrews 9:8). That is, the veil showed that while the Old Testament saints had access to God, they did not have it on the ground of their animal sacrifices; the true ground of their justification had not yet been fully revealed.

But now Christ has come and fulfilled all the Old Testament types. He has rent the veil and now welcomes us into the secret place in full assurance of acceptance through Him. Thus the New Testament assures us that we may "come boldly unto the throne of grace, that we may obtain mercy, and find grace to help in time of need" (Hebrews 4:16). It clearly identifies the basis of our confidence that we may enter into the presence of the Lord: It is because "we have a great high priest, that is passed into the heavens, Jesus the Son of God" (Hebrews 4:14). The classic statement of this confidence is given in Hebrews 10:19–22: "Having therefore, brethren, boldness to enter into the holiest by the blood of Jesus, by a new and living way, which he hath consecrated for us, through the veil, that is to say, his flesh; and having an high priest over the house of God; let us draw near with a true heart in full assurance of faith, having our hearts sprinkled from an evil conscience, and our bodies washed with pure water" (Hebrews 10:19–22). The Greek of verse 19 says simply, "Having therefore brethren confidence regarding the entrance into the holiest by the blood of Jesus." The entrance into the holiest that forms the subject of the apostle's exposition in the earlier chapters in Hebrews is Christ's entrance by His own blood (see Hebrews 9:12). We have confidence in His entrance and acceptance as our great high priest, and on that ground we may now "draw near with a true heart in full assurance of faith." Because of Christ, the way into the secret place is open to us.

The Lord has always promised to meet His people in the secret place. When He commanded Moses to erect the Tabernacle He promised, "There I will meet with thee, and I will commune with thee from above the mercy seat" (Exodus 25:22). He instructed Elijah, "Hide thyself by the brook Cherith, that is before

Jordan. And it shall be, that thou shalt drink of the brook; and I have commanded the ravens to feed thee there" (1 Kings 17:3–4). Time has not altered the Lord's promise. He still meets His people in the secret place: "For thus saith the high and lofty One that inhabiteth eternity, whose name is Holy; I dwell in the high and holy place, with him also that is of a contrite and humble spirit, to revive the spirit of the humble, and to revive the heart of the contrite ones" (Isaiah 57:15). In the secret place with the Lord we begin to enjoy the very purpose for which we were saved, namely, to hold fellowship with God. There the scales of sin and worldliness are peeled away to allow us "to behold the beauty of the Lord, and to enquire in his temple" (Psalm 27:4).

In the secret place we see things that the world cannot see. Noah walked with God. He knew the Lord in the secret place and was "warned of God of things not seen as yet" (Hebrews 11:7). Moses "endured, as seeing him who is invisible" (Hebrews 11:27). Indeed, all the Old Testament saints "died in faith, not having received the promises, but having seen them afar off" (Hebrews 11:13). Every man of prayer has a power of spiritual vision that the world in its blindness knows nothing about. For example, like the bride in the Song of Solomon, Christians see the loveliness of Christ. They testify, "Yea, he is altogether lovely" (Song of Solomon 5:16), while the ungodly say, "He hath no form nor comeliness; and when we shall see him, there is no beauty that we should desire him" (Isaiah 53:2). Like Asaph, Christians in the secret place come to see the end of the wicked (Psalm 73:17), while the ungodly carelessly plunge on to their doom, blind to the judgment that awaits them (Psalm 10:11, 13; 94:7).

In the secret place we understand things the world cannot grasp. "The secret of the Lord is with them that fear him" (Psalm 25:14). Those who know God in the secret place share the testimony of the men of Issachar who "were men that had understanding of the times, to know what Israel ought to do" (1 Chronicles 12:32). Even wicked sinners recognize the insight of people who know the God of the secret place. King Zedekiah certainly knew that if anyone knew the mind of God about affairs in his country, it would be the prophet Jeremiah, who was then being held in prison as a traitor: "Then Zedekiah the king sent, and took him out: and the king asked him secretly in his house, and said, Is there any word from the Lord?" (Jeremiah 37:17).

In the secret place we feel our lives and souls becoming submerged in the great purpose of the all-wise God. There flesh is crucified until we can honestly cry, "Thy will be done." Jacob is an outstanding example of this. "Jacob was left alone; and there wrestled a man with him until the breaking of the day" (Genesis 32:24). He was alone with God; God wrestled with him to subdue his fleshly strength and will; and thus Jacob was blessed (verse 29) so that from that day his walk bore the mark of his encounter with God (verses 31–32). This is always the way for a Christian to come under the control of the Spirit. In the secret place God does battle with the will of the flesh and so reveals Himself to us—and exercises His power upon us—that we bear the evident mark of His dealings with us in the way we walk before men. If we are not blessed through our experience of the Lord in the secret place, we will never have victory over the flesh and will never live in conformity to Christ.

All this is true because *in the secret place we behold the fullness of Christ.* The book of Revelation provides a wonderful example of the truth of this assertion. Alone with God on the Isle of Patmos, the apostle John saw Jesus before he saw God's plans for the church and the nations. Is it not always true that we see everything more clearly when we behold Christ in all His fullness? To see Him is the chief delight of saints in the secret place. Paul expounded the glory of Christ's fullness more than any other New Testament writer, and it is surely significant that he insisted that he had never learned his gospel from any man, but had received it "by the revelation of Jesus Christ" (Galatians 1:12). Where and when did he receive this revelation and learn the glorious truth of Christ's fullness that so dominates his epistles? He gives us a clue just after the statement we have quoted. Telling of his movements immediately after his conversion and initial witness in Damascus he says, "Neither went I up to Jerusalem to them which were apostles before me; but *I went into Arabia*, and returned again unto Damascus" (Galatians 1:17). The solitude of Arabia was Paul's seminary, the place where he met alone with God and came to behold the fullness and glory of his Saviour. That is the only way we can ever see the glory of Christ, for it is in the secret place that God meets with us and shows us His glory. With Moses we should pray, "I beseech thee, shew me thy glory" (Exodus 33:18). We may do so with confidence, for God meets with us in the secret place with the express intention of manifesting to us there the fullness of Christ in whom His glory fully shines.

God Sees Us in the Secret Place

"Thy Father … seeth in secret." The Lord Jesus meant this truth to be a strong source of comfort to His people and it is. "That which is the hypocrite's fear, and binds condemnation upon the heart of a wicked man, is here made to be the saints' support and ground of comfort—that they pray to an all seeing God: 1 John 3:20, 'For if our heart condemn us, God is greater than our heart, and knoweth all things (1 John 3:20). Their heavenly Father seeth in secret; he can interpret their groans, and read the language of their sighs" (Thomas Manton).

The Lord sees if we pray. When Ananias was reluctant to obey Him and to go find the newly converted Saul of Tarsus, the Lord told him, "Arise, and go into the street which is called Straight, and enquire in the house of Judas for one called Saul, of Tarsus: *for, behold, he prayeth"* (Acts 9:11).

The Lord sees how we pray. He assures us, just as He did the churches of Asia Minor, "I know thy works" (Revelation 2–3). He knows those who, like the church in Sardis, have a name that they live and yet they are dead, and those who, like the Laodiceans, are lukewarm (Revelation 3:1, 15–16).

The Lord sees why we pray. "All things are naked and opened unto the eyes of him with whom we have to do" (Hebrews 4:13). Our motives are not hidden from Him. He sees the heart and discerns what moves us to pray. Thus He can say to many of us, as He said to the people to whom James wrote, "Ye ask, and receive not, because ye ask amiss, that ye may consume it upon your lusts" (James 4:3).

The Lord sees what we pray for. It is the consistent testimony of Scripture that God sees the needs of His people, hears their cries, and answers their petitions. When Israel lay in Egyptian slavery, "they cried, and their cry came up unto God by reason of the bondage" (Exodus 2:23). The Lord's response was decisive: "The Lord said, I have surely seen the affliction of my people which are in Egypt, and have heard their cry by reason of their taskmasters" (Exodus 3:7). This is the confidence of God's people in every age. As David put it, "The eyes of the Lord are upon the righteous, and his ears are open unto their cry.... The righteous cry, and the Lord heareth, and delivereth them out of all their troubles" (Psalm 34:15, 17).

God Responds to Us in the Secret Place

Jesus promised, "Pray to thy Father which is in secret; and thy Father which seeth in secret shall reward thee openly" (Matthew 6:6). The secret place is rich in rewards. It is not that our prayers *earn* or *merit* God's favor. The only merit that earns favor for us from God is Christ's merit. We could say that attending to the secret place is our duty. It is, but God blesses that duty richly and lavishly.

God blesses the secret place of prayer personally and internally. He blesses us in our souls, giving us assurance, confidence, joy, peace, and love. He strengthens us with might by His Spirit in the inner man (Ephesians 3:16). What this means in terms of spiritual experience is clear from the verses that follow: "That Christ may dwell in your hearts by faith; that ye, being rooted and grounded in love, may be able to comprehend with all saints what is the breadth, and length, and depth, and height; and to know the love of Christ, which passeth knowledge, that ye might be filled with all the fullness of God" (Ephesians 3:17–19).

God blesses the secret place of prayer powerfully and externally: "Thy Father which seeth in secret shall reward thee openly." We have a dramatic illustration of this promise being fulfilled in the history of the early church. Following their healing of the lame man at the gate of the temple, Peter and John took the opportunity to preach the gospel to the people. The Jewish leaders were outraged and put the apostles into prison. The next day they arraigned them before the council and commanded them "that they speak henceforth to no man in this name" (Acts 4:17). In the face of the apostles' blunt refusal to be bound by such a command, the Jews threatened them with severe punishment (verse 21). But far from being frightened by such tactics, Peter and John went at once to report to their brethren in the church. They immediately shut themselves in with the Lord in a season of prayer and committed their persecutors and their threats to Him: "And now, Lord, behold their threatenings: and grant unto thy servants, that with all boldness they may speak thy word" (verse 29). The Lord's answer shows how He openly rewarded their faithful ministry in prayer: "And when they had prayed, the place was shaken where they were assembled together; and they were all filled with the Holy Ghost, and they spake the word of God with boldness.... And with great power gave the apostles witness of the resurrection of the Lord Jesus: and great grace was upon them all" (Acts 4:31, 33).

God blesses the secret place of prayer publicly and eternally. The reward of true prayer is everlasting. The Lord's promise through Isaiah extends into eternity: "Say ye to the righteous, that it shall be well with him: for they shall eat the fruit of their doings" (Isaiah 3:10). That includes the fruit of the labor of prayer, as Malachi makes plain: "Then they that feared the Lord spake often one to another: and the Lord hearkened, and heard it, and a book of remembrance was written before him for them that feared the Lord, and that thought upon his name. And they shall be mine, saith the Lord of hosts, in that day when I make up my jewels; and I will spare them, as a man spareth his own son that serveth him. Then shall ye return, and discern between the righteous and the wicked, between him that serveth God and him that serveth him not" (Malachi 3:16–18).

Such are the blessings of the secret place. It is not too late for any believer to cultivate the hidden life, the life of the secret place of God. Our Father dwells in the secret place. He waits for us there. He welcomes us there. And He blesses us there. "In [Christ] we have boldness and access with confidence by the faith of him" (Ephesians 3:12). So let us enter in and pursue an ever-deepening communion with the God of the secret place in the secret place of God.

4

The Public Reward of Private Prayer

"When thou prayest, enter into thy closet, and when thou hast shut thy door, pray to thy Father which is in secret; and thy Father which seeth in secret shall reward thee openly." Matthew 6:6

The Lord Jesus Christ tells us that there are some people who long for public acclaim as holy men, men of prayer. They do everything possible to create the illusion that they have particular intimacy with God. Yet, they will never have any reward beyond the brief, shallow admiration of easily impressible men. In the end they will stand condemned before all as hypocrites, disowned by God, with nothing good to show for their pretended spirituality.

Then again the Saviour tells us that there are others who court no public acclaim for their private devotions. Indeed, they are embarrassed by it. Their chief concern is to have real communion with God. They desire to get alone with Him. Far from human view, they rejoice in the radiance of His face and the reality of His fellowship. Yet, says the Lord Jesus, these people will have the Lord's public endorsement and acknowledgment. He will reward them *openly.*

This is a little like what happened to Solomon. He met with the Lord at Gibeon and had the opportunity to ask and obtain from God whatever his heart desired. Such an opportunity provides a great measure of a man's true state. It certainly gave an insight into the young king's soul. He did not ask for riches, personal prosperity, long life, military prowess, power over his enemies, or even for the security of his throne. What he desired was a wise and understanding heart to serve the Lord well in the sphere in which He had placed him. The Lord was well pleased with that desire and said to Solomon, "Because thou hast asked this thing, and hast not asked for thyself long life; neither hast asked riches for thyself, nor hast asked the life of thine enemies; but hast asked for thyself understanding to discern judgment; behold, I have done according to thy words: lo, I have given thee a wise and an understanding heart; so that there was none like thee before thee, neither after thee shall any arise like unto thee. And I have also given thee that which thou hast not asked, both riches, and honour: so that there shall not be any among the kings like unto thee all thy days. And if thou wilt walk in my ways, to keep my statutes and my commandments, as thy father David did walk, then I will lengthen thy days" (1 Kings 3:11–14).

Those who truly seek the Lord in the secret place do not do so for public acknowledgment. Their desire is much humbler. They deeply desire to commune with their Father; they wish to invoke His help with their needs; and they yearn to be conformed to the image of their Saviour—all to the glory of God alone. These are the ruling passions of all who truly pray. But the Lord's answer exceeds all their expectations. Not only does He give them the desires of their hearts, but He also promises them a great public demonstration of His power and favor.

This is a principle that the Lord Jesus Christ strongly emphasized in the Sermon on the Mount. For example, He said, "Seek ye first the kingdom of God, and his righteousness; and all these things shall be added unto you" (Matthew 6: 33). And again in our text He states the same principle. He emphasizes that God rewards a Christian according to what He sees in his private prayer life. There is a public reward for private prayer.

God Sees Our Private Prayers

In the context of Christ's teaching in Matthew the fact that God sees our private prayer life is meant as a comfort. For many, however, it does the very opposite. The thought frightens and alarms them. We can all understand that feeling. Every Christian feels unworthy of anything but censure for his lack of progress in personal godliness. None of us is all he should be or all he sincerely wants to be, but only hypocrites and Christ-rejecters need be alarmed by the Lord's teaching here. Any who make religion a cloak of maliciousness should tremble at the thought that the God of heaven sees even the most secret parts of their lives. Jesus shocked Nathanael with the revelation, "Before that Philip called thee, when thou wast under the fig tree, I saw thee" (John 1:48). He greeted each of the seven churches of Asia Minor with the words, "I know thy works" (Revelation 2:2) and proceeded to lay bare the true state of their souls in the sight of God. To many another He has brought home the same challenging truth. "I saw you when no one else could see you, for the secret things are not hidden from Me. I saw right into your heart and understood every secret thought." The Scripture assures us that the Lord Jesus Christ "needed not that any should testify of man: for he knew what was in man" (John 2:25).

For every religious deceiver and hypocrite this is a terrible truth. "The ways of man are before the eyes of the Lord, and he pondereth all his goings" (Proverbs 5:21); "neither is there any creature that is not manifest in his sight: but all things are naked and opened unto the eyes of him with whom we have to do" (Hebrews 4:13). But this is not meant to alarm a humble believer in Christ who, despite all his felt faults, is justified by grace and sincerely desires to get alone with His heavenly Father to have fellowship with Him. For such a person it is a glorious comfort to know that the Lord sees him in his private prayer life.

The Lord sees us in the secret place. He sees our attitude when we pray. He sees our grief over our sins and failures. He sees our weaknesses and our yearnings after Him, our faith and yet our battles with unbelief. He sees every tear we shed in secret before Him: "Thou tellest my wanderings: put thou my tears into thy bottle: are they not in thy book?" (Psalm 56:8). He sees every heartache and trouble we bear: "I will be glad and rejoice in thy mercy: for thou hast considered my trouble; thou hast known my soul in adversities" (Psalm 31:7). Most of all, He sees our praying: "When thou prayest, enter into thy closet, and when thou hast shut thy door, pray to thy Father which is in secret; and thy Father which seeth in secret shall reward thee openly" (Matthew 6:6). In the light of all this we would do well to make the psalmist's prayer our own: "Search me, O God, and know my heart: try me, and know my thoughts: And see if there be any wicked way in me, and lead me in the way everlasting" (Psalm 139:23–24).

God Rewards Our Private Prayers

The Lord is pleased when His people pray. "The eyes of the Lord are upon the righteous, and his ears are open unto their cry" (Psalm 34:15). The sound of their voices raised in prayer is a delight to Him: "The sacrifice of the wicked is an abomination to the Lord: but the prayer of the upright is his delight" (Proverbs 15:8). What the bridegroom says to his betrothed in the Song of Solomon, Christ says to His church: "O my dove,… let me see thy countenance, let me hear thy voice; for sweet is thy voice, and thy countenance is comely" (Song of Solomon 2:14).

The Lord answers prayer in the best way and at the best time. The Bible is full of this assurance. Moses told the Israelites, "If … thou shalt seek the Lord thy God, thou shalt find him, if thou seek him with all thy heart and with all thy soul" (Deuteronomy 4:29). Asaph quotes the Lord as saying, "Call upon me in the day of trouble: I will deliver thee, and thou shalt glorify me" (Psalm 50:15). Psalm 91 speaks of the man who "dwelleth in the secret place of the most High" (verse 1) and confidently promises, "He shall call upon me, and I will answer him: I will be with him in trouble; I will deliver him, and honour him" (Psalm 91:15). He may "bear long" with his praying people, but He will certainly hear their cry and "avenge them speedily" (Luke 18:8). His timing is always perfect. "As for God, his way is perfect:... and [he] maketh my way perfect" (Psalm 18:30, 32). When He calls us to "wait patiently for him" (Psalm 37:7), it is to prepare us to receive the blessing: "Lord, thou hast heard the desire of the humble: thou wilt prepare their heart, thou wilt cause thine ear to hear" (Psalm 10:17).

The Lord's answers will enrich our lives. The Lord Jesus calls God's answers to prayer a reward. He repays the honest devotion of true prayer in the coin of heaven and puts us in possession of what we could not otherwise enjoy.

- He rewards us with *His presence:* "The Lord is nigh unto all them that call upon him, to all that call upon him in truth" (Psalm 145:18).

- He rewards us with *His peace:* "They looked unto him, and were lightened: and their faces were not ashamed. This poor man cried, and the Lord heard him, and saved him out of all his troubles" (Psalm 34:5–6).

- He rewards us with *His pardon:* "If we confess our sins, he is faithful and just to forgive us our sins, and to cleanse us from all unrighteousness" (1 John 1:9).

- He rewards us with *His protection:* "The eyes of the Lord are over the righteous, and his ears are open unto their prayers: but the face of the Lord is against them that do evil" (1 Peter 3:12).

- He rewards us with *His power:* "If ye then, being evil, know how to give good gifts unto your children: how much more shall your heavenly Father give the Holy Spirit to them that ask him?" (Luke 11:13).

- He rewards us with *His full provision:* "They that seek the Lord shall not want any good thing" (Psalm 34:10). Christ's promise is clear: "Seek ye first the kingdom of God, and his righteousness; and all these things shall be added unto you" (Matthew 6:33). Thus we pray in the assurance that our God "shall supply all [our] need according to his riches in glory by Christ Jesus" (Philippians 4:19) and shall "make all grace abound toward [us]; that [we], always having all sufficiency in all things, may abound to every good work" (2 Corinthians 9:8).

It may be argued that these blessings belong to Christians by virtue of their being in Christ, not by virtue of their praying. It is true that every blessing we enjoy comes to us solely on the merit of Christ and that the privileges we have just noted are the birthright of everyone who is in Christ. But it is also true that failure in the place of prayer will rob us of the enjoyment of our birthright. It will grieve the Holy Spirit so that we lose the comforting sense of the Lord's nearness. We will forfeit the joy of living in His peace. Our sin of prayerlessness will hide His face from us, so that He will not hear us (Isaiah 59:2), and we will lose the joy of divine pardon, protection, provision, and power.

By way of contrast, maintaining the secret place of prayer will constantly enrich and refresh us. In *The Pilgrim's Progress* Bunyan describes Christian in the house of the Interpreter, where he sees "a fire burning against a wall, and one standing by it always casting water upon it to quench it; yet did the fire burn higher and hotter." Bunyan's picture represents the maintenance of grace in the soul of a believer. Satan seeks to put out the fire of grace, but it increases despite all his activity. How? Behind the wall was a man who continually threw oil upon the fire. This is the secret work of the Holy Spirit. Bunyan meant that the Spirit sustains grace in God's people in ways they can neither see nor comprehend, but it is also fair to say that the Spirit does this work in the secret place. It is as we meet with the Lord there that His Spirit will make us enjoy all the benefits and blessings of our being in Christ.

God Rewards Us According to Our Private Praying

"Pray to thy Father which is in secret; and thy Father which seeth in secret shall reward thee openly." Secret prayer is the measure of God's blessing on His people. In other words, how we pray determines the way we are blessed and how much we are blessed. Robert Murray McCheyne stated no more than the truth when he said that it is not so much great talent that God blesses as great likeness to Christ. And it is in the secret place that we become more and more like Him (2 Corinthians 3:18).

Thus, in a very real measure, it is private communion with God that gives us the capacity to receive and that fits us to enjoy every other blessing. Without it, we would turn blessings into curses. Take the office of a bishop or elder in the church as an example. To attain to this office is a great privilege. It is a good thing. But note Paul's warning: A bishop must not be a novice, "lest being lifted up with pride he fall into the condemnation of the devil" (1 Timothy 3:6). If a man achieves the office of elder without first having matured sufficiently to be capable of exercising it, the office may destroy him. And so it is with any great blessing. Our capacity to receive it and to use it aright is critical. And it is in the secret place of communion with our Lord that we receive that capacity.

Prayer is not the only virtue the Lord rewards, but since every rewardable service depends on our communion with God in the secret place, prayer is the condition and measure of all the blessings we enjoy. Our spiritual powerlessness and poverty mirror our prayerlessness. If we do not pray we will not receive the blessings we need: "Ye have not, because ye ask not" (James 4:2). Jesus promised, "Ask, and it shall be given you" (Luke 11:9). Moreover, He made it clear that as we ask, so shall we receive: "If a son shall ask bread of any of you that is a father, will he give him a stone? or if he ask a fish, will he for a fish give him a serpent? or if he shall ask an egg, will he offer him a scorpion?" (Luke 11:11–12). We receive what we ask, according to our Father's will. That is the measure of our blessings.

God Will Soon Reward Publicly What He Now Sees and Rewards in Private

"Thy Father which seeth in secret shall reward thee openly." This is the answering "exceeding abundantly" that so amazed Paul (Ephesians 3:20). The Lord will reward publicly what He now sees and rewards in private. By the same token, He will condemn publicly what He now sees and condemns in private. In other words, we all have a closet life of one kind or another. The Lord knows what we are in the secret place. Others may lavish praise upon us for what they see as impressive holiness or prayerfulness, but God does not judge by mere appearance. When He gives out His rewards, He will demonstrate how wide of the mark man's estimation of spiritual service has been. He will not act according to the imagined successes that have impressed men, nor will He reward the pomp and pageantry that sway human verdicts. He sees the heart and its attitude to the secret place. He will richly reward every lover of the secret place, but will confer no reward on the vainglorious religion of those whose devotions were calculated to court the praise of man.

We must not fail to mark the contrast between verses five and six of Matthew 6: "When thou prayest, thou shalt not be as the hypocrites are: for they love to pray standing in the synagogues and in the corners of the streets, that they may be seen of men. Verily I say unto you, They have their reward. But thou, when thou prayest, enter into thy closet, and when thou hast shut thy door, pray to thy Father which is in secret; and thy Father which seeth in secret shall reward thee openly" (Matthew 6:5–6).

Those who now enjoy the public praise of men and the private condemnation of God will soon be exposed to the public condemnation of God. That condemnation will show how ill-founded and ephemeral their reputation really was.

Those who are now commended by God, though they are ignored or condemned by men, will soon be acknowledged and acclaimed by their Lord before all. This is the judgment that matters. This is the reward that counts.

The Certainty and Nature of God's Answers to Prayer

"Pray to thy Father which is in secret; and thy Father which seeth in secret shall reward thee openly." Matthew 6:6

T hy Father will reward thee openly." This promise at once raises the important issue of answered prayer. For most Christians this is not only a matter of great importance, but frequently of confusion and even frustration. Ask any Christian if he believes that God answers prayer and he will at once answer, "Yes!" Isn't this an article of the Christian faith? And yet, if pressed, that same Christian will often admit that his own experience of prayer is unsatisfactory and that he feels that he frequently prays to no apparent effect. He has seen prayer answered, but he has also seen it go unanswered. He reads the Bible's promises regarding answered prayer and is struck with their straightforward simplicity. Their meaning is plain:

Luke 11:9–10: "I say unto you, Ask, and it shall be given you; seek, and ye shall find; knock, and it shall be opened unto you. For every one that asketh receiveth; and he that seeketh findeth; and to him that knocketh it shall be opened."

John 14:13: "Whatsoever ye shall ask in my name, that will I do, that the Father may be glorified in the Son."

John 15:7: "If ye abide in me, and my words abide in you, ye shall ask what ye will, and it shall be done unto you."

John 16:23: "Verily, verily, I say unto you, Whatsoever ye shall ask the Father in my name, he will give it you."

1 John 3:22: "Whatsoever we ask, we receive of him, because we keep his commandments, and do those things that are pleasing in his sight."

Psalm 37:4: "Delight thyself also in the Lord; and he shall give thee the desires of thine heart."

All these—and scores more like them—appear to be simple, absolute promises. Yet our typical Christian admits: "I have asked in Jesus' name and have not received what I asked. I abide in Christ and seek to obey His word, but still I have asked and not received. I believe that I delight in the Lord, but yet there are things that I greatly desire and do not receive." So for the Christian there is a recognized tension between his understanding of God's promises to answer prayer and his experience of answers to prayer.

There is nothing new in this. Even great men of prayer and faith have struggled with this tension. Job is an outstanding example. Listen to his bitter lamentation: "Behold, I cry out of wrong, but I am not heard: I cry aloud, but there is no judgment" (Job 19:7); "I cry unto thee, and thou dost not hear me: I stand up, and thou regardest me not" (Job 30:20); "Oh that I knew where I might find him! that I might come even to his seat!" (Job 23:3). David voiced a similar anxiety: "Why standest thou afar off, O Lord? why hidest thou thyself in times of trouble?" (Psalm 10:1).

We have all felt this tension between what we know to be true, because God has stated it, and what we actually experience. So there is probably no more urgently and personally important subject for God's people than the one the Lord Jesus Christ raises in our text. In this study we will seek to learn from the Saviour's words the certainty and nature of God's answers to His people's prayers.

God Answers Prayer

We must commence by reiterating the fact that God does answer prayer. Christ's words leave no room for doubt on that score. This is the testimony of the entire Bible. Speaking of the priests who were active in Hezekiah's reformation, 2 Chronicles 30:27 testifies, "Their voice was heard, and their prayer came up to his holy dwelling place, even unto heaven." It is the plain message of Scripture to encourage all believers that the same is true when they pray. So the biblical statement is incontrovertible: *God answers prayer.* But what does the Bible mean by this promise to "answer" our prayers?

Answering prayer means that *God makes a particular response to a particular request.* "Thou shalt weep no more: he will be very gracious unto thee at the voice of thy cry; when he shall hear it, he will answer thee" (Isaiah 30:19).

It also means that *God gives us the things we ask Him for.* Jesus promised, "What things soever ye desire, when ye pray, believe that ye receive them, and ye shall have them" (Mark 11:24). Again, He asked, "What man is there of you, whom if his son ask bread, will he give him a stone? Or if he ask a fish, will he give him a serpent? If ye then, being evil, know how to give good gifts unto your children, how much more shall your Father which is in heaven give good things to them that ask him?" (Matthew 7:9–11).

Answering prayer means that *God gives His people the deliverance from need or danger for which they cry to Him.* The words of Psalm 50:15 are unmistakably clear: "Call upon me in the day of trouble: I will deliver thee, and thou shalt glorify me."

Again, it means that *God will demonstrate His power on behalf of His people who cry to Him.* This is what the Lord promised Jeremiah: "Call unto me, and I will answer thee, and shew thee great and mighty things, which thou knowest not" (Jeremiah 33:3).

This is what the word of God means by its teaching that God answers prayer. Such answers to prayer are real and objective. They are not mere alterations in the believer's state of mind. They are not delusions. They are not the product of frenzied or wishful thinking. They are objectively real.

Testimony of Scripture History

Scripture history affords many examples of God's answers to His people's prayers. Three familiar passages illustrate that the history of the Bible is replete with records of God's answers to His people's prayers.

Exodus 17

When, during their wilderness wanderings, the Israelites arrived at Rephidim, they faced two enormous challenges. First, they had no water and no apparent means of obtaining it. Second, they had to endure a vicious attack from the Amalekites. In both cases Moses prayed and the Lord gloriously answered him and delivered the people. When he cried to the Lord in the face of the people's bitterness at finding no water, the Lord answered, "Go on before the people, and take with thee of the elders of Israel; and thy rod, wherewith thou smotest the river, take in thine hand, and go. Behold, I will stand before thee there upon the rock in Horeb; and thou shalt smite the rock, and there shall come water out of it, that the people may drink" (verses 5–6).

"Then came Amalek, and fought with Israel in Rephidim" (verse 8). Israel's response was twofold: Joshua chose an army to confront the attacker; Moses stood on a hilltop overlooking the battle and lifted his hands to heaven, holding up the rod of God in the sight of the Lord and of His people. "And it came to pass, when Moses held up his hand, that Israel prevailed: and when he let down his hand, Amalek prevailed. But Moses' hands were heavy; and they took a stone, and put it under him, and he sat thereon; and Aaron and Hur stayed up his hands, the one on the one side, and the other on the other side; and his hands were steady until the going down of the sun. And Joshua discomfited Amalek and his people with the edge of the sword" (verses 11–13).

2 Chronicles 20

This chapter tells the story of the Moabites joining with the Ammonites and Edomites to launch an attack on Judah. King Jehoshaphat was naturally fearful of such an alliance of powers against him, so he prayed, "O our God, wilt thou not judge them? for we have no might against this great company that cometh against us; neither know we what to do: but our eyes are upon thee" (verse 12). God answered by sending Jehaziel with this promise: "Hearken ye, all Judah, and ye inhabitants of Jerusalem, and thou king Jehoshaphat, Thus saith the Lord unto you, Be not afraid nor dismayed by reason of this great multitude; for the battle is not yours, but God's.... Ye shall not need to fight in this battle: set yourselves, stand ye still, and see the salvation of the Lord with you, O Judah and Jerusalem: fear not, nor be dismayed; to morrow go out against them: for the Lord will be with you" (verses 15–17).

God's performance is never less than His promise. Jehoshaphat and his people believed this and went forth confidently to face their powerful foes on the strength of God's word. They were not disappointed: "When they began to sing and to praise, the Lord set ambushments against the children of Ammon, Moab, and mount Seir, which were come against Judah; and they were smitten" (verse 22).

Acts 12

The fires of passion and persecution were raging against the early church. King Herod had put the apostle James to death and, seeing that it pleased the people, he proceeded to lay hold of Peter, with the intention of killing him also. As Peter lay in prison on the eve of his execution, the church met in fervent prayer. The Lord answered them and delivered Peter: "Peter therefore was kept in prison: but prayer was made without ceasing of the church unto God for him. And when Herod would have brought him forth, the same night Peter was sleeping between two soldiers, bound with two chains: and the keepers before the door kept the prison. And, behold, the angel of the Lord came upon him, and a light shined in the prison: and he smote Peter on the side, and raised him up, saying, Arise up quickly. And his chains fell off from his hands. And the angel said unto him, Gird thyself, and bind on thy sandals. And so he did. And he saith unto him, Cast thy garment about thee, and follow me. And he went out, and followed him; and wist not that it was true which was done by the angel; but thought he saw a vision. When they were past the first and the second ward, they came unto the iron gate that leadeth unto the city; which opened to them of his own accord: and they went out, and passed on through one street; and forthwith the angel departed from him" (verses 5–10).

Testimony of Subsequent History

The history of the church after the close of the canon of Scripture is replete with testimonies to God's answering the prayers of His people. In Carthage a godly mother prayed for her brilliant but profligate and heretical son. God gave her the assurance that He would answer her cry, and she boldly confessed her confidence to her boy. Nine long years passed before Monica saw him brought to faith in Christ. When he sailed from Carthage to Rome, still proudly rejecting the gospel, she bewailed his going to such a place of vice and corruption and filled the ears of God with her cries. And once again God heard her, for in Rome her son was appointed to go to Milan to teach rhetoric. There he came under the ministry of the famous Ambrose and was soundly converted to Christ. The Christian church ever since has had cause to bless God for answering Monica's prayers, thereby giving to the world the theological genius of Augustine of Hippo.

Most of us are familiar with the name of George Müller of Bristol. The story of his life of faith has become a classic. Through prayer and without acquainting friends and donors of his daily needs, Müller fed, clothed, and housed hundreds of orphan children amid the grinding poverty of nineteenth-century England. Even when there was no food in the orphanage and no money to procure it, he had the children sit at the table while he asked the Lord to meet their need. Never once did he or his orphans go without. God answered prayer.

The evangelist Charles Inglis recounted a conversation he had with the captain of the ship on which he was traveling from Britain to America. When they were off the coast of Newfoundland the captain told Inglis this story:

> The last time I crossed here, five weeks ago, one of the most extraordinary things happened that has completely revolutionized my whole Christian life. Up to that time I was one of your ordinary Christians. We had a man on board, George Müller of Bristol. I had been on that bridge for twenty-two hours, and never left it. I was startled by someone tapping me on the shoulder. It was George Müller.
>
> "Captain," he said, "I have come to tell you that I must be in Quebec on Saturday afternoon" (this was Wednesday).
>
> "It is impossible," I said.
>
> "Very well, if your ship can't take me, but I have never broken an engagement in fifty years."

"I would willingly help you. How can I? I am helpless," I replied.

"Let us go down to the chart room and pray," said Müller.

I looked at the man of God and I thought to myself what lunatic asylum he could have come from. I had never heard of such a thing.

"Mr. Müller," I said. "Do you know how dense the fog is?"

"No," he replied. "My eye is not on the density of the fog, but on the living God who controls every circumstance of my life."

He got down on his knees and prayed one of the most simple prayers. I muttered to myself, "That would suit a children's class where the children are not more than eight years old." The burden of his prayer was something like this: "O Lord, if it is consistent with Thy will, please remove this fog in five minutes. Thou knowest the engagement Thou didst make for me in Quebec for Saturday. I believe it is Thy will." When he finished I was going to pray, but he put his hand on my shoulder and told me not to pray.

He said, "First, you do not believe He will. Second, I believe He has and there is no need to pray."

And, as George Müller prayed, the fog had lifted.

Testimony of Christian Experience

David's testimony is the testimony of God's people in every age: "This poor man cried, and the Lord heard him, and saved him out of all his troubles" (Psalm 34:6). Despite the feebleness of our praying and the frequent unbelief and constant unworthiness that attend it, God has answered us. He answered when we cried to Him for salvation from sin and for deliverance from the awful dominion that sin and Satan had gained over our souls. That is a miracle of grace, a powerful answer to prayer. When you kneel with harlots, alcoholics, or drug addicts and hear their cries for mercy (as I have had the privilege of doing) and then see them rise from their knees new creatures, you know that God answers prayer.

He continues to answer prayer in keeping those whom He saves. I remember a man who was a hopeless drunkard. He was on a downward spiral that must soon have ended in destitution or even death. Then God saved him and made him a new creature in Christ. While I have known others with similar problems receive instantaneous freedom from the attraction of alcohol, I found that his case was different. He told me that there were times when his body would crave for alcohol. When that happened, he cried out to the Lord. As he put it, if he had time to drink, he had time to stop and pray. He would get alone with God and stay on his knees until God had given him the victory. Every time, God answered prayer.

God not only answers prayer in saving and keeping us, He answers by teaching us His word and showing us His will. He has given all believers the Holy Spirit to guide them into biblical truth and to enrich their lives by its application to them. He also answers by admitting us to His fellowship and by letting us see something of His power and glory. These are the most precious of all answers to prayer, for they bring us closest to experiencing heaven while we are still on earth.

But we are still on the earth and therefore tend to look on the answers to prayer that touch immediately on our earthly affairs as the most outstanding. While this is regrettable, we must confess that when we touch on matters that those around us can easily relate to, we can give powerful witness to the truth that God answers prayer. I am loath to use personal experience, for it can all too easily turn attention away from the Lord to His witness. Yet each of us should be able to give testimony to God's answering us in the day of trouble. This is not the prerogative of some elite body of Christians but of all God's people. This was borne in on me while I was just a young boy. My dad, a very ordinary working man, told me that when I was about three years old my mother became very ill. The doctor examined her and then gave my dad some chilling news. She put it in rather a strange way. She said, "I believe that you are a man of prayer," and added quite bluntly (for she was not only an unbeliever but a spiritist), "You had better be. We can do nothing for your wife; she is in the hands of God." My dad went at once to my mother's bedside and told her the news. Then he took her hand, bowed by her bed, and cried to the Lord for her life. God heard that cry and my mother lived for almost fifty years after that. I have seen God answer the prayer of church elders asking for the deliverance of a little girl from a malignant and incurable brain tumor. My wife and I have known Him to meet urgent financial needs in a totally unforeseen way, right down to the precise amount sought, when not another soul on earth even knew that the need existed.

Such experiences are common in the church of Christ. Time would fail to tell of missionaries delivered from imminent danger and death at the very moment Christians thousands of miles away were constrained to get out of bed and cry to God for them—and that without any earthly indication of any special need. Or of others who stood back in amazement while God used the roar at the scoring of a goal in an international soccer match to distract a communist border guard, so that in his hurry to get back to his radio he waved through a truck loaded with prohibited Bibles on their way to Christians behind the Iron Curtain.

God's answering prayer is not just an article of faith. It is not merely a fact of history. It is a present reality. His promises are the same as ever and just as dependable. He still undertakes to hear His people and to answer them in all the ways outlined above.

Source of Comfort and Confidence

The fact that God still answers prayer is a source of comfort. It tells us that we are not left alone to struggle with the impersonal forces of fate or chance. It reminds us that our God is sovereign. He is in control. He is all-seeing, all-knowing, and all-powerful. He *can* answer prayer.

The fact that God still answers prayer is also a source of confidence. Not only can He answer prayer, He *will* answer prayer. John assures us, "This is the confidence that we have in him, that, if we ask any thing according to his will, he heareth us: and if we know that he hear us, whatsoever we ask, we know that we have the petitions that we desired of him" (1 John 5:14–15). It is because such a confidence is well grounded that the Bible exhorts us to pray: "Having therefore, brethren, boldness to enter into the holiest by the blood of Jesus, by a new and living way, which he hath consecrated for us, through the veil, that is to say, his flesh; and having an high priest over the house of God; let us draw near with a true heart in full assurance of faith" (Hebrews 10:19–22). *Boldness* in this text means "confidence." In his famous commentary on Hebrews, John Brown suggests that Paul means that because we have confidence in Christ's entrance into the presence of God to act as our high priest, we may draw near to God in prayer with full assurance. Either way—whether Paul is referring to our confidence in entering or our confidence in Christ's having entered for us—Christians who approach God "with a true heart" should have "full assurance of faith" that He will hear them.

God Answers Us As an All-Wise Father
Answers a Needy Child

The Lord is both lavish and loving in His responses to the cries of His people. But He is also purposeful. We are mere children. At best, we see very little of the great scheme of things or of the place our particular circumstances play in it. We tend to make everything revolve around our personal feelings at any given time and to think that we must have what we feel we need and that we must have it at once. Every parent recognizes this pattern in his own children, and every good parent therefore recognizes that his response must take more than the child's keenly felt desires into consideration. A father who gives his child everything he asks for, however foolish the request may be, is abdicating his responsibility, betraying his child, and hurting rather than helping him.

God is our Father. He hears our prayers and answers them. But in doing so He follows a clearly stated purpose. He aims at more than our instant gratification. There are times when it is good and beneficial for Him to grant us precisely what we feel we need—witness the illustrations given above. However, this is not always the case. God's chief aim in all He does is His own glory, and this is His supreme end in answering our prayers. Subordinate to that end, He pursues other objectives for our true and ultimate good.

God often answers prayer in ways that are different from—and better than—what we envisage. Archibald Naismith, in his *Notes Quotes and Anecdotes,* quotes from an anonymous but wise source: "He was a Christian and he prayed. He asked for strength to do greater things, but He was given infirmity that he might do better things. He asked for power that he might have the praise of men; he was given weakness that he might feel the need of God." To produce this feeling of the need of God, not just as a source of gifts and gratification, but as the very essence and reason for our living, is one of the great ends the Lord has in answering prayer. He so deals with us that we may confess with Asaph, who had struggled with doubt in the face of the apparent ease of the wicked and the suffering of the saints: "Whom have I in heaven but thee? and there is none upon earth that I desire beside thee. My flesh and my heart faileth: but God is the strength of my heart, and my portion for ever" (Psalm 73:25–26).

Paul expressed the same sentiment when he prayed, "that I may know him, and the power of his resurrection, and the fellowship of his sufferings, being made conformable unto his death" (Philippians 3:10). A chief end of God's answering prayer is, therefore, the great work of conforming us to the image of Christ, even though it entails "the fellowship of his sufferings."

At the beginning of this chapter we posed some searching questions about the contrast between the stated faith of Christians that God answers prayer and their personal experience. Perhaps now we may begin to see that what we face in those times when God either denies our request or delays fulfilling it, is actually the loving exercise of our all-wise Father's good will as He works out the big picture of His purpose.

While there are issues that are beyond our grasp, we may nevertheless be assured that as our heavenly Father, the Lord will always hear us when we bring certain matters before Him. He promises to answer us when we cry for necessary *provision.* Jesus said, "If ye then, being evil, know how to give good gifts unto your children, how much more shall your Father which is in heaven give good things to them that ask him?" (Matthew 7:11).

He also undertakes to answer our cry for *protection:* "Fear thou not; for I am with thee: be not dismayed; for I am thy God: I will strengthen thee; yea, I will help thee; yea, I will uphold thee with the right hand of my righteousness.... Fear not, thou worm Jacob, and ye men of Israel; I will help thee, saith the Lord, and thy redeemer, the Holy One of Israel" (Isaiah 41:10, 14). It has to be said that a promise like this at once raises questions as to why then God allows some of His people to die in an accident or to be brutalized or even murdered. Foolish people often say that it must be because of some sin or unbelief in the life of the victim, but this is nonsense. Peter and Paul were murdered by enemies of Christ, and certainly it was because of godliness, not sin, that they died. Did God fail to protect them? No, for He had already made it clear that martyrdom was part of His way of accomplishing His purpose in and through them. We do not always have such a clear statement of God's purpose, but we should still believe that He has not abandoned us or failed to protect us when bad things happen to us. However difficult it is for us to grasp—and it is very difficult—these are some of the occasions when the Lord is working out a greater purpose than we can see. So we should continue to invoke His protection with confidence. Had we eyes to see, we would understand that He stands guard over us continually and delivers us from disasters and from the evil one times without number.

The Lord also always answers our prayers for *instruction*. David prayed, "Shew me thy ways, O Lord; teach me thy paths. Lead me in thy truth, and teach me: for thou art the God of my salvation; on thee do I wait all the day" (Psalm 25:4–5). That is a prayer that the Lord will answer. David was well assured of this: "The meek will he guide in judgment: and the meek will he teach his way" (Psalm 25:9). God does not undertake to give us understanding of every deep matter or the answer to every theological or philosophical complexity. Nor does He promise to give us supernaturally what we should arrive at by diligent study. What He promises is the aid of His Spirit to us as we submit to His guidance. This matter of our submitting to His guidance is, of course, the reason good men come to different conclusions, all believing that they have the mind of the Lord. None of us is perfect in his submission, none free from the prejudices of the flesh. But it is gratifying to see that for all their imperfections, God's people enjoy unanimity on the essential issues of the gospel. The Lord so supervises the instruction of His people that none of them espouses what Peter terms "damnable heresies" (2 Peter 2:1), what we may call "heresies of perdition."

Another prayer the Lord always delights to answer is our cry for spiritual *maturity*. Communion with God aims at conformity to Him and His will. Prayer is a vital part of the means to effect that conformity. When Paul prayed for the Lord to remove his "thorn in the flesh," it appeared that the Lord failed to answer. The thorn remained, but the Lord answered Paul nonetheless. This was one of those cases that we have already mentioned in which the Lord was pursuing a greater purpose. Mark carefully God's response to Paul and Paul's response to God's answer: "For this thing [the thorn in the flesh] I besought the Lord thrice, that it might depart from me. And he said unto me, My grace is sufficient for thee: for my strength is made perfect in weakness. Most gladly therefore will I rather glory in my infirmities, that the power of Christ may rest upon me" (2 Corinthians 12:8–9). Here is maturity indeed! Paul said, in effect, "If I have to choose between being freed from my suffering and continuing to suffer but having the experience of God's all-sufficient grace to sustain me, I will choose the suffering. If the means of having the power of Christ in my life is the presence of constant pain that keeps my flesh humble, I will gladly embrace that pain. If I must be kept weak that the strength of Christ may work through me to the glory of God, then I happily choose to be weak."

This gives us another way of looking at the problem of unanswered prayer in the lives of people who count it an article of faith to believe that their God answers prayer. A large part of the problem arises from the fact that we too often ask immaturely, prematurely, and even ignorantly. Nowhere more than in the place of prayer do we need to be governed and guided by the Holy Spirit. Paul called attention to the twin hindrances of infirmity and ignorance in the place of prayer and showed that it is by the ministry of the Holy Spirit that we may overcome them: "The Spirit also helpeth our infirmities: for we know not what we should pray for as we ought: but the Spirit itself maketh intercession for us with groanings which cannot be uttered" (Romans 8:26).

Only the Holy Spirit can enable us to rise above the dictates of our nature to embrace the will of God. We have thought of God's answer to the prayers of Monica for her son Augustine. It was good and right that she should cry for his salvation, but it was in ignorance that she pleaded that the Lord stop him from going to Rome. As Augustine himself noted in his *Confessions,* the Lord "denied her special request to grant her life-long request," for through going to Rome he was saved. It is only as we are brought by the Holy Spirit to embrace His will that we can truly pray, for the Father knows and welcomes the mind of the Spirit as being entirely at one with His own (Romans 8:27).

When we apply all this to a case such as Paul's prayer for the removal of the thorn in his flesh—a thorn that God allowed to remain, despite repeated prayer—we can see the wisdom of Bishop Handley Moule's remarks on the words "He that searcheth the hearts knoweth what is the mind of the Spirit" (Romans 8:27): "Knoweth—and meeteth with a corresponding answer; crossing perhaps the saint's *explicit* prayer, but granting the *implicit.*"

With this truth established we are now in a position to make one final important point.

God's Answers to Our Prayers Follow Directly from Our Communion with Him

Christ's words in our text make it abundantly clear that God's answers to our prayers follow directly from our communion with Him: "When thou prayest, enter into thy closet, and when thou hast shut thy door, pray to thy Father which is in secret; and thy Father which seeth in secret shall reward thee openly." Ultimately, this truth answers every difficulty we encounter with unanswered prayer. It will reveal where we fail in prayer through growing cold in the place of personal communion with God. It will show us where we fail because we have prayed either without knowledge of God's will or in defiance of it. Communion with God is the key to enjoying the privilege of having our prayers answered. The reasons for this have already been suggested.

When we truly commune with God we submit our understanding to His mind. He knows our need and understands everything about the matters we bring before Him. He not only knows the problem but also the best way of responding to it. He knows best how to answer us and may therefore substitute something better than what we asked of Him. Paul rejoiced that the Lord "is able to do exceeding abundantly above all that we ask or think" (Ephesians 3:20). Our great aim in prayer must be to grasp what the mind of God is on the matter and to pray accordingly. George Müller made this the secret of his whole prayer life. When we get to know the mind of God and submit to it, we will have our prayers answered.

When we truly commune with God, we will submit our will to His will. Our Lord taught us to pray, "Thy will be done." We should recognize the danger of willfulness in our praying. The Israelites were willful in their demands on the Lord, and "he gave them their request; but sent leanness into their soul" (Psalm 106:15). Sometimes the greatest good the Lord can do for us is *not* to answer us as we have asked and instead to bring our foolish wills into submission to His will. Elijah foolishly demanded to be allowed to die, but the Lord denied his prayer. Instead He slowly brought the distraught prophet to the place of hearing His "still small voice" and of being willing to do His will. As a result, instead of dying in failure and depression, Elijah lived to anoint Elisha as his successor and then was translated directly into heaven. He is eternally grateful that the Lord denied his willful request and instead brought his will into conformity to his Master's!

We should rejoice that we are not left slaves to the willfulness of our own flesh and that our God has made it possible for us to know and do His will. We have already thought of what the apostle John said about this subject (1 John 5:14–15). We may know God's will, we should know God's will, and we should pray accordingly. Such knowledge arises out of deep, personal communion with God in the diligent, prayerful study of His word under the guidance of His Spirit.

When we truly commune with God, we will aim at His glory and not merely at our own gain or comfort. "Hallowed be thy name" must permeate all our praying. Everything must serve the glory of our God. This is not only our chief purpose in praying; it is our only reason for existing. "Thou art worthy, O Lord, to receive glory and honour and power: for thou hast created all things, and for thy pleasure they are [or, *exist*] and were created" (Revelation 4:11). Aiming at the glory of God in prayer helps us to see that there is no contradiction between the Lord's unconditional and conditional promises to answer our prayers. On the one hand we read, "Whatsoever ye shall ask in my name, that will I do" (John 14:13). On the other hand we read, "But let him ask in faith, nothing wavering. For he that wavereth is like a wave of the sea driven with the wind and tossed. For let not that man think that he shall receive any thing of the Lord" (James 1:6–7). Or we read, "If we ask any thing according to his will, he heareth us" (1 John 5:14). At first it may appear that the conditional promises are meant to modify or water down the unconditional. This is not the case. In the language of true prayer, *asking* means asking in faith (which is not make-believe, or a forcing of oneself to believe, but a receptive response to something God has revealed), and *asking in faith* is just another way of saying we are asking according to God's will.

When we cannot understand why the Lord does something or why He refrains from doing something, we must say, as our Saviour did, "Even so, Father: for so it seemed good in thy sight" (Matthew 11:26). With this confidence we will see that what we have been wont to think of as unanswered prayer is God's way of giving us a better answer—one that achieves a higher purpose or that delays His answer to a better time—and all for the greater glory of His own name.

God does answer prayer. He answers us as our all-wise heavenly Father. And His answers to us follow naturally on our communion with Him. This is what encourages us to pray. Paradoxically, it is also what makes prayer so difficult, for if God answers prayer that arises out of deep communion with Him, isn't it obvious that Satan will employ every device to keep us from true prayer? He will seek to confuse us, to turn our prayer time into a "name-it-and-claim-it" recitation of a laundry list of demands, or to make it an expression of selfishness instead of a humble seeking after God. He will endeavor to get us so taken up with ourselves and our wants that we have little yearning to enter into deep and true communion with our God simply for the joy of knowing Him. Thus the place of prayer for God's people will always be a battleground, indeed the chief battleground of life here on earth. But it will also be a blessed ground, for communion with God is the birthright of all the redeemed. So let us obey the command of our Saviour and pray to our Father in the certainty that our Father answers prayer.

6

The Comfort and Confidence of Knowing That God Knows

"Be not ye therefore like unto them: for your Father knoweth what things ye have need of, before ye ask him." Matthew 6:8

The only kind of repetition in prayer that the Lord Jesus Christ condemns is vain, or empty, repetition. Not for a moment does He condemn the repeated cries of a heart in agony or of a soul that is aflame with devotion and adoration to God. As long as the lips express the active thinking of the mind and the earnest yearning of the heart, they are not uttering vain repetition. It is important to grasp this because too often God's people feel guilty about repeatedly using the same words or making the same requests in prayer. But the fact that a prayer is repeated does not mean that it is vain or condemned by the Lord. The Lord Jesus commands us to repeat the very words of the Lord's Prayer: "When ye pray, say, Our Father, which art in heaven," and so on.

The word of God supplies many examples of godly repetition in prayer. Repetition may be the continued expression of a heart's desire, thus denoting *intensity*. It may signify a *deepening awareness* of the nature and urgency of the soul's need. Or it may express the *reiterated faithfulness* of a soul in the face of repeated assaults from Satan. Take Daniel's great prayer (Daniel 9) as an example of godly repetition in prayer. Verses 5–11 show the prophet's deepening awareness of the calamitous situation of his people and record his repeated confession of sin. A carnal mind may say that it is enough to confess, "We have sinned," but in the agony of his soul and in the depths of his yearning, Daniel cries, "We have sinned, and have committed iniquity, and have done wickedly, and have rebelled, even by departing from thy precepts and from thy judgments" (verse 5). Piling one statement upon another, he proceeds to restate the sins of his people. But this is not vain repetition. Feel the intensity of Daniel's prayer as he cries, "O Lord, hear; O Lord, forgive; O Lord, hearken and do; defer not, for thine own sake, O my God: for thy city and thy people are called by thy name" (verse 19). This is certainly not vain repetition. Another example is the prayer of the Lord Jesus Christ in the Garden of Gethsemane. For long hours he agonized in prayer. His words were as few as His feelings were deep. The spiritual conflict He endured was the most acute in the history of the world as Satan concentrated every ounce of hell's energy against the mind and heart of the Son of God. Such was the intensity of the conflict that Christ's "sweat was as it were great drops of blood falling down to the ground" (Luke 22:44). Already burdened in soul almost to the point of death before He entered the severest part of His agony (Matthew 26:38), He felt that He would die unless His Father intervened. Thus He cried, "O my Father, if it be possible, let this cup pass from me: nevertheless not as I will, but as thou wilt....He went away again the second time, and prayed, saying, O my Father, if this cup may not pass away from me, except I drink it, thy will be done" (Matthew 26:39, 42). Finding His disciples asleep, He "went away again, and prayed the third time, saying the same words" (verse 44). So there is nothing wrong in repeating the words in prayer as long as they are the outpouring of the feelings and faith of the heart. All such praying is good. We can never have too much of it.

But we must never fall into the habit of the vain repetition of saying words with our minds disengaged. Repetition that is mindless and thoughtless is heathen, not Christian. It is based on a wrong view of God and on a wrong view of prayer. The heathen's entire concept of how to get something from God is shameful and has no place in a Christian's life. To heathens, God is a remote deity, one they must render willing to help them. God is one from whom they must extract a blessing as from an unwilling giver, and to do so they must seek to make a large impression on Him. One way to do that is to pray. But since they feel remote from their God, they know only the ritual of fear, the meaningless form of repetitive prayers, and by that very repetition a self-induced sense of euphoria achieved by disengaging the mind through hypnotic incantations. That is the heathen attitude to prayer, and Jesus says, "Be ye not therefore like unto them."

True prayer, Christian prayer, is not a mantra to be chanted or incanted. Some professedly evangelical leaders—notably the South Korean who boasts the world's largest church—have promoted certain Buddhist techniques as powerful prayer tools. Many people, largely found in or influenced by the Charismatic Movement, repeatedly use the name *Jesus* as if it were a charm. Such mindless incantation is not true prayer. True prayer is the humble, simple, and sincere approach of a child of God to his Father in heaven, in the confidence that his Father loves him and hears him. We do not need to convince the Lord to hear us. We do not have to extort something from an unwilling God. When we tell the Lord of our needs, we do not do so to inform Him of them. We do so that we may pray with intelligence, meaning, and purpose. But, as our Saviour made clear, He knows all about them, even before we have recognized them clearly enough to make them a matter of prayer. So we don't need to repeat ourselves like heathens in the hope of drawing God's attention to our situation.

The underlying truth of our text is that the effectiveness of prayer does not lie in the words we employ or in their repetition. Rather it depends on the Lord, His paternal relationship to us, His infinite resources, His wisdom, and His willingness to meet our needs. This is the plain teaching of the Lord Jesus Christ in Matthew 6, and His purpose in setting forth this great truth is to give us comfort and confidence in our communion with God. Thus we may say that the subject before us in Matthew 6:8 is that we may find comfort and confidence in knowing that our Father knows.

The Lord Has His People in Mind

The Lord always has His children in His mind. Without doubt the words *Your Father knoweth what things ye have need of, before ye ask him* reflect an aspect of the omniscience of God. But the Lord Jesus does not here make the general truth of God's omniscience the basis of our comfort and confidence in prayer. That is not to say that it does not afford comfort and confidence. It does. God's knowing all we need before we ask Him raises the whole question of His divine sovereignty, foreknowledge, and eternal purpose. The carnal mind argues that if God foreknows, predestinates, and purposes whatever comes to pass, there is no need to pray. Nothing could be further from the truth. Our Lord clearly teaches us that God's sovereignty is the very thing that will help us to pray. We do not pray to an impotent God, who is sitting in heaven with a furrowed brow, wringing His hands and lamenting, "O, I wish there were something I could do about the terrible situation down there on earth." No, we pray to the God of glory, the everlasting King, the Creator and Sovereign of heaven, earth, and hell, the omniscient and omnipotent Jehovah. So the idea of God's omniscience is not a hindrance but a help to prayer.

The Saviour is not making that general truth the basis of our comfort and confidence in prayer, however. He does not say, "Your Father knows all things," but, "Your Father knows what things *you* have need of." In other words, "God's mind is not just on all things, which is true, but His mind is particularly on you. He knows your needs. His eye is upon you. His heart is with you. His purpose is favorable to you. His love embraces you. His promise includes you. His grace sustains you. His power energizes you. The Father always keeps His children in mind." The psalmist David found great comfort in this truth: "I am poor and needy; yet the Lord thinketh upon me" (Psalm 40:17). What a glorious truth! Scientists are always telling us how vast the universe is, and it is incredibly vast. In comparison to the immense greatness of the universe, the earth is like a grain of sand on the seashore. And amid all the billions who have ever lived on earth each of us is infinitesimally small. In any other scheme of things but the biblical—certainly in the atheistic, evolutionary scheme—we are both insignificant and meaningless, random fragments in an endless chain of chance. The truth is far otherwise. However insignificant we may be, we may confidently affirm, "The Lord thinketh on me," not just giving me a passing thought but keeping me in His mind and surrounding my existence with His loving purpose. "Many, O Lord my God, are thy wonderful works which thou hast done, and thy thoughts which are to usward: they cannot be reckoned up in order unto thee: if I would declare and speak of them, they are more than can be numbered" (Psalm 40:5).

We are never out of our Father's thoughts: "Can a woman forget her sucking child, that she should not have compassion on the son of her womb? yea, they may forget, yet will I not forget thee" (Isaiah 49:15). "I will not forget thee"—what joy and comfort this brings when we are overwhelmed by life's troubles. When Job was suffering indescribable physical pain, mental turmoil, and spiritual conflict, he found consolation in the truth that "He knoweth the way that I take" (Job 23:10).

At times we are tempted to think that God has forgotten us. Job did. So did the psalmist Asaph. In a bleak but ultimately blessed Psalm he asks, "Will the Lord cast off for ever? and will he be favourable no more? Is his mercy clean gone for ever? doth his promise fail for evermore? Hath God forgotten to be gracious? hath he in anger shut up his tender mercies?" (Psalm 77:7–9). There are times in life when we feel we need an immediate answer and we don't receive it. We feel that we need heaven to open to us and it remains closed. Then we are prone to depressing doubts and fears like Asaph's. Why is God deaf to my cry and silent when I cry for Him to answer me? Has He given me up? Has he forgotten to be gracious? We feel that God has forgotten us.

At such a time the Lord asks a probing question: "Why sayest thou, O Jacob, and speakest, O Israel, My way is hid from the Lord, and my judgment is passed over from my God?" (Isaiah 40:27). Why do we say it? Let us face the question. Have God's word and promise changed? Has His purpose changed? Has the merit of Christ been destroyed or even lessened? Never! Why then do we say, "My way is hid from the Lord" or imagine that our Father has forgotten us? It is because of how we feel about our circumstances. Have our feelings never been wrong before? Have we never misread our circumstances before? As we noted in the last chapter, we are mere children, and as children we often think that we know what we need and when we need it, only to find out a little later that we were mistaken. Thus, whatever we are called upon to endure, we should remember our Saviour's words, "Your Father knows." He has us always in mind. Every time Israel's high priest appeared before God he bore the names of the children of Israel in two places — on his shoulders and on the breastplate over his heart. What a picture of Christ, our great high priest! With all the strength of His infinite merit and with all the love of His eternal grace, He constantly bears the names of His people before His Father. Unless the Father can ignore His Son, He must have His people ever in mind.

The Lord Has Our Situation in Hand

The Lord knows what we need, and He has our situation in hand. "Your Father knoweth what things ye have need of before you ask him." The One who rewards true prayer (verse 6) knows what we need. In His sovereign wisdom our Father is working out all our circumstances for our good and for His glory. "As for God, his way is perfect: the word of the Lord is tried: he is a buckler to all those that trust in him.... It is God that girdeth me with strength, and maketh my way perfect" (Psalm 18:30, 32). God's way is perfect and He is working in and through all the circumstances of our lives to make our way perfect. In Scripture, Joseph is perhaps the most outstanding example of this truth in operation. Joseph was a man of God, a man of prayer. He was a man to whom God revealed great things and to whom He made glorious promises. On the strength of those promises and revelations Joseph declared the mind of God to his ungodly brethren. As a result they threw him into a pit and began to plot his murder. Knowing what they were planning, Joseph piteously cried for mercy. But they callously ignored his pleas, though the memory of that voice would never leave them. Years later, long after they had sold him into slavery in place of killing him, they felt the guilt of what they had done, "and they said one to another, We are verily guilty concerning our brother, in that we saw the anguish of his soul, when he besought us, and we would not hear" (Genesis 42:21). That was a sore trial for Joseph, who had ventured all on the promise of God.

Even more trying was the fact that God also appeared deaf to his cry. We read, "Joseph ... was sold for a servant: whose feet they hurt with fetters: he was laid in iron: until the time that his word came: the word of the Lord tried him" (Psalm 105:17–19). *The word of the Lord tried him.* Joseph could not forget the promises that God made to him, but despite those promises he was cast into a pit, carried away as a slave, falsely accused, thrown into prison, and left there to rot, apparently forgotten by both God and man. But appearances were wrong, as they always are when they contradict the word of God. God had not forgotten Joseph. His word was trying him and equipping him for the great work of his life. Through all the years of trial and of suffering, slavery, false accusation, imprisonment, and neglect the Lord was working in grace. Joseph himself came to realize that his sufferings were neither accidental nor meaningless. They were not even to be attributed solely to the malice of man, for God was overruling every circumstance in His all-wise grace. As Joseph told his brothers, "Ye thought evil against me; but God meant it unto good, to bring to pass, as it is this day, to save much people alive" (Genesis 50:20). The Lord had the situation in hand. He always does. Our Father knows. This truth leads us to a third important observation.

The Lord Calls Us to Faith, Not Frenzy

Assuring us that our Father knows our needs, the Lord calls us to faith, not to frenzy. We are not to pray like heathens. At the heart of the repetition of heathen praying lies the frenzy of desperation. One of the great points that John Knox made in his helpful treatise on prayer is that prayer is not an act of desperation. True, we may reach the end of ourselves. All our resources may be removed from us so that we are cast entirely upon God. Even then, however, prayer is not desperation but the lifting up of our urgent needs to our Father in heaven in the assurance that He is our Father, that He knows, and that He will hear us. Such prayer begets faith; it does not produce frenzy. The heathen have every cause to be frenzied, but why should God's redeemed children be so? Why should we feel desperate or hopeless? The apostle Peter encourages us, "Humble yourselves therefore under the mighty hand of God, that he may exalt you in due time: casting all your care upon him; for he careth for you" (1 Peter 5:6–7). The psalmist assures us, "The steps of a good man are ordered by the Lord" (Psalm 37:23). Some of those steps may be steps of suffering or steps into the dark unknown, but they are ordered by the Lord. "He knoweth the way that I take" (Job 23:10).

Thus at times when the heathen naturally feel the frenzy of desperation, believers in Christ have the comfort of faith. David, who had more trouble in his life than most men, used his experience to encourage us: "Cast thy burden upon the Lord, and he shall sustain thee: he shall never suffer the righteous to be moved" (Psalm 55:22). In a home I once visited I saw a needlepoint script that read, "The Lord is able to remove the burden from your shoulders, or He is able to strengthen your shoulders to bear the burden." Either way, He will not suffer the righteous to be moved. D. L. Moody liked to use Isaiah 12:2 as a motto text and was probably inspired to do so by learning of a conversation between two old Scots believers that went something like this: One said to the other, "I love Psalm 56:3, 'What time I am afraid, I will trust in thee.'" His friend replied, "Yes, that is good, but personally I prefer Isaiah 12:2, 'Behold, God is my salvation; I will trust, and not be afraid: for the Lord Jehovah is my strength and my song; he also is become my salvation.'" It is the privilege of every Christian to be delivered from the frenzy of the heathen and to live in the confidence of such faith.

A Comfort that Sustains

In the light of all this, praying in the knowledge that our Father knows will comfort and sustain us as God deals with us in great wisdom and grace. It will enable us to endure the burden we are called to bear. It will encourage us to rest assured that God will answer wisely and well. It will equip us to receive the answer that He sends.

God knows our needs; often we do not. We need to have our viewpoint changed so that we look at things from the perspective of eternity, not of time. Often, we need to have our desires modified; that is, we need to get beyond merely expressing the desires of the flesh. To do that we must have our understanding brought into line with our Father's knowledge. We need to have our wills submitted to His will. And we need to have a single eye to the glory of God, so that even our own suffering or comfort will take second place to the glory of God. Remember how Job suffered and complained bitterly that God was afflicting him without cause. Then the Lord began to speak to Job. He did not tell him why He allowed him to suffer. Rather, He showed him something of the greatness of His wisdom, power, and glory. As the Lord spoke to him, Job was still suffering—the boils had not gone away, the wracking physical pain had not been alleviated, he was still bereft of all his wealth and all his children, and God had not spoken a word about restoring any of his losses to him. Physically, he was as badly off as when he had been complaining. But now he was so taken up with the glory of God that he had no complaints. Confession, yes; complaint, no. He knew his Father knew.

For the same reason the apostle Paul said, "[I] now rejoice in my sufferings for you, and fill up that which is behind of the afflictions of Christ in my flesh for his body's sake, which is the church" (Colossians 1:24). When people tried to keep him back from going to Jerusalem because they feared that he would suffer and die there, he said, "What mean ye to weep and to break mine heart? for I am ready not to be bound only, but also to die at Jerusalem for the name of the Lord Jesus" (Acts 21:13). Paul had great comfort and confidence, whatever his situation or surroundings. Writing to the Philippians he said, "To me to live is Christ, and to die is gain" (Philippians 1:21). For Paul, living meant affliction, suffering, pain, and being stoned until he was bloodied, broken, and left for dead. It meant being ostracized by his fellow countrymen and disowned by many of the Christian churches that he had established. Finally, it meant shipwreck, imprisonment, and death. But to Paul, living meant much more than all of these. It meant Christ. John Calvin understood Paul's words as meaning, "Whether I live or die, Christ is my gain." Having such an assurance, the apostle had no complaints. He knew that God was dealing with him in perfect wisdom and grace. He knew that the Lord knew all about him, and that knowledge enabled him to live, not in despair, but in Christian confidence and joy.

We can experience that same confidence and joy as the fruit of knowing that our Father knows.

The Structure of the Model Prayer

"After this manner therefore pray ye: Our Father which art in heaven, Hallowed be thy name. Thy kingdom come. Thy will be done in earth, as it is in heaven. Give us this day our daily bread. And forgive us our debts, as we forgive our debtors. And lead us not into temptation, but deliver us from evil: for thine is the kingdom, and the power, and the glory, for ever. Amen."
Matthew 6:9–13

How we pray depends on how well we learn the lessons that the Lord Jesus Christ teaches us in Matthew 6:5–8, where He tells us not to pray like hypocrites or heathens. He commands us to pray without ostentation, without calling public attention to our secret devotions. He instructs us to get alone with God and seek true communion with our Father who is in secret and who sees in secret. Now the Saviour says, "After this manner therefore pray ye" (verse 9), and goes on to give us what we generally call the Lord's Prayer. If we should ask *how* we should pray, *what* we should pray, and *why* we should pray, here is Christ's answer.

This prayer is a pattern for all our praying. The Lord Jesus Christ clearly intended it to be so. In many ways it covers all the ground that we need to cover in prayer, not exhaustively but suggestively or representatively. It introduces us to categories of praying, patterns of thought in prayer that, properly understood, will cover all our earthly experience. This means that no matter how well we know the familiar words of the Lord's Prayer, we have much more to learn about it. However deeply we have entered into it, we have yet greater depths to plumb. The Lord's Prayer, then, will repay a lifetime of study and of diligent application.

The Lord's Prayer is peculiarly a prayer for the children of God, as is plain from its opening words, *Our Father.* Only God's children, those born of His

Spirit and rightly related to Him through Jesus Christ, have an assured access to God. To them alone belong the Bible's great prayer promises. That is not to say that God never hears the cry of an ungodly man. To say that would be unscriptural and untrue, for the grace of God is greater than men deserve and even than Christians can conceive. But the comfort of access to the throne of grace amid the trials and troubles of life belongs exclusively to God's children, to those who can honestly address Him as "Our Father."

It is so obvious that the Lord's Prayer is to be prayed by God's children that it comes as a shock to realize that there are some who deny it any place in Christian worship, whether public or private. Some dispensationalists maintain a determined opposition to placing this prayer in the mouths of Christians. A prominent evangelist of this school who is personally known to me was indignant when he found that his mother had taught his children the words of the Lord's Prayer. To him, it has no place in the "church age" but belongs to the "kingdom age." He says it is Jewish, not Christian. Those who adopt such views use two main arguments—though their main argument is their theory of its place in their preconceived dispensational scheme. First, they argue that this cannot be a Christian prayer because it contains no mention of the name of Christ. Secondly, they argue that this prayer places those who use it on the ground of law rather than grace because it says, "Forgive us our debts, as we forgive our debtors" (verse 12).

There is no merit in either argument. As to the first—the absence of the name of Christ—remember that the pattern is not exhaustive but suggestive. The Lord Jesus left His specific instruction on the matter of praying in His name until the end of His ministry, until the time His disciples could benefit from it. Furthermore, it would be a dangerous misinterpretation of Scripture to remove from the church the seminal teaching of the Saviour on a subject by isolating it from the fuller treatment He and His apostles later gave it. For example, on the subject of divorce Paul specifically states that he is addressing aspects of the subject that the Lord did not deal with (1 Corinthians 7:12; compare verse 10). No one would dream of saying that because the Lord Jesus did not mention the aspects of the subject that Paul later introduced, His teaching has no place in the Christian church. Yet that is the very logic that is employed with reference to the Lord's Prayer: Because the name of Jesus is not specifically mentioned in it—and we know that later Christ and the apostles teach us to pray in that name—the Lord's Prayer cannot be admitted as Christian. The idea is as devoid of logical force as it is of theological merit. Also, it fails to note that the very formula it insists on, praying in the name of Christ, is not at all foreign to the Lord's Prayer. Praying in Christ's *name* includes the idea of doing so on His *authority*—and certainly we have His express authority for praying these words.

A final consideration shows that the rejection of the Lord's Prayer as a Christian prayer because it does not mention the name of Jesus is without merit. The last word of the prayer is *Amen*. We will consider the significance of this word in its proper place, but for now we should remember that it is given in Revelation 3: 14 as a name or title of Christ: "These things saith the Amen, the faithful and true witness." *Amen* was the common ending for a prayer for a Jew, and at the time the Lord first taught this prayer, neither the Jews nor the disciples knew that *Amen* was actually a name of Christ. But Christ certainly knew it and knowing it, He included it in the prayer He taught His disciples to pray. Possessing the completed revelation of Scripture, we also know it, so that when we conclude the Lord's Prayer as the Lord Jesus commanded us — with the *Amen* — it is tantamount to saying, "We ask these things in His name." That is true Christian praying.

The second objection — that the Lord's Prayer teaches us to seek forgiveness for our sins on the basis of law not grace — is even further from the truth. If it were not for the fact that Christians are often better than their stated theology, I would be tempted to write off such a charge as blasphemous. To say that Christ taught His people to pray for forgiveness on the ground or merit of their own forgiving spirit is repugnant to the whole of Scripture. To state this assertion is to refute it. There never was a time when God forgave people on the basis of law or when any man could obtain pardon because of his personal obedience to the law.

Forgiveness has always been on the ground of grace. It has always been imparted according to the covenant of grace that God eternally established in His Son and that He executed in history on the merits of Christ's atoning blood. Pardon has always been on the ground of grace. That was so throughout the period of the Old Testament. "Without shedding of blood" there never was remission of sins (Hebrews 9:22). Nor was it the merit of the blood of animal sacrifices that procured forgiveness. The law "can never with those sacrifices which they offered year by year continually make the comers thereunto perfect.... For it is not possible that the blood of bulls and of goats should take away sins" (Hebrews 10:1, 4). All forgiveness has always been on the merit of the blood of Christ. The Bible knows no other merit on which God remits the sins of men (Romans 3: 25). So in the Lord's Prayer the Lord Jesus does not teach pardon on the basis of law. This is not some sub-Christian prayer. The very idea that Christ could teach anything that is sub-Christian is preposterous. So let us make it abundantly clear that this prayer does not belong to some past or future Jewish dispensation, but to the people of God throughout the ages.

The Lord's Prayer is a *model* prayer and the Lord Jesus meant us to use it in two ways. First, He meant us to pray it as He gave it, that is, to use it word for word. The parallel passage in Luke 11:2 records His command, "When ye pray, say," followed by the words of this prayer. Dr. Martyn Lloyd-Jones said,

"I have always been comforted by this thought, that whatever I may forget in my own private prayers, as long as I pray the Lord's Prayer I have at any rate covered all the principles. On the condition, of course, that I am not merely mechanically repeating the words, but am really praying from my heart and with my mind and with my whole being" (*Studies in the Sermon on the Mount,* Eerdmans, [1981], vol. 2, p. 50). This last point is well worth emphasizing.

While we are to use the words of the Lord's Prayer, we are to *pray* them, not mindlessly recite them. We are not meant to repeat them while our minds are engaged on some other subject. We are to come to God with our minds fully engaged in our praying, and if we do so we will benefit greatly from using the very words of the Lord's Prayer. That is the first way in which the Lord meant us to use it. The second way in which He meant us to use this model prayer was as a basis for all our praying: "After this manner therefore pray ye." According to Luke 11:1, Jesus gave His disciples the Lord's Prayer in response to their request, "Lord, teach us to pray." This model prayer, then, is a lesson in praying from the greatest master of prayer of all time, the Son of God Himself, the one who could say, "I [know] thou hearest me always" (John 11:42), the one who never had a prayer unanswered.

The Master here teaches us how to engage in the most important spiritual work that any man can do. In Matthew 6 the Lord Jesus speaks of a number of important matters, such as the giving of alms and fasting, but prayer is our most important engagement with God. It is prayer that gives validity to those other spiritual exercises. It is prayer that is the measure of our maturity and the gauge of our spiritual growth. We cannot be greater in any area than we are on our knees. Yet must we not confess that this is the very place where we feel weakest? Some people speak of prayer as if it were the easiest thing in the world. It is not. Indeed, it is the most difficult. It is more difficult than Bible study or preaching or taking the most difficult seminary course. It is in the place of prayer that the flesh most needs curbing, for it is there that it will be most active. It is there that the old man will rise up in all his depravity to hinder our doing business with God. And it is in the place of prayer that Satan most needs crushing. Indeed if we truly learn to pray and get real victory here, we will be able to live victoriously and usefully in every other phase of life.

All this makes the subject matter of the Lord's Prayer one of vital significance for every Christian. Here we have His pattern for our praying. In this chapter we will take an overview of the prayer, noting its structure. In the next chapter we will continue the overview by noting the prayer's leading features.

Fact of Structure

The Lord's Prayer is structured, very beautifully structured. In our first study we noted the force of Christ's command in verse 7, "Use not vain repetitions, as the heathen do: for they think that they shall be heard for their much speaking." To use vain repetitions is to gabble, as when we become what Americans picturesquely term a "motor mouth," when we multiply words with little or no thought of what we are saying or why we are saying it. Some evangelicals have such a detestation of read or formal prayers that even in public worship they eschew all structure in their praying. Preachers who would count it sacrilege to stand before men without a thoughtful and structured sermon think nothing of standing before God without the slightest thought or preparation of what they are to say to Him. We must not make the mistake of equating sincerity with gabbling or wandering incoherently in prayer. The Scriptures command us, "Be not rash with thy mouth, and let not thine heart be hasty to utter any thing before God: for God is in heaven, and thou upon earth: therefore let thy words be few" (Ecclesiastes 5:2). The psalmist had a similar thought when he prayed, "Set a watch, O Lord, before my mouth; keep the door of my lips" (Psalm 141:3).

Three Deductions from Structure

The fact that Christ gives us a structured model for our praying teaches us that prayer is the result of deep thought, deep feeling, and deep faith. Consider these principles.

First, true prayer is the result of deep thought. It is not haphazard. It is spontaneous, which does not mean that it comes without thought, but that it is the product of our own will or volition. It is free, not forced; thoughtful, not trifling. We should guard true spontaneity in prayer. The practice of reducing either our private or public praying to the formulas of a prayer book carries real danger. Reading prayers (usually written by others) may easily numb the mind and may degenerate into vain repetition. It is all too easy to wallow in vague generalizations in prayer or to let beauty of expression replace passion. Spontaneity is essential to true prayer. But true spontaneity means that our praying comes from the depths of our soul and that it is the product of deep thought. That is why the reading and devotional study of God's word should precede our praying. According to his assistant minister, the great English Baptist preacher Dr. Alexander Maclaren set aside an hour every morning to saturate his soul with the devotional message of a passage of Scripture. Having allowed the words of Scripture to penetrate his heart and guide his thoughts, he was ready to pray.

Second, true prayer is the result of deep feeling. It confesses our need and expresses our desire. It comes from the heart and burns with the passion of genuine spiritual longing. Proceeding from the depths of our being, it can never be reduced to a cold, mechanical ritual. In the place of prayer, "deep answers unto deep," as out of the depths of our need we cry to our Father who hears us out of the depths of His compassion.

Third, true prayer is the result of deep faith. This is evident from how the Lord Jesus climaxes the Lord's Prayer: "For thine is the kingdom, and the power, and the glory, for ever. Amen" (Mathew 6:13). Notice the word *for* at the beginning of this ascription. Why do we pray? Because we believe that God is and that He is our Father. Because we believe that God is and that He has the kingdom. He has the power and He has the glory. That is our faith. It is our vision of God—the grasp we have of His greatness, glory, purpose, and power—that enables us to pray. A person with little idea of what God is will have little idea how to pray. But the person who has come to God's word and thought deeply upon it will have such a spiritual vision of God that his prayer will proceed from genuine faith.

Three Parts of the Structure

While we must not make the mistake of reducing prayer to a merely mechanical, or even a literary, composition, we should not fail to give our full attention to the things that make up real prayer. According to the example Christ gives in the Lord's Prayer, there are three parts to a prayer.

Part One: Invocation

First, there is an invocation. *Invocation* comes from two Latin words, *in,* meaning "in" or "into," and *vocare,* meaning "to call." An invocation is a solemn address to God to call Him into the situation about which we are praying. It focuses on the one we address before considering the things we need. This is a fundamental law of all true prayer: Our hearts and minds must first be taken up with our great and glorious God before we can pray effectively about the matters that burden us. Many of the great prayers recorded in Scripture arose out of circumstances of extreme need or danger and were prayed by people facing life-and-death situations. Given their dire situations, we would expect them to rush into God's presence without much preamble and to clamor for an immediate intervention. But this is not the case. They start by taking time to consider Him to whom they come. Before they present their desires, they worship and let the glory of the God they invoke fill their souls. This is indeed the secret of the greatness of their praying.

In many ways, the beginning of a prayer is the most important part of it. How a man approaches God, how he worships at the beginning of his prayer, reveals a lot about his whole attitude as he comes to God and has a lot to do with his effectiveness in prayer. This does not mean that before we can pray effectively we must be profound theologians. Some of the greatest prayer warriors of all time prayed with great simplicity. John Hyde of India, usually known as "Praying Hyde," and George Müller of Bristol are striking examples of men who prayed very simply, but anyone who has read much about their lives will be struck with the fact that they were men whose minds were saturated with the greatness and glory of God. The American evangelist J. Wilbur Chapman told about meeting John Hyde. Knowing Hyde's power in prayer, Chapman asked the great prayer warrior to pray for him. For five minutes they knelt together and Hyde did not utter a word. Then he lifted his face to heaven and uttered just two words, "O God." He relapsed into silent meditation for some time and then began to pray. Chapman said that Hyde prayed such a prayer for him as he had never before heard, and that God answered the petitions of that prayer in a way that permanently changed his ministry. Hyde took time to have the glory of God fill his soul so that when he made his request it was effective because it was the prayer of faith.

In the British navy it used to be that every ship had its bugler. When a crisis arose the bugler blew a piece that was called "The Still," so named because it was the captain's command for every man to stop and take measure of the situation, to consider and not just react, because much depended on the wisdom of the reaction. The beginning of every prayer is when God as it were puts the bugle to His lips and plays "The Still." As Psalm 46:10 says, "Be still, and know that I am God." Or, as Isaiah 41:1 puts it, "Keep silence before me." When we come to God we should never be in such a hurry that we cannot take time to address God in a way that is worthy of His great name.

Part Two: Supplication

The second part in the structure of prayer is supplication, or *asking*. Asking is the very essence of prayer. We must never forget this. When we pray we bring all our spiritual, physical, and material needs to the Lord to plead with Him to grant us "grace to help in time of need" (Hebrews 4:16). Prayer must not degenerate into a vague statement of generalities, asking for nothing in particular. By its very nature, prayer presupposes weak, needy souls urgently pleading their case before the throne of grace, pouring out their petitions with passionate urgency and asking for definite answers to definite requests. Jesus said, "Ask, and it shall be given you; seek, and ye shall find; knock, and it shall be opened unto you" (Luke 11:9). James's criticism is all too true of many of us: "Ye have not, because ye ask not" (James 4:2).

It is a sobering exercise for a Christian, immediately after he has prayed, to ask himself, "Precisely what have I just asked of the Lord?" Many will find it surprising how difficult it is to give a satisfactory answer, for they have allowed their prayer times to become barren exercises in uttering pious-sounding but empty phrases. They may have lectured God about some point of theology or kept up a flow of words that they cannot recall because they spoke them while their active thoughts were engaged elsewhere. They "ask not," and therefore they do not really pray at all.

I knew a retired missionary who exercised a powerful ministry in prayer and support of God's work around the world. She kept a book in which she listed all the things for which she asked the Lord. She noted down the souls whose salvation she was praying for, the financial needs of mission stations she wanted the Lord to meet, and the people in distressing circumstances whom she wanted Him to touch and bless. Beside these petitions were two columns for dates, the first for the date on which she had begun making request of the Lord and the second for the date on which He had answered. She believed in getting definite answers to definite asking.

The place of asking in prayer is important. As we have seen, it follows invocation. In other words, when we have recognized something of the greatness and glory of God, when we have been moved to deep feeling and faith as we have contemplated and worshiped Him, then we are ready to make our supplication. Stirred to lively faith by meditating on the Lord we will say to ourselves, as John Newton did,

> *Thou art coming to a King; Large petitions with thee bring;*
> *For His grace and power are such, None can ever ask too much.*

Our asking arises immediately out of our address to God. It will be directed and moderated or emboldened, as the case may be, by how we have been gripped and overwhelmed by the person and perfections of the Lord. It will be humble but not fawning, bold but not brash, confident but not presumptuous. And it will be effective, for this is the kind of praying that God answers.

Part Three: Ascription

The third part of the Lord's Prayer is the glorious ascription with which it ends. Having covered every area of human need, the Lord Jesus reminds us not to leave the place of prayer without rejoicing in the truth that no need of ours taxes the greatness and power of God. He is "able to do exceeding abundantly above all that we ask or think" (Ephesians 3:20). He has all authority to command heaven, earth, and hell to do His will, for His is the kingdom. He has all ability—the actual power—to insure that His authority is respected by friend and foe.

The Lord Jesus reminds us of something else. By ending the prayer with an ascription of glory to God, He teaches us never to leave the place of prayer without realizing just how deeply God has pledged Himself to hear and answer us. God's glory is at stake in answering prayer because He who has magnified His word above all His name (Psalm 138:2) would suffer shame if He failed to do all that He has promised.

Thus the ascription with which the prayer ends stirs us to greater faith and expectancy. If we get up from our knees rejoicing in the truth that "Thine is the kingdom, and the power, and the glory, for ever" (verse 13), we will wait patiently and confidently for the answer. He who truly makes this ascription to the Lord knows that He cannot and will not fail him.

Full Circle

The Lord's Prayer comes full circle. It commences with worship and it concludes with worship. This is another key to true prayer. Recognizing the glory of God leads us to ask with confidence. Asking deals with every aspect of our need and emphasizes our utter weakness. Realizing our weakness forces us to return to the reality of the surpassing greatness of God. With that in mind, not only can we *take* our burden to the Lord; we can *leave* it there. If our praying does not come full circle back to the greatness and glory of God, we will most likely get up from our knees defeated and dissatisfied. Fear and doubt will seek to usurp the place of faith, causing us to wonder whether we have been in touch with God at all. If this happens to us we are missing the main point of prayer.

Obtaining answers to our asking is important and it will come in God's time and in God's way, but the most important aspect and effect of prayer is our being completely wrapped up in the wonder of fellowship with the Lord. Whereas the flesh would seek to turn the place of prayer into an exercise in selfishness—*I* demand that God hear *me* and give me *my* desire and satisfy *my* need—the Lord Jesus Christ teaches us to focus on our God: "Thy name be hallowed, Thy kingdom come, Thy will be done, for Thine is the kingdom, and Thine is the power, and Thine is the glory, for ever." Until we learn that prayer begins and ends with worship, and that God, not ourselves, is the great focus of our praying, we will not be able to pray for ourselves at all.

Here then is the structure of the model prayer. It starts with invocation, proceeds to supplication, and climaxes with a great ascription of praise and worship because our praying must begin and end with God.

The Features of the Model Prayer

"After this manner therefore pray ye: Our Father which art in heaven, Hallowed be thy name. Thy kingdom come. Thy will be done in earth, as it is in heaven. Give us this day our daily bread. And forgive us our debts, as we forgive our debtors. And lead us not into temptation, but deliver us from evil: For thine is the kingdom, and the power, and the glory, for ever. Amen." Matthew 6:9–13

The Lord Jesus Christ gave us the Lord's Prayer as a pattern for all our praying. As we have seen, it directs us as to the way we should structure our prayers. But it goes further and gives us valuable instruction on the leading features of all true prayer. In all, we may trace seven features of true prayer, seven glorious truths to encourage us to pray and to fill us with a well-grounded confidence that God hears and answers us when we pray.

The Access We Enjoy

The first outstanding feature of prayer that the Lord's Prayer emphasizes is the access we enjoy in prayer. Jesus said, "When ye pray, say," or, "After this manner pray ye: Our Father which art in heaven." The familiarity of these words must not dull our minds to the glorious truth they teach us: We have access to God the Father in heaven. Here on the earth, facing all the difficulties of earthly existence, burdened by our own sinfulness and weakness, challenged by great needs and surrounded by daunting problems, we have an assured entrance to the throne of the God of heaven.

Twice in his Ephesian epistle—the epistle that expounds the doctrine of the believer's position seated "in heavenly places in Christ Jesus" (2:6)—Paul sets forth this privilege. In Ephesians 2:18 he says, "Through him we both [Jewish and Gentile Christians] have access by one Spirit unto the Father." Then in chapter three verse twelve he states, "In whom we have boldness and access with confidence by the faith of him." *Boldness* carries the idea of liberty of speech, of being free to open our hearts to the Lord, without the restrictions that manmade religion tends to put on us. False Christianity has interposed a host of alleged saints as intermediaries through whom the faithful may present their prayers, but the word of God destroys the need for them. It tells us that every Christian has access directly to the Father Himself.

Every Christian has the right of entrance into the holiest. Christ earned that right for us, and it is solely through Him and on His merit that we can approach God. That means that the efforts of the devotees of all other religions to gain access to God must fail. The ecumenical dogma that all religions ultimately lead to God is a lie: Outside of Christ there is no way to God. In Christ, however, we have access to God. As Paul wrote to the Hebrews: "Having therefore, brethren, boldness to enter into the holiest by the blood of Jesus, by a new and living way, which he hath consecrated for us, through the veil, that is to say, his flesh; and having an high priest over the house of God; let us draw near with a true heart in full assurance of faith" (Hebrews 10:19–22). We have an open door to the Lord, a standing invitation from the God of heaven to come before Him. His promise is, "Draw nigh to God, and he will draw nigh to you"(James 4:8). Having an open door to God, we are assured that we have the ear of the Almighty. Peter, quoting David, says, "The eyes of the Lord are over the righteous, and his ears are open unto their prayers" (1 Peter 3:12).

Thus, we may come to God our Father at all times, in all places, and with all our needs. We may come to Him in perfect confidence that He will not refuse His children an entrance and a hearing. This is the access we enjoy.

The Assumptions We Entertain

The familiar words of the Lord's Prayer are built on certain assumptions. They are based on things that we believe to be true and because of which we engage in prayer. Without these fundamental assumptions we could never pray with confidence. Examining the Lord's Prayer we may note four such assumptions or beliefs that form the foundation for all true prayer.

The First Assumption

The first assumption is that our Father is absolutely sovereign. This is clear from the Saviour's instruction as to how to pray and what to pray for. He bids us remember that our Father is "in heaven." In other words, He rules over all. He is, as Jewish prayers frequently say, "the King of the universe." If this title were the only way we had of addressing God, it would place an impenetrable barrier between Him and us and eradicate all hope of personal communion. Nevertheless, it emphasizes a scriptural truth: Our God is King of kings and Lord of lords. Nehemiah kept this in mind as he prayed, addressing the Lord as the "Lord God of heaven, the great and terrible God" (Nehemiah 1:5). Our Father reigns in absolute power, His will invincible, and His actions irresistible. Nebuchadnezzar, Babylon's mightiest monarch, confessed this, having found it out the hard way: "He doeth according to his will in the army of heaven, and among the inhabitants of the earth: and none can stay his hand, or say unto him, What doest thou?" (Daniel 4:35).

God's sovereignty, then, is the first assumption we make as we pray. If we are not convinced of this, our praying can amount to nothing more than the desperate cries of the heathen addressing their impotent idols. In prayer, all Christians are what the world calls Calvinists. It is difficult to find any Arminians in the place of prayer. I am not saying that Armninians do not pray, for some of them have been mighty in prayer. However, when they pray they are as convinced of the absolute sovereignty of God as Calvin himself. They ask the Lord to intervene in human affairs, to act according to His infinite wisdom, grace, and power. Every cry to God from a believer's heart expresses his assumption that God is absolutely sovereign.

It is commonly believed that deep theological truth is not very practical. Indeed, many analyses of the New Testament epistles follow a basic division of the contents into doctrinal and practical sections—as if the doctrinal section were not practical. But biblical doctrine is eminently practical, as is obvious from the case before us. Every believer feels instinctively that prayer is essential to all Christian living. That means that the first assumption we make in prayer—the sovereignty of God—is of immediate practical value. We can see this clearly in the Lord's Prayer where it underscores a vital practical truth: Our grasp of the truth of God's sovereign greatness is the measure of all our praying. To put it another way, our praying can never outstrip our conviction of God's all-powerful sovereignty. The more we are overwhelmed by this conviction, the more we will be encouraged and enabled to pray. The larger our vision of God, the greater our praying will be.

This first assumption that we make every time we pray expresses what theologians call the transcendence of God. This is a doctrine we must never lose sight of or we will fall into the error of making God after our own image or conception, which is idolatry. However, alongside the transcendence of God, the Bible sets the truth of the immanence of God. The word *immanence* expresses the idea that God enters and is active in the events and processes of our world.

The Second Assumption

It is this truth of God's immanence that underlies the second assumption we make every time we pray: Our sovereign God is interested in our affairs both small and great. If this were not so, the Lord's Prayer—indeed, every biblical exhortation and promise connected with the subject of prayer—would be a mockery. The Lord's Prayer is based on the truth that the sovereign God of heaven is our Father, and "like as a father pitieth his children, so the Lord pitieth them that fear him" (Psalm 103:13). He is interested in our affairs. David was much comforted by this truth: "I am poor and needy; yet the Lord thinketh upon me: thou art my help and my deliverer; make no tarrying, O my God" (Psalm 40:17). "The Lord thinketh on me." For that reason we can pray not only for the great worldwide success of the gospel, but also for such an apparently insignificant matter as our daily bread. Our God upholds all things and is working "all things after the counsel of his own will" (Ephesians 1:11). Yet He cares for His people individually and bears the burden of all their cares (1 Peter 5:7). He tells us, "Even the very hairs of your head are all numbered" (Luke 12:7).

We may be tempted to think that God is interested only in the great cosmic events to effect His eternal purpose, but we should never forget that the salvation of every child of God is a vital part of that purpose (Ephesians 1:4–5). That means that our needs, however insignificant they may appear to others, are not outside of our Father's interest. A homely (or *homey,* as Americans say) illustration will help us to see the beautiful intimacy this interest reveals. All over the world people are dying in the most harrowing circumstances imaginable. Looking at the reports of such suffering we are naturally moved with compassion. Then the cries of our own little child reach us. He has suffered a slight nick on the end of his finger or has fallen on the grass and grazed his knee and is calling for our attention. In comparison to the great events in the world, what is his little crisis? It is nothing. But when such a thing happens do we ignore our child's cry and tell him that we are too busy considering the great events that are transpiring across the world? No, no. Parents stand ready to address even the small needs of their children. Jesus asked, "If ye then, being evil, know how to give good gifts unto your children, how much more shall your Father which is in heaven give good things to them that ask him?" (Matthew 7:11). Will our heavenly Father be less interested in His children than depraved men are in theirs? Our God is in control of the important things concerning the world such as the rise and fall of kingdoms and empires, but He still has time for his children, even when what concerns them seems insignificant to others.

The tender reality that the Lord cares is a powerful incentive to pray. It gives us boldness and confidence to carry our burdens to the Lord. Frank E. Graeff wrote a beautiful hymn that asks the question, "Does Jesus care?" and gives a resounding answer:

> Does Jesus care when my heart is pained,
> Too deeply for mirth or song,
> As the burdens press and the cares distress,
> And the day grows weary and long?

> Does Jesus care when my way is dark
> With a nameless dread and fear?
> As the daylight fades into deep night shades,
> Does He care enough to be near?

> Does Jesus care when I've tried and failed
> To resist some temptation strong;
> When in my deep grief I find no relief,
> Tho' my tears flow all the night long?

> Does Jesus care when I've said goodbye
> To the dearest on earth to me,
> And my sad heart aches till it nearly breaks,
> Is it aught to Him? Does He see?

> O yes, He cares; I know He cares;
> His heart is touched with my grief.
> When the days are weary, the long nights dreary,
> I know my Saviour cares.

This is the knowledge that inspires a Christian to pray. Our God is interested in us and in all that concerns us.

The Third Assumption

There is a third assumption underlying the Lord's Prayer: Our Father can and will do the things that we request. When we pray, we deliberately do not ask what we know is either unworthy of His name or contrary to His revealed will. We recognize that to do so would place us on dangerous ground. The experience of the ancient Israelites witnesses to this. They grumbled and murmured against God in their impatience to indulge their fleshly appetites. He heard their petulant demands, "and he gave them their request; but sent leanness into their soul" (Psalm 106:15). So we do not pray for what we know is unworthy of God or contrary to His will. He commands us, "Acknowledge my might" (Isaiah 33: 13), and we gladly do so. We also acknowledge His right to do as He wills, but we believe that He can and will do the things that we humbly request of Him.

The Scriptures are full of divine promises that God is both able and willing to hear our prayers. "Call unto me, and I will answer thee, and shew thee great and mighty things, which thou knowest not" (Jeremiah 33:3). The Lord Jesus Christ urged His people to pray in the confidence that God could and would hear them: "All things, whatsoever ye shall ask in prayer, believing, ye shall receive" (Matthew 21:22); "Whatsoever ye shall ask in my name, that will I do, that the Father may be glorified in the Son. If ye shall ask any thing in my name, I will do it" (John 14:13–14); "Ye have not chosen me, but I have chosen you, and ordained you, that ye should go and bring forth fruit, and that your fruit should remain: that whatsoever ye shall ask of the Father in my name, he may give it you" (John 15:16). These are wonderful promises and they should create in us the same certainty that they created in the apostle John: "This is the confidence that we have in him, that, if we ask any thing according to his will, he heareth us: and if we know that he hear us, whatsoever we ask, we know that we have the petitions that we desired of him" (1 John 5:14–15).

The Fourth Assumption

The final assumption in the Lord's Prayer is that we exist for God, not God for us. God is for us, and "if God be for us, who can be against us?" (Romans 8:31). When we say that God is for us, we mean that He graciously exercises His favor toward us. When we say that we exist for God and not God for us, we address the question of the purpose of life. God's purpose in all He does is His own glory. The chief purpose of our existence is His glory, and as His creatures we can have no other or higher end. "Thou art worthy, O Lord, to receive glory and honour and power: for thou hast created all things, and for thy pleasure they are and were created" (Revelation 4:11). This is what we express when we pray.

The first three petitions of the Lord's Prayer focus on God's glory: "Hallowed be thy name. Thy kingdom come. Thy will be done." The three ascriptions of honour that end the prayer have the same focus: "Thine is the kingdom, and the power, and the glory, for ever." When we pray, we express the same commitment to promote the ultimate glory of our Father. Although we rejoice in His watch-care over us, we fully accept that His glory is what is of paramount importance, not only to Him but also to us as His children. The glory of God draws a large circle around what we may properly pray about. We assume that we may pray with confidence for anything within that circle, and that whatever is outside the circle, and therefore not for His glory, is not a fit matter for prayer at all.

These four assumptions are the presuppositions, the starting point, of all true praying—so we need to learn them well.

The Attitude We Exhibit

A third feature of all true prayer that we learn from the Lord's Prayer is the attitude that we should exhibit in coming to God. There are five clearly defined attitudes to be adopted by all who pray—attitudes that are all evident in the Lord's Prayer.

Attitude of a Son

From the words *Our Father* we gather that in prayer we come to God as His *sons*. This is one of the most precious truths about prayer revealed in Scripture. When God saves a sinner, He adopts him into His family, so that thenceforth he has a right to the name and privileges of His sons. As Paul says, "Ye have not received the spirit of bondage again to fear; but ye have received the Spirit of adoption, whereby we cry, Abba, Father" (Romans 8:15). Again, "Because ye are sons, God hath sent forth the Spirit of his Son into your hearts, crying, Abba, Father" (Galatians 4:6). As the sons of God, we are "heirs of God, and joint-heirs with Christ" (Romans 8:17). Thus we may pray with confidence, coming to our Father with a sense of freedom, assured of our welcome at His throne.

Attitude of a Subject

The words *Thy kingdom come* remind us that we are *subjects* of the King of glory. He is the absolute sovereign of all His creation. "The Lord hath prepared his throne in the heavens; and his kingdom ruleth over all" (Psalm 103:19). When we approach Him we come with a spirit of submissiveness, acknowledging His all-wise government of all His creatures and asserting that our highest aim in all we seek is the establishment and advancement of His cause.

Maintaining the attitude of a subject does not conflict with or in any way lessen the joy and privileges of sonship. It does, however, save us from the outrageous familiarities that some people utter to God. Some teach that *Abba*, which is the word a child uses for "Father," expresses the idea of tender relationship and therefore may be rendered, "Dad," or "Papa." To speak to God in this way is blasphemous. *Abba* expresses the intimacy of sons. Remembering that we are also God's subjects will keep us from allowing intimacy to degenerate into familiarity (see pages 86, 131).

Attitude of a Servant

The words *Thy will be done* tell us that we pray as God's *servants*. Acknowledging that our Father "knoweth what things [we] have need of" (verse 8) and that He does all things well, we have no other desire than that we should know and do His will. We recognize that earth is different from heaven and that here we face opposition to and rebellion against God's will. Instead of giving us an excuse for ignoring God's will, this realization ignites in us a burning desire for the day when earth will be as free from every trace of rebellion as heaven is. Until then, as God's servants, we pray that we may be willing instruments to do our Father's will.

Attitude of a Suppliant

The words *give us* remind us that we appear before God as *suppliants*. We come to God empty-handed. We pray out of a deep sense of need and a conviction that our Father is able to meet our need. We realize that we have no merit that deserves the blessing for which we pray. We are dependent on divine grace; we are pleading for God's gifts. And we realize that even those things that most people take for granted, such as "our daily bread," are really God's gifts. Without Him and apart from His generous giving, we would have nothing. All living things depend on Him: "These wait all upon thee; that thou mayest give them their meat in due season. That thou givest them they gather: thou openest thine hand, they are filled with good. Thou hidest thy face, they are troubled: thou takest away their breath, they die, and return to their dust" (Psalm 104:27–29). When we pray we gladly confess that we are dependent on the goodness of our Father and that "every good gift and every perfect gift is from above, and cometh down from the Father of lights, with whom is no variableness, neither shadow of turning" (James 1:17).

Attitude of a Saint

When we pray, "forgive us," "lead us," and "deliver us," we use the language of *saints*. Each of these supplications emphasizes our preoccupation with personal holiness. As saints we must know that there is "nothing between my soul and the Saviour," no unforgiven sin to mar our fellowship or hinder our praying. We recognize that sin hides God's face so that He refuses to hear our prayers (Isaiah 59:2; Psalm 66:18), and we therefore desire to keep short accounts with Him. While the carnal mind stridently asserts its claim to independence from God, as saints we wholeheartedly submit our wills to His. We long to walk in close communion with Him, knowing His constant guidance, protection, and deliverance from sin and Satan.

These are the attitudes that must govern us in our praying. In other words, prayer consists of a lot more than what we say. It must reflect the attitudes of our hearts. The beautiful expressions of carefully composed prayers are worthless—indeed, we could argue that they are abominable—in the sight of

God if they do not spring from the hearts of those who pray as sons of God, as subjects of His kingdom, as servants who are dedicated to His will, as suppliants who are coming to Him empty-handed, pleading for His fullness, and as saints who are seriously interested in personal holiness. Nobody likes a hypocrite and neither does the Lord. As we have seen, He specifically warns us against praying hypocritically, and to say prayers without the proper attitude of heart is hypocrisy at its worst.

The Ambitions We Evince

The fourth feature of true prayer that the Lord's Prayer deals with is the ambitions we evince in prayer. When we pray we give expression to certain deeply held ambitions.

Rising above Our Circumstances

The first is the ambition to rise above the world and its circumstances. We let our circumstances—whether they pose physical, emotional, relational, or material challenges—drive us to God and not to sin, despair, or spiritual carelessness. When facing difficult situations we often feel that no one else suffers as we do. Such feelings tend to isolate us from the rest of the body of Christ. The devil's ultimate purpose in plying us with such ideas is to isolate us from the Lord Himself. We must remind ourselves of the truth of the sovereignty of God our Father and of His paternal care for us. Keeping these truths in mind will provide us with the power to fulfil our ambition of rising above our circumstances to meet with God at the throne of grace.

Enjoying Family Fellowship

We may describe the ambition we evince in prayer another way: We yearn to enter into the fullness of family fellowship with God. The opening words of the Lord's Prayer are *Our Father*. The most obvious reason for commencing in this way is to emphasize the family fellowship that we have with God in prayer. It is true that prayer is asking. Some make asking the exclusive essence of prayer and hold that worship, thanksgiving, and confession are not really parts of prayer. They do not deny the need or validity of these things, but they deny that they are parts of prayer, for prayer is asking.

While asking is essential to all true prayer, it is not true that it is the only element in praying. Before there can be effective asking there must be something much deeper. Prayer is much more than rushing into God's presence with a wish list. Prayer is a deep yearning to meet with God and to enter into the fullness of the intimacy suggested by His being our Father. Every time we come to pray, we must carry in our hearts the fundamental desire to experience real communion with God, not merely to obtain a list of things from Him. It is the Blesser, not the blessing, that is uppermost in our minds.

Days of Heaven on Earth

According to the Lord's Prayer, the ambition that possesses our souls when we really pray is to enjoy "days of heaven upon the earth" (Deuteronomy 11: 21). The phrase "on earth as it is in heaven" governs the first three petitions. Evidently the Saviour is instructing us to pray that while we are on this earth with all its sin and suffering, we may through fellowship with God know days of heaven upon the earth. The Lord's promise to the children of Israel holds good for all His people: "Thou shalt write [my words] upon the door posts of thine house, and upon thy gates: that your days may be multiplied, and the days of your children, in the land which the Lord sware unto your fathers to give them, as the days of heaven upon the earth" (Deuteronomy 11:20–21). According to Paul's epistle to the Ephesians, believers walk and war in the heavenlies, where they are blessed with all spiritual blessings in Christ (Ephesians 1:3). Every true prayer is based on the longing to "possess the land which the Lord God hath given us," to borrow the language of Joshua 18:3.

The Manifestation of God's Power

Another ambition that drives true praying is the desire to witness a mighty manifestation of God's power to further His kingdom and to defeat His enemies: "Thy kingdom come, thy will be done." We have heard of what the Lord did in former times and we long to see Him work with almighty grace and power in our times. We read how He used others and we strongly desire that He would use us. David gave a testimony that every prayer warrior longs to be able to give: "As we have heard, so have we seen in the city of the Lord of hosts, in the city of our God" (Psalm 48:8). In other words, our experience does not fall one whit short of all we have heard of God's doings in former times. True prayer cannot be content without the manifestation of the power of God. It is driven to see Him act with power in and through His servants.

Living Out What It Means to Be "in Christ"

In summary, we may say that the ambition we evince in prayer is that we may be brought to the place where our character and experience are true expressions of our position in Christ. The gospel conveys to us "the unsearchable riches of Christ" (Ephesians 3:8), whose "divine power hath given unto us all things that pertain unto life and godliness" (2 Peter 1:3). Sadly, though we are spiritual millionaires, we often live as paupers. Our experience is far short of what our position in Christ implies.

As a thirty-seven year old missionary in China, J. Hudson Taylor felt convicted of his irritability and lack of control over his temper. Harassed and under immense pressure, he found himself being ungracious to his helpers and cried to God for forgiveness. As he prayed, he learned from Scripture that he was *in Christ* and felt that glorious truth take control of his entire being. It transformed his life and energized his service. The great missionary had discovered the fundamental ambition that must possess a Christian as he prays: the desire that his character and experience be brought into line with his position in Christ. That is an ambition worthy of a Christian and certain to be fulfilled by our Father in heaven.

The Address We Employ

The fifth feature of true prayer set before us in our Lord's pattern prayer is the address that we employ in prayer. The Lord Jesus instructed us to pray, "Our Father which art in heaven." We approach God with terms of peculiar intimacy and humility. He is "our Father," but we must never forget that He is "in heaven." Paul describes the intimacy we enjoy in prayer: "Ye have not received the spirit of bondage again to fear; but ye have received the Spirit of adoption, whereby we cry, Abba, Father" (Romans 8:15). *Abba* is the word for father used by a child of the family, but not by a servant. It is a word that expresses the most tender intimacy. However, it also carries the idea of respect and reverence. Some Charismatics have fastened on this word as an excuse to refer to God as "Dad" or "Papa." This is a scandalous misapplication of the biblical term.

When Paul came to employ the Aramaic *abba* in Greek, he did not translate it *papa*, but simply transliterated it. *Abba* is an intimate but deeply respectful address to God who is our *pater*. Peter emphasizes the need for reverence in coming before our Father: "If ye call on the Father, who without respect of persons judgeth according to every man's work, pass the time of your sojourning here in fear" (1 Peter 1:17). "The fear of the Lord is the beginning [or principal part] of wisdom" (Proverbs 9:10), so that we never address God wisely unless we address Him with godly fear.

God is in heaven, the sovereign Lord of all creation. In coming to Him we must never forget what Abraham said in a prayer that proved his unique closeness to God: "Behold now, I have taken upon me to speak unto the Lord, which am but dust and ashes" (Genesis 18:27). Boldness in addressing God must never be allowed to degenerate into brashness. True intimacy will produce true humility, the deep sense that "though the Lord be high, yet hath he respect unto the lowly" (Psalm 138:6). We must never forget that it is *God* whom we address. Who was closer to the Father than the Lord Jesus Christ, His only begotten Son? He stood in the closest possible intimacy with Him. How did Christ express this intimacy with His Father? He addressed Him as "Holy Father" and "Righteous Father" (John 17:11, 25). In Christ's address there is none of the flippant language or arrogant brashness that is so evident in the performances of many televangelists and their misguided followers.

Our address to God celebrates the privilege He has given us to "draw near" (Hebrews 10:22), but it never loses sight of the unspeakable glory of the one we approach. We are never closer to Him than when in deep humility we cry with the seraphim that surround His throne, "Holy, holy, holy, is the Lord of hosts: the whole earth is full of his glory" (Isaiah 6:3).

The Answers We Entreat

The sixth feature of true prayer that the Saviour emphasizes in His model prayer is the answers we entreat when we pray. The petitions of the Lord's Prayer cover the widest range of Christian desire and need. First, we lift up our spiritual concerns. In the first three petitions, we express our zeal for the Lord's name, the Lord's kingdom, the Lord's will. In praying for forgiveness and in asking the Lord, "Lead us not into temptation, but deliver us from evil," we express our zeal for our personal sanctification. We ask that we may walk in company with the Lord and be kept from anything that would lead us away from Him or that would grieve His Spirit. These are the spiritual concerns that are of overriding importance to every Christian as he gives himself to real prayer. We also lift up our temporal needs. We ask, "Give us this day our daily bread," and with it the Lord's provision for our every physical need.

True prayer entreats God's gracious intervention in these matters of spiritual and material concern to us. These are all legitimate matters for prayer. They are all issues on which we should expect the Lord to hear us, for our Saviour has commanded us to bring them before the throne of grace. In every case the governing motive is the glory of God and the performance of His will. Seeing these accomplished will be the chief part of every answer to our prayers. Whatever our situation, if we may but see God glorified, His kingdom advanced, and His will accomplished, we will be able to rejoice that He has heard our cry. We can be encouraged that He is glorified in sanctifying and providing for His people. Thus, we may with boldness bring our petitions to our Father, knowing that He has chosen to glorify Himself by hearing our prayers and sustaining us, even in the most trying circumstances of life.

The Assurance We Express

The last feature of true prayer that the Saviour teaches us in His model prayer is the assurance we express in prayer. The Lord's Prayer has a glorious conclusion, a majestic climax: "For thine is the kingdom, and the power, and the glory, for ever. Amen." This is the note on which to end our prayers. True prayer is not a cry of desperation but a cry of faith. It sees the difficulties, it traverses the vale of tears, but it comes to God's throne. It sees His glory and confesses, "Thine is the kingdom, Thine is the power, Thine is the glory."

Occasionally the prayers recorded in the Bible end on what sounds like a depressed note. We should be grateful to God that He has left them in His word for our consolation because they show us that even great men of God were "subject to like passions as we are" (James 5:17). We can identify with their feelings and failures in the place of prayer. Often we rise from our knees with no more feeling of assurance of God's answer than when we started to pray. When we realize that much greater prayer warriors than we are have experienced the same kind of feelings, we are comforted that we may rise above such failure and reach true assurance in prayer. And we should be led to an assurance, for the general rule is that having met with our Father and brought our burdens to Him, we should be overwhelmed with the thought of His absolute greatness, grace, and glory — truths that create in us a confident assurance that we have not prayed in vain.

This is clear from the correspondence between the beginning and the end of the Lord's Prayer. We pray, "Hallowed be thy name" and feel the assurance of the Saviour's words, "Thine is the glory." We pray, "Thy kingdom come" and are gripped by the confidence that "Thine is the kingdom." We pray for our Father to ensure that His will prevail on earth, and we hear our Lord's assurance, "Thine is the power." Here is why we pray. Here is the ground of our faith, the basis of our assurance.

In the Lord's Prayer the Lord Jesus leads us to face up to all the varied circumstances of life, all the needs, desires, and pitfalls we may encounter. He raises the thought of the challenge of temptation, trial, and calamity as well as the very real enmity of the devil. He makes us face up to all these things in prayer. But in the stirring conclusion to the prayer He says in effect, "You have brought these concerns to your Father. He is on the throne. He is able to answer prayer. Leave your burden with Him in the assurance that He will not fail you, for were He to do so, He would fail Himself. His glory must be seen, His kingdom must prevail, and His power must be victorious." This is the assurance that should grip our hearts when we have prayed to our Father in heaven.

The Lord's Prayer is Christ's answer to the disciples' request, "Lord, teach us to pray." It provides the pattern for all our praying and reveals the features that should be present when we approach God's throne. We are meant to learn these lessons well and diligently put them into practice. Our Lord has thrown open to us the door into the holiest of all. We have His warrant to enter in; let us not fail to do so "in full assurance of faith" (Hebrews 10:22).

9

What It Means to Call God Our Father

"Our Father" Matthew 6:9

We should be careful to heed Christ's warning against all vain repetitions in prayer, but especially in the way we address God. As we take His holy name on our lips, we should make sure that we do not use empty or meaningless words and that we do not speak thoughtlessly to or about Him. Above all, we should not lie by reciting words to Him that we really do not mean. Yet we are commanded to use a given form of address to God repeatedly. Jesus said, "When ye pray, say, Our Father which art in heaven" (Luke 11: 2). How are we to repeat such words each time we pray without sinking into vain repetition? Thomas Manton, the great Puritan divine, points us in the right direction: "We should begin prayer with awful thoughts of God." By "awful thoughts" he means thoughts that inspire us with a deep awe of God.

Here is the key to all successful praying: getting a clear view of the one whom we approach. This is what the words *Our Father which art in heaven* are intended to give us. They invite us to stand still awhile at the threshold of prayer and to consider the *mercy* of God, as expressed by the words *Our Father,* and the *majesty* of God, as expressed by *which art in heaven.* Thinking on God's mercy begets confidence in prayer, while pondering His majesty produces reverence.

Both these elements must always be found in our approach to God. We must come with confidence. The New Testament is full of texts that deal with the theme of our coming boldly to the throne of grace to speak freely to the Lord. But that boldness must not degenerate into brashness. It must always be accompanied by deep and godly reverence. In this chapter our emphasis will be on the confidence-building words *Our Father*, and we will explore what it means to Christians to be able to address God in this manner.

Never Alone

The first truth that the words *our Father* teach us is that we never stand alone before God. There are two wonderful reasons for saying this. The first highlights our union with Christ, and the second highlights our communion with our fellow believers.

Union with Christ

Christians never stand alone before God because we always appear before Him in union with the Lord Jesus Christ. It is interesting to note that our Lord's characteristic way of referring to God was "Father." He constantly emphasized that God was His Father. He claimed, "I and my Father are one" (John 10:30) and He told His disciples, "I am in the Father, and the Father in me" (John 14:11). He called heaven "My Father's house" and said that He came forth from the Father to do the will and work of His Father and that when He had finished His appointed task, He was going back to His Father. This strong emphasis upon God as His Father is particularly clear in the praying of the Lord Jesus Christ.

High Priestly Prayer

John 17 provides the longest and most detailed record of any of Christ's prayers. This prayer is often called His high priestly prayer, for in it He is seen exercising His high priestly function of interceding specifically for His own people. Throughout this prayer the Saviour addresses God as "Father." "Jesus … lifted up his eyes to heaven, and said, Father, the hour is come; glorify thy Son, that thy Son also may glorify thee" (verse 1); "Now, O Father, glorify thou me with thine own self with the glory which I had with thee before the world was" (verse 5); "Holy Father, keep through thine own name those whom thou has given me, that they may be one, as we are" (verse 11); "Thou, Father, art in me, and I in thee" (verse 21); "Father, I will that they also, whom thou hast given me, be with me where I am; that they may behold my glory, which thou hast given me: for thou lovedst me before the foundation of the world. O righteous Father, the world hath not known thee: but I have known thee, and these have known that thou hast sent me" (verses 24–25). Again and again as Christ prayed for His church in all ages He constantly used the terms *Father, Holy Father,* and *Righteous Father.*

Gethsemane

Follow the Lord Jesus Christ into Gethsemane. A solitary figure, with the blood oozing through His skin, suffering the deepest anguish He had ever experienced, forsaken by His three most intimate disciples (they had fallen asleep), and facing all the fury of the powers of hell, He prayed, "O my Father, if this cup may not pass away from me, except I drink it, thy will be done" (Matthew 26: 42). Or, as Mark records His petition, "Abba, Father, all things are possible unto thee; take away this cup from me: nevertheless not what I will, but what thou wilt" (Mark 14:36). Clearly, even in that time of extreme agony and affliction, the Saviour cherished the truth that God was His Father.

Calvary

Following Christ on to Calvary, we find the same truth gripping His mind. He uttered seven significant sayings from the cross. He commenced with a prayer, "Father forgive them," and finished with another prayer, "Father into thy hands I commit my Spirit." Calling God "Father" was Christ's characteristic way of addressing Him.

It is significant that when the Lord Jesus used a possessive adjective before the word *Father,* it was always *my,* never *our.* Almost sixty times He used the phrase *my Father.* Clearly His sonship is a unique sonship, but we may gather more than that from *my Father.* When Christ stood before God, He stood alone. He stood on His own merit and dependent on no righteousness but His own. Because He prayed, "My Father," we are able, in union with Him, to pray, "Our Father."

Thus when we pray, "Our Father," we take our stand alongside the Lord Jesus Christ. He made this clear when He spoke to Mary Magdalene after His resurrection: "Go to my brethren, and say unto them, I ascend unto my Father, and your Father; and to my God, and your God" (John 20:17). Paul touched on the same truth in his epistle to the Ephesians: "I bow my knees unto the Father of our Lord Jesus Christ, of whom the whole family in heaven and earth is named" (Ephesians 3:14–15). This sharing of Christ's peculiar name for God is vitally important. It is essential for us to recognize this union with Him every time we pray. Christ has purchased every blessing of the covenant of grace, one of which is that we have Him for our great high priest and advocate with the Father. Because of His perfect righteousness, He always receives what He prays for. As He Himself asserted, "I [know] that thou hearest me always" (John 11:42). When we pray, "Our Father," we pray in Jesus' name, on Jesus' merit, and through Jesus' blood. In other words, when we come to God with the address, "Our Father," we consciously express the fact that we stand in union with His Son.

There is a further thought to consider. Recognizing that our Lord prays, "Father," we pray, "Our Father," in the assurance that as we pray, He prays for us and His Spirit prays in us (Hebrews 4:14–16; 10:19–22; Romans 8:14–15, 26). What strength and encouragement this gives us in prayer! We never pray alone. We have the constant guidance and grace of the Holy Spirit, and "we have an advocate with the Father, Jesus Christ the righteous" (1 John 2:2). There is One who is always pleading our cause, who, like the Jewish high priest, bears His people on His heart and on His shoulders, that is, with all the tenderness and strength of His being. As soon as He had risen from the dead He gave His disciples the promise, "I ascend to my Father, and to your Father" (John 20:17). In other words, we can pray, "Our Father," because we have a risen Saviour who has returned to His Father to plead our cause at His throne.

Amid the dark trials and troubles of life let us never lose sight of this glorious truth, and we will be able to pray effectively through every challenge. We never stand alone before God, for we are in union with Christ who constantly intercedes for us and who assures us, "I will never leave thee"; "I am with you alway" (Hebrews 13:5; Matthew 28:20). He will not leave us in the battles of life. That includes what is perhaps our greatest spiritual battleground, the place of our greatest weakness—namely, the place of prayer. But the Lord Jesus comforts us by directing us away from dependence on our own strength in prayer and by reminding us that He is praying for us and that His Spirit is working in us, strengthening us to pray effectively. Every time we pray, "Our Father," we should remember these truths that flow from our union with Christ.

Communion with the Saints

There is another sense in which Christians never stand alone in prayer: We come to God not just as individuals but as part of a great communion of saints. That is another good reason we always pray, "*Our* Father." As we have seen, the Lord Jesus prayed, "*My* Father," because He stood absolutely alone in the great work that He came to do. There was none who could help Him bear the sin of the world. He had to bear the burden of human guilt and pay the price of our salvation alone. But in our work and experience we are never alone. This is true not only because the Saviour is with us but because He never leaves us without others of His people on the earth.

Feelings of isolation are powerful hindrances to prayer and to all spiritual joy and usefulness. Even the intrepid prophet Elijah was reduced to a depressed shadow of his former self because he came to believe that he was the last of God's faithful people: "He said [to the Lord], I have been very jealous for the Lord God of hosts: for the children of Israel have forsaken thy covenant, thrown down thine altars, and slain thy prophets with the sword; and I, even I only, am left; and they seek my life, to take it away" (1 Kings 19:10). But he was not the only one left. The Lord had reserved for Himself seven thousand faithful souls in Israel. Elijah lost his joy and his powerful ministry in prayer (James 5:17–18) because he believed a lie.

Most Christians know the story of Elijah, and yet we are slow to learn its lesson. We easily feel ourselves isolated, if not in the sense of feeling that we are the only believers left, at least in the sense that our sufferings or circumstances are unique. This feeling of isolation is based on a falsehood. The word of God plainly declares, "There hath no temptation taken you but such as is common to man" (1 Corinthians 10:13). We are never placed in a situation in which we stand alone. That is why the Saviour reminds us to pray, "*Our* Father," for we are part of a vast fellowship of saints who have proved God under the very circumstances that cause us so much concern. What a comfort this is when we are in distress! And what a cause for confidence in prayer!

There is another comfort here. The emphasis on *our* Father reminds us that prayer is constantly being offered to God from His children all over the world. The Lord's Prayer is without doubt the most prayed prayer wherever Christians are found. Probably it is lifted up every minute of every day by a Christian or group of Christians somewhere. Does God hear them? Can He possibly fail to hear the very prayer that His people pray in obedience to the express command of the Lord Jesus Christ? Undoubtedly He will hear His people when they address Him as His Son directed. But consider this. When Christians pray, "Our Father," their petition takes in all who are included in the word *our,* that is, the entire body of God's people. The answer that God gives them must be equally extensive, and all of us who are "the children of God by faith in Christ Jesus" (Galatians 3:26) benefit from the faithful praying of brethren all around the world, as they do from ours.

Here is a glimpse into the beautiful mystery of the unity and communion of the family of God. There are people who will never know us or realize that we need to be prayed for, who are honestly pouring out their hearts to God, praying, "Hallowed be thy name. Thy kingdom come. Thy will be done in earth, as it is in heaven. Give us this day our daily bread. And forgive us our debts, as we forgive our debtors. And lead us not into temptation, but deliver us from evil." As our Father looks down upon His praying church interceding in these general but nonetheless powerful terms given by the Lord Jesus Christ Himself, He moves to answer, and His answer is as broad as the prayer. It is not merely a personal answer, but one that reaches to the entire body of Christ. There is a benefit that flows to the whole body when any of God's people pray as Christ directs us to pray in the Lord's Prayer.

What a blessing it is to be part of a great family, the family of God! Let us never fail to appreciate the privilege. We participate in the life, fellowship, and welfare of the family when we pray, "Our Father." We never stand alone before God. We are never left without the prayer support of an army of His people who are ceaselessly petitioning His throne.

Intimately Related to God

The second truth that the words *our Father* teach us is that we stand in a very intimate relationship with God. He is our Father. In Scripture, that is a title of peculiar tenderness and beauty.

Widest Meaning of *Father*

There is a sense in which God is a Father to all His creation. The broadest significance of *Father* as a name for God is simply "Creator." For example, the angels are called His sons, making Him in a sense their Father. It was with angels in mind that the Lord spoke to Job of the time before He had laid the foundations of the earth as a time "when the morning stars sang together, and all the sons of God shouted for joy" (Job 38:7). Not only are the angels His sons, but so are all His human creatures. In Isaiah 64:8 we read, "O Lord, thou art our father; we are the clay, and thou our potter; and we all are the work of thy hand." In this text the words *we are the clay, and thou our potter; and we all are the work of thy hand* explain the meaning of "Thou art our father." Thus in Luke 3:38 we read, "Adam . . . was the son of God" because God created him. Paul terms God "the Father of spirits" (Hebrews 12:9) for the same reason: He created them. So the broadest use of *Father* as applied to God reminds us that He is our Creator.

Clearly, the idea of God as Creator is not the chief truth the Saviour has in mind when He instructs His disciples, "When ye pray, say, Our Father." But while it is not the leading idea, it should not be entirely overlooked. When we pray, we should remember that we are God's creatures. It will help us to pray if we keep in mind how we came to be here in the first place and why we are here. We are not accidents of evolutionary processes; we are the products of the thoughtful purpose of a gracious Creator, placed here as instruments for His glory. We will pray all the more effectively if we keep in mind what we learn in Revelation 4:11: "Thou art worthy, O Lord, to receive glory and honour and power: for thou hast created all things, and for thy pleasure they are and were created." Here we may reiterate a great theological truth: God is the infinite Creator; we are His finite creatures—yet we may approach Him. He is transcendent yet approachable, and He is approachable because the transcendent God has become immanent. He has revealed Himself to and in His creation, and He has done so fully and finally in the incarnation of His Son, Jesus Christ. This is how lowly creatures have a way "into the holiest" (Hebrews 10:19) and how they may with humble confidence address their great Creator.

There is an added reason we should not overlook the idea of God as Creator in the title *Father*. Some people who have not attained assurance of salvation, when they hear that addressing God as Father is the sole prerogative of the sons of God, wonder if they have any right to pray. They ask, "May I not cry to God?

Have I no entrance to His presence? Will He not hear me at all? If God will not hear me until I am a Christian, and I can become a Christian only by calling on God, can I never be saved?"

These are legitimate questions, but the case is not as bleak as they make it sound. The question has a simple answer: As God is the Father of all men—in the sense that He created and sustains them—you are His creature and you should cry to Him. This is not to say that an unsaved person may make a convenience of God while he lives in willful defiance of Him and in rejection of His Son. What it means is that an unsaved man may and should cry out to his Maker, saying, "I acknowledge that Thou art our Father and that I am the work of Thy hand. I desire to enter into the full meaning of the fatherhood of God and of my sonship. Lead me to an assured faith in Christ that I may know what it is to receive Him and through Him the power to be called one of the sons of God, not merely as a creature, but as one redeemed to Thee by Jesus Christ."

Redeemer in Christ

This reference to our being called the sons of God through receiving Christ as Saviour introduces us to the true and full meaning of the opening words of the Lord's Prayer. Here *Father* refers to the special relationship that God has with those who are redeemed and reconciled to Him by the blood of Christ. Contrary to the sentimental notions of liberal theology, spiritually unregenerate sinners are not the children of God. In its highest sense, *Father* speaks of God's relationship to those who have been brought into His family and who are rightly related to Him by faith in Jesus Christ—for as Paul said, "Ye are all the children of God by faith in Christ Jesus" (Galatians 3:26). The Lord Jesus Christ declared the spiritual parentage of the ungodly when He said to the Jews, "Ye are of your father the devil, and the lusts of your father ye will do" (John 8:44).

The fact is that in the sense of spiritual relationship, God is Father only to those to whom He is a redeemer. "Thou, O Lord, art our father, our redeemer" (Isaiah 63:16). Thus we read, "As many as received him [Christ], to them gave he power to become the sons of God, even to them that believe on his name" (John 1:12). Paul combines these twin ideas of divine redeemer and fatherhood in Galatians 4:4–6: "When the fulness of the time was come, God sent forth his Son, made of a woman, made under the law, to redeem them that were under the law, that we might receive the adoption of sons. And because ye are sons, God hath sent forth the Spirit of his Son into your hearts, crying, Abba, Father." John had the same thought in mind when he wrote, "Behold, what manner of love the Father hath bestowed upon us, that we should be called the sons of God" (1 John 3:1). This special kind of love that makes us sons of God is the love that John describes in the next chapter: "In this was manifested the love of God toward us, because that God sent his only begotten Son into the world, that we might live through him. Herein is love, not that we loved God, but that he loved us, and sent his Son to be the propitiation for our sins" (1 John 4:9–10).

When we pray, "Our Father," we are saying, "Lord, we are thine by redemption. We stand reconciled by the cross of Christ. We approach Thee, clothed in the merits of our Saviour. Thou hast begotten us [1 Peter 1:3; James 1:18]. Thou hast given us Thy name [Daniel 9:19]. And Thou hast destined us to eternal communion with Thee through Thy Son, for Thou hast said that Thou hast 'given unto us exceeding great and precious promises: that by these [we] might be partakers of the divine nature, having escaped the corruption that is in the world through lust'" (2 Peter 1:4).

What a testimony! God has saved *us*! Consider what we are by nature: "I have said to corruption, Thou art my father: to the worm, Thou art my mother, and my sister" (Job 17:14). Commenting on this verse Thomas Manton said that we are "cousins to worms, a handful of enlivened dust." Yet by the grace of God we can honestly say to Almighty God, "*Thou* art our Father." How can such a thing be? The answer is astounding and awe-inspiring: We worms become the sons of God because the Son of God made Himself a worm for us. This is the witness of Scripture. Psalm 22:6 describes the confession of Christ on the cross in these words: "I am a worm, and no man; a reproach of men, and despised of the people." With such an intimate relationship with God, based on such a union of Christ with us, we know that praying "our Father" assures us that God will hear us.

Richly Endowed

The third truth that the words *our Father* teach us is that we stand before God as people who are richly endowed. We enjoy unique privileges as the sons of our Heavenly Father, and this is something we must keep in mind as we come to pray. Too often we feel the pressure of our difficulties and needs so keenly that we lose sight of the privileges we possess. If we can honestly address God as our Father, whatever our current circumstances, we are already richly blessed. God is our Father and He has richly endowed His children. The Bible supplies us with a full list of the blessings and privileges the Lord confers on us because we are His children.

The Indwelling Spirit

First and foremost among the privileges of the children of God is this: Our Father gives us His Holy Spirit to dwell in us. "Ye have not received the spirit of bondage again to fear; but ye have received the Spirit of adoption, whereby we cry, Abba, Father" (Romans 8:15). In Galatians 4:6 Paul returns to this theme:

"Because ye are sons, God hath sent forth the Spirit of his Son into your hearts, crying, Abba, Father" (Galatians 4:6).

The Father gives us the indwelling Holy Spirit to lead us. Paul says, "As many as are led by the Spirit of God, they are the sons of God" (Romans 8:14). It is the prerogative of the sons of God to be led by the Spirit of God. In fact, according to Paul, being led by the Holy Spirit is a definitive mark of God's true sons. In the context of Romans 8, "As many as are led by the Spirit, they are the sons of God" is tantamount to saying, "As many as are the sons of God, they are led by the Spirit of God." There are no exceptions to the rule. All the sons of God are led by the Spirit of God. If this definition of the sons of God is accurate—and obviously it is, for it is inspired—there is something radically wrong with the experience of most professing Christians, who live without the vital reality of the leading of the Holy Spirit and the consciousness of the divine fellowship that it brings.

The whole idea of divine guidance has become a matter of intense controversy. Some, following the subjective, extra-biblical teachings popularized by the Pentecostal and Charismatic movements, glibly claim divine guidance for their own whims and wishes. Others swing to the opposite extreme and practically deny that there is such a thing as divine guidance or knowing the will of God for one's life, beyond making our own decisions in keeping with the moral commandments of Scripture. But the leading of the Holy Spirit is surely something of which we must be conscious. As He leads His people into all the truth that has been revealed in the gospel and as He makes Christ a living reality to them, He communicates with them. This is not mysticism, as some falsely claim, but Bible Christianity.

The Father also gives us His Spirit to comfort us by teaching us the fullness He has for us in Christ. "Now we have received, not the spirit of the world, but the spirit which is of God; that we might know the things that are freely given to us of God" (1 Corinthians 2:12). Knowing the things that are freely given to us by God is probably the single most important key to a Christian's sanctification and happiness, and yet it is one of the most neglected areas of New Testament teaching. Instead of all the "how-to" books that have become so popular among us; instead of the psychological gimmicks that masquerade under misapplied texts of Scripture; and instead of the promotion of so-called "principles" (usually human theories, often dredged from the thinking of atheists or agnostics and refurbished in Christian-sounding language) that bring God's people back under legal bondage—instead of these things, we need a clear understanding of the objective reality of what we are and have in Christ. This is what we need in order to live the life of faith, for as Peter says, "His divine power hath given unto us all things that pertain unto life and godliness, through the knowledge of him that hath called us to glory and virtue" (2 Peter 1:3). To live in the light of what we believe is to allow the gospel to govern our behavior, or to put it another way, it is to live by faith. Clearly, to live by the faith of the gospel we need to know as much as possible of what our Father says about it, and to help us in this He has given us His Spirit.

Our Father gives us His Spirit also to supply us with power for service. "If ye then, being evil, know how to give good gifts unto your children: how much more shall your heavenly Father give the Holy Spirit to them that ask him?" (Luke 11:13). God's work must be energized by God's power: "This is the word of the Lord,...Not by might, nor by power, but by my spirit, saith the Lord of hosts" (Zechariah 4:6). In this text, *might* signifies "armies" or great numbers, and *power* denotes human strength or ability. These are not the necessary instruments for the success of God's work. What is needed is His Spirit and the working of His power. The early church proved this and so must we. Having received the Spirit of our Father, we cannot settle for anything less than the full experience and enjoyment of His ministry of guidance, instruction, and power.

Supply of Needs

In exercising His fatherhood, our Father in heaven also supplies all our needs. Fathers are to be providers for their children. This is God's law. He tells human parents that "the children ought not to lay up for the parents, but the parents for the children" (2 Corinthians 12:14). In doing so, they act according to the manner of our heavenly Father toward His children. The Lord Jesus emphasized the Father's provision for us in His Sermon on the Mount. He tells us first that God knows our need: "Your Father knoweth what things ye have need of, before ye ask him" (Matthew 6:8). Then He assures us that we may trust our Father to meet the needs He sees we have: "Therefore take no [anxious] thought, saying, What shall we eat? or, What shall we drink? or, Wherewithal shall we be clothed? (For after all these things do the Gentiles seek:) for your heavenly Father knoweth that ye have need of all these things. But seek ye first the kingdom of God, and his righteousness; and all these things shall be added unto you" (verses 31–33).

The history of the Christian church gives us outstanding examples of this provision. Think again of George Müller, who depended solely on the Lord so that without appeals to any human agency, he saw God provide all the finances and food to build and run his orphan homes. But Müller was not unique. He got his inspiration to prove God in this way from what he learned about the work of the eighteenth-century German Pietist Augustus Hermann Francke. Such men are only particularly visible examples of something all Christians prove in their own lives: God looks after His children.

When Paul was in want and the believers at Philippi sent him some much-needed supplies, he took it as God's provision, for he had appealed to none but the Lord. In writing to thank the Philippians, who had given not out of abundance but out of their own need, the apostle said: "I have all, and abound: I am full, having received of Epaphroditus the things which were sent from you, an odour of a sweet smell, a sacrifice acceptable, wellpleasing to God. But my God shall supply all your need according to his riches in glory by Christ Jesus" (Philippians 4:18–19). *God shall supply all your need.* That is the assurance our Father gives His children.

The Lord stands by His people, ready to fend for them and feed them. Because He is our shepherd we shall not want (Psalm 23:2), and He will furnish for us a table in the wilderness (verse 5; Psalm 78:19). When He redeems His people, He brings them into His promised land, a place of milk and honey (Exodus 3:8; Deuteronomy 8:7), which is a plain type of our salvation rest in Christ (Hebrews 4). So our Father does not forsake His children; He feeds them. This is a major doctrine of the Scriptures, repeated often to comfort the people of God in all their afflictions.

Consider the following statement: "The Lord will not forsake his people for his great name's sake: because it hath pleased the Lord to make you his people" (1 Samuel 12:22)—there are two reasons here for assurance: first, the honor of the Lord's name, and second, the relationship His people enjoy with Him. Consider also, "The Lord loveth judgment, and forsaketh not his saints; they are preserved for ever" (Psalm 37:28); and "The Lord will not cast off his people, neither will he forsake his inheritance" (Psalm 94:14). These assurances hold good even in the midst of trouble and affliction, as Paul testifies, "We are troubled on every side, yet not distressed; we are perplexed, but not in despair; persecuted, but not forsaken; cast down, but not destroyed" (2 Corinthians 4:8–9). This certainty of our Father's never-failing presence and provision is what makes the apostle's exultant cry in 2 Corinthians 2:14 more than wishful thinking: "Thanks be unto God, which always causeth us to triumph in Christ" (2 Corinthians 2:14).

Comfort in Trouble

As our Father, God comforts us in all our trouble. David expressed this confidence in Psalm 103:13: "Like as a father pitieth his children, so the Lord pitieth them that fear him." Our God has a true father's heart toward His children. He understands them even better than they understand themselves. And He is not harsh and demanding. This is a truth that is all too often forgotten or tacitly denied, even by Bible believers. Jesus said, "My yoke is easy, and my burden is light" (Matthew 11:30). As David proceeded to say in Psalm 103, "He knoweth our frame; he remembereth that we are dust" (verse 14). To hear some preachers, you would think that God is standing behind His children with a big stick, ready to come down hard on them at the slightest provocation. Sitting under such guilt-ridden preaching, many a Christian has such a faulty view of the Lord that he lives in cowering insecurity, always remembering his own failures and forgetting the Lord's fatherly pity.

Commenting on Psalm 103:14, E. W. Bullinger remarks in his *Companion Bible*, "God *remembers* what man forgets (i.e., our infirmities); and He *forgets* what man remembers (i.e., our sins)." What a lovely thought—and what a comfort! It is true that our Father is holy and calls us to holiness (1 Peter 1:14–16), but He has pardoned our sin and buried it beyond His remembrance for ever (Hebrews 8:12). Even when He has to correct us, He does it in love to preserve us, not to destroy us. He is never vengeful or implacable to His children but is the ever-present help and comfort of our souls. Describing a period of intense personal trial and physical danger, Paul rejoiced, "Blessed be God, even the Father of our Lord Jesus Christ, the Father of mercies, and the God of all comfort, who comforteth us in all our tribulation, that we may be able to comfort them which are in any trouble, by the comfort wherewith we ourselves are comforted of God" (2 Corinthians 1:3–4). God is our Father, and even if we forget it, He never does.

Chastening

As our Father, God chastens us for our good. Chastening is part of child rearing (Proverbs 3:12). The English word carries the idea of making chaste or pure, and that is certainly the object of parental discipline. This idea is present in the scriptural representation of the Lord's dealings with His children (Deuteronomy 4:10; Psalm 94:12; 1 Peter 1:14–16). However, the Greek terms used by the New Testament have the central idea of child rearing or discipline. The picture is of the Lord acting as our Father to form in us a character becoming those who bear the name of the sons of God. "We have had fathers of our flesh which corrected us, and we gave them reverence: shall we not much rather be in subjection unto the Father of spirits, and live? For they verily for a few days chastened us after their own pleasure; but he for our profit, that we might be partakers of his holiness" (Hebrews 12:9–10).

Here is the divine purpose of chastening. Chastening is not a case of God losing His temper with us, as earthly fathers are wont to do with their children. God cannot do that. Divine chastening is never an orgy of wrathful passion. Rather, it is the peculiar work of God in those who are truly His sons by which He produces in them an image of Himself: "If ye endure chastening, God dealeth with you as with sons; for what son is he whom the father chasteneth not? But if ye be without chastisement, whereof all are partakers, then are ye bastards, and not sons" (Hebrews 12:7–8). Scripture honestly admits that chastening is not something that normal people like to endure. But it is essential and is a mark of the special care our Father in heaven takes of His people: "No chastening for the present seemeth to be joyous, but grievous: nevertheless afterward it yieldeth the peaceable fruit of righteousness unto them which are exercised thereby" (Hebrews 12:11).

Spiritual Enrichment

We may mention one further way in which God deals with us as a Father: He enriches us beyond all comprehension. It was a special burden on Peter's heart to get this truth over to the suffering saints of his day: "Blessed be the God and Father of our Lord Jesus Christ, which according to his abundant mercy hath begotten us again unto a lively hope by the resurrection of Jesus Christ from the dead, to an inheritance incorruptible, and undefiled, and that fadeth not away, reserved in heaven for you, who are kept by the power of God through faith unto salvation ready to be revealed in the last time" (1 Peter 1:3–5). Here is a familiar New Testament theme. Our Father has "blessed us with all spiritual blessings in heavenly places in Christ" (Ephesians 1:3), given us "the riches of his goodness and forbearance and longsuffering" (Romans 2:4), and redeemed us "according to the riches of his grace" (Ephesians 1:7). While the words Paul uses in 1 Corinthians 2:9 are by many pressed into service as a description of heaven, the apostle intended them as a description of the believer's present possessions in Christ: "Eye hath not seen, nor ear heard, neither have entered into the heart of man, the things which God hath prepared for them that love him. But God hath revealed them unto us by his Spirit" (1 Corinthians 2:9–10).

Here is a rich endowment indeed, and it is but the beginning: "Behold, what manner of love the Father hath bestowed upon us, that we should be called the sons of God: therefore the world knoweth us not, because it knew him not. Beloved, now are we the sons of God, and it doth not yet appear what we shall be: but we know that, when he shall appear, we shall be like him; for we shall see him as he is" (1 John 3:1–2). Our Father's future enrichment of His people beggars human vocabulary, but we know that He has "raised us up together, and made us sit together in heavenly places in Christ Jesus: that in the ages to come he might shew the exceeding riches of his grace in his kindness toward us through Christ Jesus" (Ephesians 2:6–7).

With such a rich endowment, when we come to pray, we must not allow our immediate circumstances to blind us to the blessings of having God as our Father. We must not allow the things or events of earth to rob us of the joy of the rich blessings of the sons of God. The more we enjoy these blessings, the better equipped we will be to deal with the hardships of life. This is the secret of the strength to persevere when every earthly circumstance echoes the shrill call of Job's wife to abandon God and die (Job 2:9).

Sooner or later all of us must face this trial and we will do so when our human resources are at their lowest ebb, when we are physically and emotionally drained. However, we have a way of certain victory in such a situation. It is not a matter of human courage or determination. It is a way that is open to every Christian. Peter tells us of it in 1 Peter 1:6: "Wherein ye greatly rejoice, though now for a season, if need be, ye are in heaviness through manifold temptations." By human standards, it appears incongruous, to say the least, to speak of people who "are in heaviness through manifold temptations"—literally, "who have been put to grief in or by various trials"—"greatly rejoicing," or *exulting*. But that is what Peter does, and he is not indulging in religious hyperbole or whipping up some sort of hermit-like carelessness of earthly surroundings or sufferings. The people he addresses actually feel the pain of suffering, but there are certain things in which they rejoice and which remain true whatever is going on around them or happening to them. Peter has listed these things in the opening verses of his epistle, which we have already quoted. It is the remembrance that our Father has, in abundant mercy, begotten us again to a living hope through our risen Saviour and has appointed us an inheritance that will never fade away and has guaranteed to preserve us unto that eternal kingdom—it is this remembrance that gives believers both joy and strength to persevere amid the trials of life.

If we can honestly address God as "our Father" in the knowledge of the full significance of the phrase, even in those times when we are so weak that we cannot compose a prayer of high-sounding expressions, we will feel the sunlight of heaven beaming into our hearts, enabling us to see beyond the fogs of our immediate troubles and trials and to exult in the glorious realities of being the children of God.

Obligations of Sons

There is one more truth that the opening words of the Lord's Prayer lead us to consider, namely, our obligations as the children of God. With every privilege there comes a responsibility. When we pray, "Our Father," we are professing to be His children. If God is our Father, there are some things that Scripture sets before us as our filial duties.

Gratitude

We should show true gratitude. God our Father is the "Father of mercies" (2 Corinthians 1:3), the one whom David praised in Psalm 68:19: "Blessed be the

Lord, who daily loadeth us with benefits, even the God of our salvation." The metric version of Psalm 136 carries the same message:

> Praise God, for He is kind:
> His mercy lasts for aye.
> Give thanks with heart and mind
> To God of gods always:
> For certainly His mercies dure
> Most firm and sure eternally.

We should manifest this spirit of thankfulness for the unspeakable goodness of God to us. We must not be like greedy, grasping children who take our Father's rich grace for granted. We must never allow the very multitude of God's mercies, which are new every morning (Lamentations 3:23), or the certainty of their supply to dull our sense of gratitude. The thoughtless ingratitude of the nine lepers whom Jesus cleansed but who did not return to say thank you (Luke 17:17) should have no place in the heart of a child of God. All we are and have — or ever will be or have — we owe to our Father's sovereign goodness and grace. We above all others should be thankful people.

Holiness

The second obvious filial duty of those who call God their Father is to flee sin and follow righteousness. We have already noted Peter's command that "as obedient children" we should not fashion ourselves by the lusts of the ungodly but should be holy as our Father is holy (1 Peter 1:14–16). In Deuteronomy 32:5–6 we read: "They have corrupted themselves, their spot is not the spot of his children: they are a perverse and crooked generation. Do ye thus requite the Lord, O foolish people and unwise? is not he thy father that hath bought thee? hath he not made thee, and established thee?" What Moses says here is, "If God is your Father, then you must not corrupt yourselves. If you bear the *name* of God, you should bear the *mark* of God, which is holiness. If you are numbered among the *sons* of God, you must live as the *saints* of God." Men become like the one they worship. Idolaters become like their idols: "They that make them are like unto them; so is every one that trusteth in them" (Psalm 115:8; 135:18). God's children should become more and more like Him (2 Corinthians 3:18), partakers of His holiness (Hebrews 12:10).

Honor

If God is our Father, we should honor Him. The "first commandment with promise" is the fifth commandment: "Honour thy father and thy mother" (Exodus 20:12; Ephesians 6:2). If such honor is due our fathers on earth, how much more should we honor our Father in heaven? If we reverence our fathers after the flesh, "shall we not much rather [reverence] … the Father of spirits" (Hebrews 12:9)? God expects no less, though often those who claim to be His children fail to honor Him: "A son honoureth his father:… if then I be a father, where is mine honour?" (Malachi 1:6). Where is the regard for His "worthy name by which ye are called" (James 2:7)? Where is the happy obedience to His will? Or the dedication of our substance to the furtherance of His work that Proverbs 3:9 commands? And where is our Father's honor when it comes to our treatment of the Lord's Day, the Christian Sabbath? These are serious and searching questions. Do we call God our Father? Unless we honor Him, we give the lie to our profession.

Godly Fear

We may mention one more filial duty that is made clear in Scripture. We should spend our lives in godly fear: "If ye call on the Father, who without respect of persons judgeth according to every man's work, pass the time of your sojourning here in fear" (1 Peter 1:17). There is a popular fallacy that fear and love are mutually exclusive—that is, if we love God, we need not fear Him, and if we fear Him, we have not progressed as far as loving Him. Sometimes 1 John 4:18 is quoted to support this view: "There is no fear in love; but perfect love casteth out fear: because fear hath torment. He that feareth is not made perfect in love." But John is not speaking of godly fear. What he is dealing with is a slavish dread of judgment, as is clear from the immediate context—the fear he excludes from Christian love is the opposite of "boldness [confidence] before him in the day of judgment" (verse 17). That this is the apostle's meaning is further proved by his statement, "Fear hath torment," or "Fear has to do with (or has in it) *punishment*," as the Greek word *kolasis* is translated in its only other appearance in the New Testament (Matthew 25:46). To use this text to teach that the fear of God is an inferior attitude, unworthy of our relationship with "our Father" is a flagrant misuse of Scripture.

The idea that love and fear cannot co-exist could not be further from the truth. Concerning the Son of God Himself, the Lord Jesus Christ, we read, "When he had offered up prayers and supplications with strong crying and tears unto him that was able to save him from death, [he] was heard *in that he feared*" (Hebrews 5:7). Far from being mutually *exclusive,* fear and love to God are mutually *inclusive.* Only those who have godly fear have any true love for God. A godly fear, a deep, reverential awe, goes right along with calling God, "Abba Father." We should always recognize who our Father is. He is the God of glory. Angels veil their faces and cover their feet in His presence. Heaven and earth await His commands. He is the almighty. He is not a tyrant whom we must approach with slavish dread but our Father whom we adore with reverential awe. As John Newton found, this is one of the keys to enjoying the place of prayer:

> How sweet and awful [awe inspiring] is the place
> With Christ within the doors,
> While everlasting love displays
> The choicest of her stores.

Our Father—to most people it is just an empty phrase, something they say by rote, without thought or appreciation of its glorious implications. We must never fall into this error that is so demeaning to God and so costly to us, for it robs us of the comforts our souls' need. Therefore, let us ponder the glorious significance of these words *our Father*. They teach us that we never stand alone in God's presence, that we enjoy the most intimate relationship with Him, and that we have received a rich endowment from His hand to enable us to live in a manner that is worthy of His name. By leading us into deep and sweet communion with Him, they are a major part of Christ's answer to the cry of every believing heart: They teach us what it really is to pray.

Praying to the King of Heaven

"Our Father which art in heaven" Matthew 6:9

One of the Lord Jesus Christ's favorite ways of referring to God was to call Him "my [or *your*] Father which is in heaven." The Gospels record His using it seventeen times, with the equivalent phrase *heavenly Father* occurring a further six times. Our Lord used this title with a clear purpose. As a brief survey of the relevant texts will show, He intended that from His use of the title His disciples would learn lessons that would shape their entire lives.

- They were to live before men so as to "glorify your Father which is in heaven" (Matthew 5:16).

- They were to be imitators of God in His kindness toward men—even His enemies—so that they would show themselves "the children of your Father which is in heaven" (Matthew 5:45).

- They were to practice true holiness, not as men-pleasers, but in the sight of God, so that they would gain the "reward of your Father which is in heaven" (Matthew 6:1).

- They were to prove the reality of their profession of faith in Him by doing "the will of my Father which is in heaven" (Matthew 7:21).

- And, of course, they were to pray to "our Father, which art in heaven."

Understanding the significance of this title is vital to all true prayer. What does it mean? What does *heaven* signify in this connection? The simplest answer to this question is that *heaven* tells us *where* God is and *what* God is.

Heaven Is God's Dwelling Place

In his prayer at the dedication of the temple, Solomon prayed, "Hear thou in heaven thy dwelling place" (1 Kings 8:43). This language does not suggest that any place can *contain* God. He is not included within the bounds or compass of any place. Solomon recognized this and so must we: "Behold, the heaven and heaven of heavens cannot contain thee" (1 Kings 8:27). As the Lord Himself says, "Do not I fill heaven and earth?" (Jeremiah 23:24). God is omnipresent. Theologians use the term *immensity* to describe His relation to space. They mean that He fills all space. For good measure they sometimes add the word *repletively*. It is redundant to say that He fills it fully, but the truth is that human minds and human language are inadequate to describe God. The best theologians can do is to emphasize that God is the uncontained, unbounded, unlimited, and illimitable Creator.

There is no exact illustration of the immensity of God available to us, but the presence of the human soul in its body comes closest. Where is the soul located? Is it in the head any more than in the feet or fingers? No, it is equally in every part of the body—and yet it is not distributed throughout the body. That is, we do not have part of the soul in one area of the body and another part in a different area. If we lose a limb we do not with it lose part of the soul. The soul fills the body but, to use precise theological terminology, not by extension. We may look on this mystery as a reflection of the greater mystery of the greatness of God and His relation to space.[1] He fills infinite space and time so that He is equally present in every specific place at every particular time. This is His omnipresence. However, His creatures, even the angels of heaven, are not omnipresent. Every creature is bound by time and space and can be in only one place at one time. So, in relation to His creatures God has chosen "the heaven of heavens," as Solomon termed it, as the place of the fullest manifestation of His power and glory.

Heaven Describes the Character of God

Heavenly Father obviously means that God is our Father in a way that distinguishes this use of the term *father* from every earthly use of it. We must not

---

[1] Using this illustration has nothing to do with the heretical notion adopted by so-called Process Theology that God is the soul of the universe. He is not. He is the Creator of the universe, and His existence, consciousness, and perfections are in no sense dependent on the universe He created. What we are discussing as the immensity of God is not His relation to the universe but His relation to *infinite space*. The distinction is important. The universe of created things exists within—but is distinct from—infinite space. Samuel Clarke, an early eighteenth-century Church of England theologian whose speculations are not always to be trusted, may have come nearest to the truth with his view that infinite space is not a creation but an attribute of God. If this is true, it opens an important line of thought on the subject of the necessity of God's existence and gives a more radical meaning than has been usually accorded to Paul's statement that "in him we live, and move, and have our being" (Acts 17:28).

judge God by any earthly experience of fatherhood. Even the best earthly fathers are weak and flawed. Others are downright wicked. To many whose earthly fathers have been monsters, the news that God is their Father sounds more threatening than thrilling. But this is to judge by mere earthly standards. It loses sight of the all-important word *heavenly*. God is our "heavenly Father" and heavenliness marks all His dealings with His children. His fatherhood is a glorious spiritual revelation of His relationship with His redeemed. The relationship is one of peculiar intimacy, marked by a closeness that even archangels have never experienced.

As our heavenly Father, God shows Himself to be all-perfect and all-powerful. In the prayers recorded in Scripture the mention of God's being in the heavens stirs the worshippers to magnify His righteousness and sovereign power. For example, the psalmist rejoices, "Righteousness and judgment are the habitation of his throne.... The heavens declare his righteousness" (Psalm 97:2, 6). Jehoshaphat prayed, "O Lord God of our fathers, art not thou God in heaven? and rulest not thou over all the kingdoms of the heathen? and in thine hand is there not power and might, so that none is able to withstand thee?" (2 Chronicles 20:6). The Lord Jesus Christ intended to include these ideas when He taught His disciples to pray, "Our Father which art in heaven," but He obviously included another glorious truth: Because He is our Father, this holy and all-powerful God of heaven is accessible to us on earth. Our Father is the most high God, the king of heaven and the ruler of earth, and He will hear the prayer of us His children. This is the central message that Jesus teaches when He instructs us to pray, "Our Father which art in heaven." This central truth of the text carries within it many implications about prayer. It sets before us what we may call lessons about prayer from the transcendent greatness of God our Father.

Lesson One: Lay Hold of Our Father's Absolute Sovereignty

The words *which art in heaven* signify our Father's total, absolute, complete, and unbounded sovereignty. He testifies of Himself, "Thus saith the Lord, The heaven is my throne, and the earth is my footstool" (Isaiah 66:1). The psalmist expressed the faith of every believer who approaches the throne of God: "Our God is in the heavens: he hath done whatsoever he hath pleased" (Psalm 115:3). The meaning could not be clearer: Our God possesses total sovereignty over all His creation.

We must be honest and say that we cannot explain what is happening in the world and why it is happening. We can only confess our faith that our Father is in total control, that He does what He pleases, and that what He pleases is good and right. We hear a lot about the "problems" of evil and suffering. How and why does a holy God allow such things? There is no easy answer—that is, no answer that we can easily comprehend. We can say that the world is not in the state in which God created it, but has fallen under the curse of sin. It lies under the judgment of God. That is part of the answer, but it does not enable us to address every tragic situation.

While suffering and death are traceable to the entrance of sin into the world (Romans 5:12), there is often no immediate connection between a person's sins and his circumstances. The Lord Jesus made this clear when He answered the question His disciples put to Him on meeting a man who had been born blind. They assumed that his affliction was the direct result of sin in him or in his parents, but Jesus told them that they were wrong: "Neither hath this man sinned, nor his parents: but that the works of God should be made manifest in him" (John 9:2–3). The Saviour made no attempt to go any further with His answer. He did not address the question of why God would allow suffering for His own glory. He leaves us with the bald assertion that the glory of God is good and sufficient reason for anything that occurs. Every creature exists for God's good pleasure and all-wise purpose: "Thou art worthy, O Lord, to receive glory and honour and power: for thou hast created all things, and for thy pleasure they are and were created" (Revelation 4:11). We must confess that we cannot understand what God is doing. He alone is infinite and He alone can understand His own ways: "O the depth of the riches both of the wisdom and knowledge of God! how unsearchable are his judgments, and his ways past finding out!" (Romans 11:33).

As we pray we must actively lay hold of this truth and rest on the assurance that while we cannot understand what God is doing, He does; and He knows that it is good and worthy of Himself. When a mine shaft collapsed in northern England and the frantic families gathered around the pit demanded of their vicar an explanation of God's purpose, the good man was at a loss for a while. Then he noticed that an old woman had brought her needle work with her. Borrowing it, he held up the "wrong" side so that all could see the ragged ends and the apparently meaningless jumble of colored threads. Then he turned it around and showed them a picture of planning and beauty, wrought with great skill. He explained that at the moment, all we can see are the threads of God's purpose. Not only are we looking at an unfinished work, we are looking at it from the "wrong" side, not from God's side. Could we see the "problem" circumstances of life as our Father does, we would see a picture of perfect beauty with every thread in its ordained place. Our Father does all things well.

When we pray we must keep the absolute sovereignty of our Father ever before us. The assurance of this truth gives great strength to God's people when, passing through the depths of trial and trouble, they complain as Jacob did, "All these things are against me" (Genesis 42:36). When that happens, the thing that sustains them is that they can come to the throne of the God of glory who "worketh all things after the counsel of his own will" (Ephesians 1:11). It brings peace to the troubled soul just to confess, "Lord, I do not know what is happening. I cannot understand Thy purpose, but I know that it is the purpose of my Father who works all for His glory and for my good." Paul wrote out of a deep personal experience of suffering and yet he exulted, "We know that all things work together for good to them that love God, to them who are the called according to his purpose" (Romans 8:28). This does not mean that a Christian does not feel the pain of human suffering and loss. He does, but he also feels the assurance that in the midst of all his perplexities His heavenly Father is sovereignly working out His perfect purpose and that this present situation is one of the threads He is weaving into the perfect picture of His final purpose.

Our Father is the One who is in heaven. As God taught the haughty Babylonian king Nebuchadnezzar, "The most High ruleth in the kingdom of men, and giveth it to whomsoever he will.... The heavens do rule" (Daniel 4:25–26). Nebuchadnezzar learned this truth the hard way, for he lost his own throne before he submitted to God's. Later, when he had learned the truth of God's sovereignty, he confessed, "I blessed the most High, and I praised and honoured him that liveth for ever, whose dominion is an everlasting dominion, and his kingdom is from generation to generation: and all the inhabitants of the earth are reputed as nothing: and he doeth according to his will in the army of heaven, and among the inhabitants of the earth: and none can stay his hand, or say unto him, What doest thou?... Now I Nebuchadnezzar praise and extol and honour the King of heaven, all whose works are truth, and his ways judgment: and those that walk in pride he is able to abase" (Daniel 4:34–35, 37).

Christians should pray in all the circumstances of life, when things are pleasant as well as when they are trying. However, given the all-pervasive reality of sin and suffering in the world, it is inevitable that most of our praying will be against the backdrop of things that vex or perplex us. Then, more than ever, is the time to cry from the heart, "Our Father which art in heaven." Trust in the absolute sovereignty of our God is not a glib philosophy for fair-weather theorists, but rather the battle-tested comfort of the saints in all ages. As the Lord said to Isaiah, "The Lord of hosts hath sworn, saying, Surely as I have thought, so shall it come to pass; and as I have purposed, so shall it stand" (Isaiah 14:24). This will always be a source of peace and comfort to praying hearts.

Lesson Two: **Remember Our Father's Majestic Holiness**

When Jesus tells us to pray, "Our Father which art in heaven," He means to impress on us the truth of our Father's majestic holiness. When we pray, we should never for a moment forget that we are coming to a holy God. The phrase *in heaven* certainly implies this. "Thus saith the high and lofty One that inhabiteth eternity, whose name is Holy; I dwell in the high and holy place, with him also that is of a contrite and humble spirit, to revive the spirit of the humble, and to revive the heart of the contrite ones" (Isaiah 57:15). God says, "I dwell in heaven, but I also dwell on earth in the hearts of those who are contrite and humble," that is, with those who have a deep sense of His holiness and of their own sin.

Failure to live in the light of God's holiness robs us of His presence, as the history of Israel illustrates. One of the Jews' worst crimes was that while they paid lip service to the truth of God's holiness and hypocritically employed the pious language of Moses and the prophets on the subject, they flaunted their wickedness in His sight. Thus He denounced their worship as arrogant and wearisome: "Thou hast made me to serve [i.e., burdened me] with thy sins, thou hast wearied me with thine iniquities" (Isaiah 43:24). In many ways this is a frightening text, for it shows the depths to which even those who profess and possess revealed truth may sink, especially in their religious exercises. What those Jews were doing was to continue to approach the Lord in their usual forms of prayer and worship, using the same hallowed formulas, but with the attitude that He would have to take them as He found them. He would just have to put up with their sins. But while God is merciful and slow to anger, He will not acquit the wicked (Nehemiah 9:17; Nahum 1:3)—He does not ultimately put up with peoples' sins. His name is holy and His only earthly dwelling place is in the hearts of those who are of a humble, contrite spirit.

Thus we need to learn humility and godly fear, especially in our approach to God in worship. Solomon stressed this: "Be not rash with thy mouth, and let not thine heart be hasty to utter any thing before God: for God is in heaven, and thou upon earth: therefore let thy words be few" (Ecclesiastes 5:2). One of the greatest prayer warriors who ever lived was Abraham. God spoke freely with him, and he with God. When he learned from the Lord that Sodom and the other cities of the plain were on the verge of an annihilating judgment, he interceded with God and pleaded with Him to spare them. He started by asking the Lord to spare them if He could find fifty righteous people in them. The Lord answered his prayer and he was emboldened to plead his case for an even greater degree of mercy. In the end he asked God to spare the entire cities if He could find a mere ten righteous people in them. Again God answered his prayer. Clearly, Abraham was on intimate terms with the Lord. Indeed, the Lord called him "Abraham my friend" (Isaiah 41:8). Yet notice how he prayed: "Behold now, I have taken upon me to speak unto the Lord, which am but dust and ashes" (Genesis 18:27). In prayer he could never forget that he was an unworthy sinner in the presence of the Holy God.

As the church of Christ has lost the vision of the holiness of God, it has lost power in prayer. There was a time when this nation felt the power of churches meeting to pray. That is hardly true any longer. Has God changed? No, He has not, but professing Christians have almost entirely lost the sense of His awe-inspiring holiness. They make God serve with their sins. The thinking seems to be, "God is our Father. Surely He understands us and wants us to be comfortable and happy. Therefore, what makes us comfortable and happy, not what holiness and godly fear demand, determines what is right and acceptable. If what we are doing is wrong, He will forgive or overlook it." It is the old story of the Jews' presumption all over again: God will put up with our sins. But He will not. Now, as then, sin will deprive us of the comfort of His presence and power: "Behold, the Lord's hand is not shortened, that it cannot save; neither his ear heavy, that it cannot hear: but your iniquities have separated between you and your God, and your sins have hid his face from you, that he will not hear" (Isaiah 59:1–2). God forgives sin, but forgiveness always follows confession that comes from a contrite heart—and contrition always follows a spiritual perception of the holiness of God.

When we pray, "Our Father which art in heaven," let us remember the holiness of God. Let the realization of that holiness permeate our thinking, and it will determine our whole outlook on life and give us the desire so well expressed by the prayer attributed to the saintly Robert Murray McCheyne: "O God, make me as holy as it is possible for a redeemed sinner to be." Or as Peter put it, "As he which hath called you is holy, so be ye holy in all manner of conversation; because it is written, Be ye holy; for I am holy. And if ye call on the Father, who without respect of persons judgeth according to every man's work, pass the time of your sojourning here in fear" (1 Peter 1:15–17).

Lesson Three: **Trust Our Father's Perfect Wisdom**

From the fact that the Lord is in heaven and we are on the earth, we should learn that we have very limited knowledge and should therefore trust His all-wise purpose. We gather this from His well known statement in Isaiah 55:8–9: "My thoughts are not your thoughts, neither are your ways my ways, saith the Lord. For as the heavens are higher than the earth, so are my ways higher than your ways, and my thoughts than your thoughts." The meaning is clear: the Lord is the all-wise, eternal, sovereign God. He dwells in heaven. We, on the other hand, are a microscopic part of a world that is itself a microscopic part of creation. We are severely limited; our vision is narrow and we tend toward surface reactions based on immediate experience; we jump to large conclusions from inadequate and usually misconstrued premises. We are on the earth and of the earth. By contrast, the Lord is in heaven. Thus when we look into the heavens and see them high above the earth, we should remember that He who dwells there and who sees and knows all things simultaneously has a purpose far beyond our puny comprehension. While we may not know what He is doing, He does.

Here is a truth that is calculated to bring comfort and stability to all who can honestly pray, "Our Father which art in heaven." They derive strength from the knowledge that their Father is acting according to an often hidden but always good purpose. They will not be overwhelmed in the time of crisis but will find strength in their Father's assurance: "I know the thoughts that I think toward you, saith the Lord, thoughts of peace, and not of evil, to give you an expected end [or, a future and a hope]" (Jeremiah 29:11). Thus when we pray, surrounded as we are by all the perplexities and troubles of life, it is vitally important to keep before us the truth that God is our Father and that He is in heaven. That confidence will sustain us as it did David so that we will be able to rejoice, "As for God, his way is perfect:… It is God that girdeth me with strength, and maketh my way perfect" (Psalm 18:30, 32).

Sadly, there are times when Christians renounce such submission to their Father's wisdom, demand their own will, and live to regret it. Dr. M. R. de Haan told the story of an incident in his medical practice when he went to visit a woman whose three-year-old daughter was on the point of death. The woman was terribly distracted; instead of bowing humbly to her Father's wisdom, she rebelled violently and accused God of cruelty. She demanded that the Lord spare her daughter and told Him that she could never trust Him again if He did not do so. Despite the doctor's predictions, God healed her daughter. The little girl grew up in the normal way, and perhaps her mother learned to forget her rebellion against her Father's wisdom. Her complacency did not last long, however. When her daughter was seventeen, after four years of evil companionships, she died of suicide. The mother's tears were now more bitter than when the girl had lain at the point of death as a child. Convulsed with grief, the mother sobbed out to Dr. de Haan, "O Doctor, how I wish God had taken her when she was three years old!" That mother felt that she had come to experience what the Scriptures record of how the Lord responded to the Israelites' rebellious demands: "He gave them their request; but sent leanness into their soul" (Psalm 106:15). We cannot say that she was right in her assessment, but we can say that she learned the value of submission to her Father in heaven the hard way. We can understand her pleas for the life of her child—what parent would not earnestly cry for God's healing touch? However, in such times we should never fail to submit our desire to our Father's will.

As a boy I was fascinated by an American singer's rendition of the spiritual "Steal Away," during which he recited the following story in verse. I have never forgotten its message:

I was walkin' in Savannah,
Past a church decayed and dim,
When there slowly through the window
Came a plaintive funeral hymn.

And as sympathy awakened,
A wonder quickly grew
Till I found myself environed
In a little Negro pew.

Out in front a young couple,
Sad in sorrow and nearly wild,
On the altar was a coffin,
In the coffin was a child.

Rose a sad old Negro preacher
From a little wooden desk,
With a manner grandly awkward
And a countenance grotesque.

And he said: Now don't be weepin'
For this pretty bit of clay,
For the little boy who lived there,
He done gone and run away.

And he's doin' very finely,
And he 'preciates your love,
But he's sure enough Father want him
In the large house, up above.

Now He didn't give you that baby,
By a hundred thousand miles;
He just think you need some sunshine
And He lent him for a while.

And He let you love and keep it
Till you hearts were fuller grown,
And these silver tears you're sheddin'
Is just interest on the loan.

So, my poor dejected mourners,
Let your hearts with Jesus rest,
And don't go criticizin'
The One who knows the best.

He's give' us many comforts,
He has the right to take away.
To the Lord be praise and glory,
Now and ever, let us pray.

Lesson Four: **Rely on Our Father's Almighty Power**

Our Father is *in heaven*. He is *the King of Heaven*. His authority extends over all creation: "The Lord hath prepared his throne in the heavens; and his kingdom ruleth over all" (Psalm 103:19). So when we pray, "Our Father which art in heaven," we express our faith that He is omnipotent, that He is on the throne, and that He not only has the *right* to rule, but also the *power* to exercise that right. This is a truth of surpassing importance to us at all times, but especially when we pray. We come to our Father to ask for great things, things that are beyond the ability of man to achieve. Thus we must be conscious that we are coming to one who has said, "Behold, I am the Lord, the God of all flesh: is there anything too hard for me?" (Jeremiah 32:27). Bowing at the throne of grace, we must recognize that our Father in heaven possesses all power. Furthermore, we must remember that He exercises that power through our Lord Jesus Christ, who declared, "All power is given unto me in heaven and in earth" (Matthew 28: 18). If we have access to the throne of God through the mediation of Christ, then however dark or difficult the circumstances under which we are called to pray, we should be encouraged by the Lord's challenge to our faith: "Is anything too hard for me?" Absolutely not.

It was the assurance of this truth that burned in the heart of William Carey, the father of the modern missionary movement, and that led him to embrace the motto, "Attempt great things for God and expect great things from God." As he launched his mission in a heathen land, Carey was gripped by the thought that his God was omnipotent. Our God is not an idol. He is not like the gods of the heathen, which have eyes that see not, ears that hear not, hands that work not, and feet that walk not. Our God is the living and true God, the everlasting King (Jeremiah 10:10). He has *all* power, so that, as Jesus explained to His disciples about that greatest of all God's acts among men—the conversion of sinners—"With men this is impossible; but with God all things are possible" (Matthew 19:26).

Christians should not be satisfied with assenting to the general proposition that God is omnipotent. The Bible does not set this truth before us as a mere point of doctrine, but as a reality that should so grip our hearts as to drive us to prayer for the experience of God's sovereign power. In other words, it is not enough for us to acknowledge that God possesses all power. We must do that, for Isaiah 33:13 commands, "Acknowledge my might." We must also prevail with God in prayer for such demonstrations of His power as He sovereignly wills to give us. It is His will that His people enjoy the power of the gospel in their everyday lives (2 Peter 1:3–8), serve in the power of the Holy Spirit (Ephesians 5:18), and pray with the power of genuine effectiveness (Hebrews 4:16).

Such power cannot be produced by any decision we make. It is not the result of any course of human action. It is the fruit of faith, which must be understood as the response of a regenerate heart to a positive revelation of divine truth. Thus the Lord Jesus commanded His disciples, who were at the time amazed at a display of His power in cursing the fruitless fig tree, "Have faith in God" (Mark 11:22). What does that mean? It means, "Get to know what God says about His person, His purpose, and His promise. Then take God at His word. Fashion your living and your praying on what God has said." This is how we progress from marveling at the truth that our Father is omnipotent to experiencing His exercise of that power through us. Thus the Lord Jesus added a promise to His command to have faith in God: "Therefore I say unto you, What things soever ye desire, when ye pray, believe that ye receive them, and ye shall have them" (Mark 11:24). This promise, like all the other prayer promises of Scripture, assumes that we pray "according to His will" (1 John 5:14). Think of what Christ has laid down for us here. In effect He has said: "You acknowledge my sovereign power; that is good. But you may go further and experience the exercise of my power in your ministry. Have faith in your almighty God and pray according to His will, and you will receive His powerful response."

George Müller used to say that when we are praying, there are three things to ask ourselves. First, Is this God's work? Second, Is this God's way? Third, Is this God's time? If we pray for God's work to be done in God's way and in God's time, we will certainly receive the answer. He has the power to do whatever He pleases and no opposition of earth or hell can stop Him.

When we pray, then, we must keep before us the glorious truth that our Father is in heaven. With that conviction burning in our souls, our praying will transcend the feeble, faithless incantations that too many mistake for true prayer. We will pray joyfully and effectively in the certainty that our Father has all power to answer the cries of His children.

Lesson Five: **Pray from the Heart**

Another lesson of a different kind arises from the words *our Father which art in heaven.* It is that we must make prayer a matter of the heart and not merely a matter of the lips. We must never use these words to "the high and lofty one who inhabiteth eternity, whose name is Holy" (Isaiah 57:15) in a thoughtless manner. To do so is utterly useless. Thomas Manton was right to insist, "[It] is not the sound of the voice that can pierce heaven and enter into the ears of the Lord of Hosts, but sighs and groans of the spirit." Our Lord's condemnation of the Jews may just as truly be made of many who profess to pray the Lord's Prayer: "This people draweth nigh unto me with their mouth, and honoureth me with their lips; but their heart is far from me" (Matthew 15:8).

Hypocrisy is never more obscene than when, not content to seek to deceive men, it carries its pretense into the very presence of God. But God is not mocked (Galatians 6:7), and He is not moved by the multitude of words or by the beauty of our diction. As David learned, "Behold, thou desirest truth in the inward parts.... The sacrifices of God are a broken spirit: a broken and a contrite heart, O God, thou wilt not despise" (Psalm 51:6, 17). God desires truth in the heart. He pays no attention to the religion of the lips, except to condemn it. He detests religion that is all words and no heart.

The Scriptures show that often He blesses when the words leave a lot to be desired, but the heart is right. At times some of God's servants—Job, Elijah, and Jeremiah spring to mind—in the agony of their passion for God and His glory, uttered words to God that would be difficult to justify, but their hearts were right, and the Lord blessed them. This does not condone the use of ignorant or intemperate language to God. We should seek to have both our words and our hearts controlled by the Spirit through the word—and we must make sure that for us, our address to our Father in heaven is always the expression of our hearts and not merely of our lips.

Lesson Six: **Set Our Affections on Things Above**

There is another lesson that we must learn from the address, "Our Father which art in heaven," and that is that we must set our affections on things which are above. Our Father whom we approach in prayer is in heaven. John Chrysostom, the "Golden-Mouthed" minister of the church in Constantinople, commented in his *Homilies on St. Matthew,* "When He saith, 'In heaven,' He speaks not this as shutting up God there, but as withdrawing him who is praying from earth, and fixing him in the high places, and in the dwellings above" (Homily 19.6). Chrysostom here applies to the specific act of praying the general truth that Paul taught the Colossians: "If ye then be risen with Christ, seek those things which are above, where Christ sitteth on the right hand of God" (Colossians 3:1).

Here is a fundamental law of true praying. We are coming to our Father *in heaven,* and therefore our souls must be withdrawn from all earthly or selfish considerations. This is so even though much of what we pray for has to do with things that are the stuff of everyday life. What the phrase *in heaven* emphasizes, however, is that while we legitimately bring the concerns of our life and service to the Lord in prayer, our focus must be for His great power and glory. In doing this we pray so that God's answers to our prayers about our earthly needs and concerns will glorify His name rather than gratify our lusts. People who pray to consume the answer on their own lusts (James 4:3) cannot truly pray, "Our Father which art in heaven."

Heavenly-mindedness is seldom recognized for what it is worth. We have often heard the sneer against some Christian, "He is so heavenly-minded that he is of no earthly use." This is a travesty of the truth, for the one whose mind is most purely fixed on Him who is in heaven will have the greatest ability to live successfully on earth. This is the one whose life will be most productive of good that will stand the test not only of time but of eternity. Thus we must learn to pray as our Saviour here commands us. We must proceed beyond the carnal level of most of what passes for prayer—that selfish recitation of a list of demands that evidences no spirit of worship, submission, or devotion to God's glory. It simply seeks to use God as a means of gratifying the cravings of the flesh.

This is the chief error of the "name-it-and-claim-it" approach of many Charismatics. We have all seen and heard children demanding that their parents give them some toy or candy or other item they imagine necessary to their happiness. At times the children become very insistent and even sulk or scream or otherwise exhibit bad manners and behavior. Some people act the same way with the demand lists they bring before God. It is fine to have a prayer list, but we must never forget that true prayer, that is, prayer modeled after the commands of our Saviour in His word, is marked by the withdrawing of the soul from earth and fixing our thoughts and interests in the heavenly places.

Perhaps no better example of this is to be found in the New Testament than in the prayers of Paul. No man faced more urgent or insistent temporal needs, but when he prayed, he was drawn up into the heavens. Withdrawn from earth, he beheld the sovereign power of his God and the glorious exaltation of his Saviour, and that gave him all the confidence he needed to get through whatever ordeal he was facing. Furthermore, Paul found that his Father never failed to meet his every need. He knew this even when, for a time, he suffered want: "I have learned, in whatsoever state I am, therewith to be content. I know both how to be abased, and I know how to abound: every where and in all things I am instructed both to be full and to be hungry, both to abound and to suffer need. I can do all things through Christ which strengtheneth me" (Philippians 4:11–13). So much for the Charismatic delusion that it is never God's will for His people to be impoverished! We should pray with this heavenly-mindedness.

Take the prayers Paul prayed for the Ephesian Christians as an example of calling on our Father in heaven. In Ephesians 1 the apostle records his prayer "that the God of our Lord Jesus Christ, the Father of glory, may give unto you the spirit of wisdom and revelation in the knowledge of him: the eyes of your understanding being enlightened; that ye may know what is the hope of his calling, and what the riches of the glory of his inheritance in the saints, and what is the exceeding greatness of his power to usward who believe, according to the working of his mighty power, which he wrought in Christ, when he raised him from the dead, and set him at his own right hand in the heavenly places, far above all principality, and power, and might, and dominion, and every name that is named, not only in this world, but also in that which is to come" (Ephesians 1:17–21). In chapter 3 Paul says that he prayed "that [Christ] would grant you, according to the riches of his glory, to be strengthened with might by his Spirit in the inner man; that Christ may dwell in your hearts by faith; that ye, being rooted and grounded in love, may be able to comprehend with all saints what is the breadth, and length, and depth, and height; and to know the love of Christ, which passeth knowledge, that ye might be filled with all the fulness of God" (Ephesians 3:16–19). Here is prayer that ascends to Him who is "in heaven."

He who genuinely prays, "Our Father which art in heaven," in effect cries with David, "As the hart panteth after the water brooks, so panteth my soul after thee, O God. My soul thirsteth for God, for the living God" (Psalm 42:1–2). Or as David expressed it in Psalm 84:2, "My soul longeth, yea, even fainteth for the courts of the Lord: my heart and my flesh crieth out for the living God." When we enter into the experience of the saints of God in both Testaments as recorded in these prayers, our lives will be what Moses called "days of heaven upon the earth" (Deuteronomy 11:21). As our praying becomes first and foremost a pursuit of God, and not just of what He can do for us, we will be able to "let our requests be made known unto God" (Philippians 4:6) and to obtain His gracious response.

Lesson Seven: **Expect the Father's Answer**

The final lesson we must learn from the initial address of the Lord's Prayer is that we must expect our Father's bountiful answer. When we pray, "Our Father which art in heaven," we are using language which our Lord Jesus deliberately employed to teach His people that God is not only all-powerful, all-wise, and absolutely sovereign, but also all-willing to answer prayer. This is a truth to which all Christians give assent. God answers prayer. We feel that we could not be Christians at all if we could not affirm this basic conviction. However, in practice, many who affirm the truth live as if it were not so. Our unbelief has led us to the feeling that while we are willing to pray, God is somehow unwilling to answer us. It is undoubtedly true that much of what most professing Christians call prayer goes unanswered. So, is God unfaithful to His promises? Absolutely not: "There hath not failed one word of all his good promise, which he promised" (1 Kings 8: 56). What then is the problem?

Let us recall the three questions George Müller asked when he was seeking to determine how to pray according to God's will: Is it God's work? Is it God's way? Is it God's time? God's timing is all important. Müller, who saw innumerable immediate answers to prayer as he cared for his orphan homes, prayed for sixty years for the conversion of two of his friends, but God answered his prayers nonetheless. Our Father is willing to answer prayer. Being assured of the truth of Christ's statement, we must trust that, "If ye then, being evil, know how to give good gifts unto your children, how much more shall your Father which is in heaven give good things to them that ask him?" (Matthew 7:11).

The best of earthly fathers are sinners, yet they know how to give good gifts to their children. If a child cries out to his earthly father to meet his need, what would hinder that father from doing what his child asked? Perhaps lack of means, or such a limitation on his resources that to do this thing would hinder him doing something else that he deems more important. Or perhaps the father may believe that responding as his child desires would do the child no real good. Of course, it is always possible that, being a sinner, the father may be hindered from helping by sheer selfishness or lack of love, but in most cases a lack of response will be for some reason like those we have just listed.

Since our Father in heaven suffers from no such limitations as earthly fathers do, we may be more certain of His favorable response to our cries than we would expect from the best of earthly fathers. That is the powerful assurance Christ gives His people, and it is with this in mind that we pray, "Our Father which art in heaven."

Our heavenly Father will give good gifts to His children. It is interesting that in the parallel passage in Luke, Christ promises not only that the Father will give us "good things," but that He will also give us the gift of His Spirit: "If ye then, being evil, know how to give good gifts unto your children: how much more shall your heavenly Father give the Holy Spirit to them that ask him?" (Luke 11: 13). Here is the greatest of all the gifts that our Father gives to His people, the powerful fullness of His Spirit to impart all the grace and strength they need in every part of their Christian life and service—and He gives this all-important gift in answer to prayer.

When we pray to our Father in heaven, we must never lose sight of the fact that He is not only able to answer us but is altogether willing to do so. Our God loves to answer prayer. "The eyes of the Lord are over the righteous, and his ears are open unto their prayers" (1 Peter 3:12). God is eager to hear the cries of His people. Because He is their Father, He loves to hear their voices lifted up to Him in sincere and earnest prayer. This is an amazing thought. God is in heaven. He is "the Lord, the most high God, the possessor of heaven and earth" (Genesis 14:22). He is so great that we cannot begin to conceive of His greatness—but He is our Father and is willing and waiting to hear the cries of even the weakest of His children.

The address at the beginning of the Lord's Prayer is full of vital instruction for those who are in earnest about learning to pray as they should. As our hearts are gripped by the truth it presents and as we learn the lessons it teaches, we will "enter into [God's] gates … with praise" (Psalm 100:4) and enjoy fellowship with Him through a prayer life that is real and effective.

11

Our First Concern in Prayer

"Hallowed be thy name." Matthew 6:9

This is the first petition in the Lord's Prayer. Commentators dispute over whether there are six or seven petitions in the prayer, depending on whether they treat "Lead us not into temptation, but deliver us from evil" as one petition or two. Thankfully the matter is not one of great importance to our understanding of the prayer. Whatever the total number of the petitions, they are clearly divided into two categories. The first three evidently belong together: "Hallowed be thy name. Thy kingdom come. Thy will be done." They are not only directed to God but also are concerned wholly with Him, not with us. The next group of petitions deals in a summary fashion with us, our needs, and the entirety of our physical and spiritual experiences here on earth. So there are two distinct sets of petitions in the Lord's Prayer.

In setting this structure for the Lord's Prayer, the Lord Jesus establishes what our first concern in prayer must be. It is not sin, or Satan, or self, or even the situation we face at the moment. We cannot ignore these matters, nor should we try. We will reach them at the right time and in the right way, but they must not be permitted to dominate our thinking so that we forget the fundamental concerns that must underlie all Christian praying. We often rush into God's presence with the thought of some sin that we have committed uppermost in our minds. We know that we must have sin dealt with or it will ruin our fellowship with God, but unless our hearts are alive to the truth presented in the first three petitions of the Lord's Prayer, we will find it difficult to obtain peace and a sense of pardon.

As a young man I read an article in a respected Christian magazine that advised God's people to list all the commandments of God and then take the time to ponder every way in which they had broken them. With this list of sins drawn up, they were then to labor to come to a spirit of true contrition and repentance as a preparation for being able to pray and to obtain God's power in life and service. I earnestly desired God's fullness in my life and so I set out to follow the advice of the writer, but I made a startling discovery. I found that far from helping me to pray, this drove me to despair and spiritual debility. Where the writer went wrong was that he set the initial focus on sin and self instead of on our Father and our Saviour. If we have a genuine concern for the subjects Christ raises in the first three petitions of the Lord's Prayer, we will turn from our sin with loathing and will obtain not only the assurance of pardon but also the assurance of power to live in Christian victory.

When we pray, we have larger considerations than anything concerning ourselves.[1] Fundamentally, we are concerned with our Father's name, kingdom, and will. Our requests concerning these govern or modify every other request. In reality they are three aspects of the same fundamental desire. We may say that they make the same request in three ways. "Hallowed be Thy name" is concerned with honoring the Lord's person; "Thy kingdom come," with the Lord's program of grace through the Lord Jesus Christ; and "Thy will be done," with the Lord's purpose. Though distinguishable, these are obviously inseparable. In answering one, our Father necessarily fulfills the other two. But it is necessary for us to treat them separately so that we may grasp the full measure of the fundamental burden of all true prayer.

The first petition is "Hallowed be Thy name." It stands at the head of the list because it is in every way the chief petition of all true prayer. It is the most important request we can ever make to God. If only we could really pray this one petition with a full understanding of its meaning and significance, we would pray all we need to pray about any situation and we would be sure of receiving the best answer. In some ways, this petition includes every other thing we may ask of God. Or, to put the matter another way, it establishes the great *end* of all our praying, while all other petitions deal with the *means* of gaining that end. "Hallowed be Thy name" stands at the head of the list of petitions not only because it is the most important, but also because the Lord intends it to act as a corrective of any foolish notions we may entertain on the basis of the fact that we are told to address God as "Father."

---

[1] This is not to say that on entering God's presence a believer cannot at once make confession of sin or raise a plea for immediate divine intervention in an urgent situation. Psalm 51 and Nehemiah 2 sufficiently prove this. The point made here is that all such crisis praying is a response to a prior and ongoing interest in and commitment to the Lord's honor. This can be experienced only by making His honor the primary focus of our daily times of prayer.

I mentioned this in an earlier chapter, but I want to really drive home the point here. People tend to sentimentalize and to trivialize the whole idea of the fatherhood of God. Noting that believers are instructed to call God "Abba, Father" (Romans 8:15), and that *Abba* is a child's name for father (as distinct from *pater,* which a servant may employ), some preachers tells us that we should really address the Lord as "Dad" or "Papa." Such a flippant mode of addressing God may well be accounted blasphemous. It is certainly without Scripture warrant. The fact that our Lord immediately followed the reference to God as "our Father" with the petition "Hallowed be Thy name" indicates that we must never sink to the level of sentimental familiarity in the place of prayer. The Jews—and remember that the disciples were Jews—would have understood this to be the force of Christ's teaching. It would never have occurred to them to imagine that He was giving them license to speak to God in any such manner. The prayers of the Jews referred to God as "Father," but alongside that title they always used additional ones such as "King of the universe" or "Ruler of all." It is this balance between intimacy and profound awe—this sense of nearness and yet of God's transcendent glory—that the Lord Jesus sets before us by teaching us first to pray, "Hallowed be thy name."

Our Lord lays it down that our first and greatest concern in prayer is that the Lord's name should be hallowed. We must never forget that. Our first concern is not to feel better or even to feel blessed. The blessing of God is a wonderful thing that enriches us and He adds no sorrow with it (Proverbs 10:22), but the true value of God's blessing is that it hallows His name. This is the ultimate reason for God's doing anything, and it should also be our ultimate reason for what we do.

David Brainerd, the brilliant and godly young American pioneer of missionary outreach to the Indians, discovered this as he sought God for the assurance of His pardon and acceptance. On July 12, 1739, Brainerd was seeking God with great fervor. He earnestly desired this gospel blessing, and he prayed almost incessantly. Then the words of John 7:37 gripped his soul: "In the last day, that great day of the feast, Jesus stood and cried, saying, If any man thirst, let him come unto me, and drink." As he pondered this beautiful invitation, the young seeker realized that in all his seeking his emphasis had been on himself, his comfort, and his peace. These were not unworthy desires, but Brainerd suddenly understood that until then he had been so full of self and sin that even in praying for salvation, he had had no desire beyond himself and his comfort. As soon as he saw that even in pleading the promise of Christ for salvation his desire had to be that God would hallow His own name, he entered into the peace of assurance of faith. If the first petition of the Lord's Prayer lies at the heart of even our cry for saving mercy, it must be our chief concern in everything we pray.

God's Name

In this petition, "name" is more than a title by which men conveniently refer to God. Literally it signifies God Himself in the perfections of His nature as He has been pleased to reveal them to us in His word. When Solomon said that he had built a house for the name of the Lord, he explained that "the name of the Lord" meant neither more nor less than the Lord Himself: "Behold, I build an house to the name of the Lord my God, to dedicate it to him" (2 Chronicles 2:4). When we praise God's name we praise *Him*: "Wherefore glorify ye the Lord in the fires, even the name of the Lord God of Israel in the isles of the sea" (Isaiah 24:15). When the Bible promises that the Lord Himself will hear the prayer of His people and protect them, it uses His name as a synonym for God in all His perfections and power: "The Lord hear thee in the day of trouble; the name of the God of Jacob defend thee…. Some trust in chariots, and some in horses: but we will remember the name of the Lord our God" (Psalm 20:1, 7). Here "the Lord" and "the name of the God of Jacob" are parallel expressions. Thus when David says, "We will remember the name of the Lord," he means that we will remember the Lord in all the revealed perfections of His nature.

The same thing is clear from the revelation the Lord gave of Himself to Moses, as it is described in Exodus 34:5–7: "The Lord descended in the cloud, and stood with him there, and proclaimed the name of the Lord. And the Lord passed by before him, and proclaimed, The Lord, The Lord God, merciful and gracious, longsuffering, and abundant in goodness and truth, keeping mercy for thousands, forgiving iniquity and transgression and sin, and that will by no means clear the guilty; visiting the iniquity of the fathers upon the children, and upon the children's children, unto the third and to the fourth generation." Here the name of the Lord is the equivalent of His attributes, particularly His mercy, grace, goodness, truth, and justice.

It would be easy to multiply texts that show that the name of the Lord means God in all the perfections of His nature as He has revealed them in Scripture. Thus when the Lord Jesus teaches us to pray, "Hallowed be thy name," He is referring to the person of God as set forth in the word of God.

Hallowed Means Sanctified

The word *hallowed* means "sanctified," so that the first petition of the Lord's Prayer is "Let Thy name be sanctified." What does it mean to sanctify the Lord's name? Ordinarily, *sanctify* means "to make holy." However, that cannot be its meaning here. "Thus saith the high and lofty One that inhabiteth eternity, whose name is Holy; I dwell in the high and holy place, with him also that is of a contrite and humble spirit, to revive the spirit of the humble, and to revive the heart of the contrite ones" (Isaiah 57:15). The Lord's name is holy; it cannot therefore be *made* holy or *become* holy, but it may be *declared* to be what it is. Thus, *hallowed* or *sanctified be Thy name* means, "Display or proclaim Your holiness."

The fundamental idea in the Greek verb *hagiadzo,* translated "hallowed," is separation or difference. When we pray, "Hallowed be thy name," we ask the Lord to set His name apart from—and to set it above—every other name. This then is our prayer: "Let the person and character of our God declared in Scripture be fully set forth—let Him be exalted in all His holiness."

Praying the Lord to Hallow His Name

Those who have a concern for the Lord's name must make it a matter of earnest prayer that He would declare it in all its fullness of glory. We should never forget that this is our first concern. Yet must we not confess that this petition usually receives the least attention in most Christians' praying? It is all too easy for us to be so consumed with ourselves—our work and worries, our homes and families, our bodily and material needs—that what the Lord Jesus sets before us as our chief concern gets hardly a mention. This must not be allowed to continue, for we live in a world in which it is common for men to profane the Lord's name, not only by using it in vain swearing, but also by despising His person and character as they are revealed in Scripture. Israel was guilty of this sin. Thus the Lord said, "I will sanctify my great name, which was profaned among the heathen, which ye have profaned in the midst of them" (Ezekiel 36:23).

Here is a word to the professing people of God. The charge against Israel may as justly be laid at the door of the professing church today. It is an alarming thought that the name of the Lord is profaned, not merely by professed atheists and secular humanists, but by professing Christians. His name is profaned by false doctrine. Apostasy from biblical truth is a form of blasphemy. So is unholy living. We read that David by his adultery and murder caused the enemies of God to blaspheme, or as the Masoretic record of the original Hebrew text at 2 Samuel 12:14 puts it, he "greatly blasphemed Jehovah" by his sin.

Men often profane God's name by the things they profess to do in His name and for His glory. When people get away from the Bible and start inventing ways in which to serve God in the flesh, it is likely that they will not serve Him but will rather profane His name. That is why Protestants, following the example of the Reformers, observe what is called the Regulative Principle of worship—that is, they regulate how they worship by the precepts, prohibitions, principles, and patterns of Scripture. What we do in worship must be commanded by, must be permitted by, or must arise as a necessary consequence of what is said in God's word.

To depart from this standard is to risk installing what God terms profanity for worship. Nadab and Abihu did that and God judged them for offering "strange fire before the Lord, which he commanded them not" (Leviticus 10:1). King Saul was another who profaned God's name by acting professedly in His name when, willing to wait no longer for Samuel to arrive, he invaded the priest's office and offered burnt offerings (1 Samuel 15: 9–14). Isaiah prophesied to the Jews that even their brethren would imagine they were glorifying God by persecuting them: "Hear the word of the Lord, ye that tremble at his word; your brethren that hated you, that cast you out for my name's sake, said, Let the Lord be glorified: but he shall appear to your joy, and they shall be ashamed" (Isaiah 66:5). The Lord Jesus warns us of a direct parallel: "They shall put you out of the synagogues: yea, the time cometh, that whosoever killeth you will think that he doeth God service" (John 16:2).

History is full of shameful spectacles of people profaning the Lord's name even as they profess to act by His authority and for His glory. The Crusades are a case in point. Starting out as a zealous attempt to regain the ascendancy over Islam and to take control of the Holy Land, they quickly became a tool of cynical popes and in time were unleashed not only against the Turks but also against those whom Rome decreed to be heretical, such as the Albigenses and the Waldenses. Such Crusades, whatever their professed motive or political justification, profaned the Lord's name and have brought shame on the cause of Christ. Many of the religious wars that attended and followed the Reformation fall into the same category. All too often unscrupulous men made use of the name of the Lord and of the cause of the gospel to further their own ungodly ends. Today it is not uncommon to hear Ku Klux Klansmen cover their vicious program with protestations of faithfulness to God and to the Christian gospel.

There are also more subtle ways of using God's name in a profane way. It may be done simply by mixing a personal, social, or political agenda with that holy name. We glorify God when we allow what we know of Him to form our views and actions in these spheres, but we profane His name when we equate our agenda with it.

Nothing so vexes a believer so much as men dishonoring the Lord's name. The psalmist David says, "As with a sword in my bones, mine enemies reproach me; while they say daily unto me, Where is thy God?" (Psalm 42:10). To David, the mockery of the Lord by the ungodly was like a sword in his bones. Every Christian must have felt something of this anxiety. But, other than feeling grieved at the defamation of the Lord's name, what can we do about this profanity? We must fervently seek our Father's face and plead, "Hallowed be thy name."

A Petition with Far-Reaching Implications

"Hallowed be Thy name" is perhaps the petition in the Lord's Prayer to which many people find it most difficult to ascribe any precise meaning. Yet it has a clearly defined meaning. The command to hallow or sanctify the Lord occurs frequently in Scripture, and a study of the biblical references will help us grasp the fullness of Christ's thoughts in this petition.

Glorify Thy Name

This is the first and most obvious meaning of the petition. Thus Chrysostom says, "Hallowed is *glorified*." The Bible is equally emphatic: "Then Moses said unto Aaron, This is that the Lord spake, saying, *I will be sanctified in them that come nigh me, and before all the people I will be glorified*" (Leviticus 10:3). The psalmist sang, "Give unto the Lord the glory due unto his name" (Psalm 96:8) or as the Hebrew puts it, "Give [ascribe] unto the Lord the glory of his name." The idea is that the glory inheres in His name, and we cannot use His name aright without declaring His glory. When we come to God to lay before Him the issues that concern or perplex us, we therefore commence with this: "Hallowed be thy name." Our first and overriding concern, the primary desire of our hearts, must be "Lord, in everything glorify Thy name." To quote Chrysostom again: "Worthy of him who calls God Father, is this prayer to ask nothing before the glory of his Father, but to account all things second to the work of praising Him."

This is a prayer then that is worthy of a Christian; it is truly expressive of the relationship he has with his heavenly Father. To anyone who has ever entered into the experience of becoming God's child by faith in Jesus Christ (Galatians 3:26), nothing comes before the glory of his Father's name. Everything else must be secondary. In this the Lord Jesus Christ is our great example. As He approached the awful agonies of the cross He prayed, "Father glorify thy name" (John 12:28). This is or should be the testimony of every child of God: "The desire of our soul is to thy name, and to the remembrance of thee" (Isaiah 26:8). Our prayer is not merely "Dispose all things for Thy glory" but "Enable us to glorify Thee by what we teach and by how we live. "

Our first aim in Christian service must be the Lord's glory: "Hallowed be Thy name," with the emphasis on *Thy*. George Whitefield, the man God first used to commence the great eighteenth-century revival that gave birth to the Methodist church, grasped this truth. With the introduction of the Arminian/Calvinist controversy by John Wesley, and with Wesley's increasing organization of Methodist societies as Wesleyan, friends asked Whitefield to lend his name to the Calvinistic societies. He refused, saying, "Let my name perish." His sole desire was that the name of his Lord be exalted, and he was unwilling to add his name to Christ's, even to distinguish the societies that owned his leadership.

That was an entirely biblical attitude. It reflected the plea of the psalmist: "Not unto us, O Lord, not unto us, but unto thy name give glory, for thy mercy, and for thy truth's sake" (Psalm 115:1).

"Glorify Thy name." The words come easily, but a genuine, wholehearted desire to see the Lord's name glorified does not come easily. It is of the utmost importance, however, because until we can honestly place this desire at the head of all our praying, we cannot learn to pray at all. When we ask our Saviour, "Teach us to pray," the first petition He gives us is, "Father, let thy name be glorified." This must be our consuming passion.

Cause Thy Name to Be Known and Confessed

In Ezekiel 36:23 the Lord says, "I will sanctify my great name, which was profaned among the heathen, which ye have profaned in the midst of them; and the heathen shall know that I am the Lord, saith the Lord God, when I shall be sanctified in you before their eyes." Again He declares, "Thus will I magnify myself, and sanctify myself; and I will be known in the eyes of many nations, and they shall know that I am the Lord" (Ezekiel 38:23). According to these statements, for the Lord to sanctify His name is for Him to have it known and confessed. So when Jesus gave us the petition, "Hallowed be Thy name," He taught us to pray, "Let the truth of our God be spread abroad on the earth and received among the nations."

This prayer includes a plea for the Lord to destroy false religion. "Let Thy name be known" means, "Defeat Satanic confusion, take away the darkness of false doctrine, and declare the pure truth about Thine own being, nature, word, and work. Do this all across the world, bringing people to an understanding of the gospel. Do it in this nation and in this community—indeed do it in my own heart. Declare Thy name there that I may know Thee in ever-deepening fellowship, and then make me Thy witness to make Thee known to others."

Cause Us to Worship Thee with Holy Reverence

"Holy and reverend [or, to be feared] is his name" (Psalm 111:9). When we pray, "Hallowed be thy name," we ask, "Cause us to worship Thee with holy reverence, with holy fear." Such is God's majestic holiness that even the sinless angels in heaven cannot contemplate Him without reverent worship. Isaiah records his vision of "the Lord ... high and lifted up" (Isaiah 6:1): "One [seraph] cried unto another, and said, Holy, holy, holy, is the Lord of hosts: the whole earth is full of his glory" (Isaiah 6:3). At the sight of that vision Isaiah was at once smitten with godly fear and cried out, "Woe is me! for I am undone; because I am a man of unclean lips, and I dwell in the midst of a people of unclean lips: for mine eyes have seen the King, the Lord of hosts" (Isaiah 6:5). This holy reverence is the very essence of worship, and we recognize that this is so every time we pray, "Hallowed be thy name." In giving us this petition the Lord Jesus instructs New Testament believers to do what He had long before commanded Israel: "Sanctify the Lord of hosts himself; and let him be your fear, and let him be your dread" (Isaiah 8:13).

The urgent need for Christians to recapture the element of reverent worship in prayer cannot be overstated. The fear of God seems to be largely absent from much of what passes for prayer, both public and private. Mistaking brashness for boldness, many approach God with unseemly familiarity, speaking of the eternal Father as "The Man Upstairs" or some similar flippancy. Such inanity is usually followed by an almost total absorption with themselves, with little or no attention given to the greatness and glory of God. "The fear of the Lord is the beginning of knowledge" (Proverbs 1:7) and "the beginning of wisdom" (Proverbs 9:10). Until we grasp this we cannot really pray.

Everything in our prayer lives depends on this holy reverence that humbles the pride of man and centers all our worship on the transcendent greatness of our great God and Saviour. Some think that this sense of awe or dread in prayer will destroy its warmth and intimacy. The opposite is the case, as a study of the prayer warriors of Scripture will demonstrate. Moses was a man closer to God than any other, one with whom God did not communicate in dreams or visions but "face to face." But when Moses described his feelings at being in the presence of God he said, "I exceedingly fear and quake" (Hebrews 12:21). Isaiah was God's chosen instrument for a great work, yet as we have noted from his own words (Isaiah 6:5), he greatly feared before the Lord. Imprisoned on the Isle of Patmos, John the apostle received his glorious vision of the risen Christ, and its effect on him was overwhelming: "When I saw him, I fell at his feet as dead" (Revelation 1:17). It is clear that the sweetest possible intimacy and the deepest possible reverence go hand in hand in prayer.

Cause Us So to Fear Thee that We Will Never Fear to Honor Thee Before Men

When we pray, "Hallowed be thy name," we are asking the Lord to give us such a sight of His face that we will never again fear the face of man. Genuine boldness before men in the cause of Christ comes from having such a conviction of the glorious greatness of our God that we see men in their true perspective. The Lord Jesus taught us not to fear what men can do to us, but to fear God (Luke 12:4–5).

Peter encouraged the young believers to whom he addressed his first epistle to grasp what hallowing the Lord's name really means and thereby to escape the fear of man: "But and if ye suffer for righteousness' sake, happy are ye: *and be not afraid of their terror, neither be troubled; but sanctify the Lord God in your hearts:* and be ready always to give an answer to every man that asketh you a reason of the hope that is in you *with meekness and fear*" (1 Peter 3:14–15).

Those young Christians were faced with the combined malevolence of Jewish and Gentile opposition, and it threatened their very lives. Peter says, however, "Be not afraid of the fear with which they seek to intimidate you." Is this realistic? Is it a case of whistling in the dark? Not at all; it is the voice of a man who had proved that when a Christian has learned to fear God, it releases him from the fear of puny men.

The fear of God is the key to a life of spiritual purity and power. It leads us to liberty and victory. Seeing God for what He is and men for what they are, we will be able to take our stand for Him despite all the opposition of the world. This is something every Christian longs to have the faith and courage to do. In teaching us to pray, "Hallowed be thy name," the Lord Jesus shows us how to obtain that faith and courage.

Cause Us to Honor and Obey Thee

Disobedience to God is ultimately a failure to hallow or sanctify His name. The Lord explained this to Moses as He spoke of his exclusion from Canaan: "Ye rebelled against my commandment in the desert of Zin, in the strife of the congregation, to sanctify me at the water before their eyes" (Numbers 27:14). We should never fail to remember this connection. Disobedience is a refusal to hallow God's name. It is an attack on His holiness, and He therefore deals with it in strict and severe terms.

King Saul failed to grasp this and it cost him his kingdom. The prophet Samuel silenced Saul's protests that he had provided sacrifices for the Lord with this statement: "Hath the Lord as great delight in burnt offerings and sacrifices, as in obeying the voice of the Lord? Behold, to obey is better than sacrifice, and to hearken than the fat of rams. *For rebellion is as the sin of witchcraft, and stubbornness is as iniquity and idolatry*" (1 Samuel 15:22–23). Thus disobedience is more than an isolated act; it betrays an attitude that fails to give the Lord the honor due His name.

When we pray, "Hallowed be thy name," we mean, therefore, "Let us not do anything to profane Thy name by disobedience." We desire to fulfill the command of the Lord recorded in Leviticus 22:32: "Neither shall ye profane my holy name; but I will be hallowed among the children of Israel: I am the Lord which hallow you." When we pray, "Hallowed be thy name," we also ask, "Let us not do anything that is unworthy of the great and holy name that we bear." We express our desire to walk worthy of our God, as the Thessalonians did in obedience to Paul's instructions: "We...charged every one of you, as a father doth his children, that ye would walk worthy of God, who hath called you unto his kingdom and glory" (1 Thessalonians 2:11–12). In praying the first petition of the Lord's Prayer we ask our Father to enable us to "let [our] light so shine before men, that they may see [our] good works, and glorify [our] Father which is in heaven" (Matthew 5:16).

Execute Thy Holy Judgments Against Thine Enemies.

As we have already seen, "Hallowed be Thy name" includes the idea of pleading for the Lord's judgment against His enemies, whether they are apostates from the truth or heathens. After the apostate priests Nadab and Abihu offered false fire before Him, the Lord slew them. This gives us some idea of how seriously God takes the matter of spiritual apostasy. Israel had an army of over six hundred thousand men and therefore numbered probably as many as three million souls in all. To serve the needs of this vast company, He anointed Aaron and his four sons to act as priests. Theirs was an immense task. Their tiny numbers meant that they were stretched to the limit to do their work, and yet when two of these five people fell into apostasy, the Lord slew them at once. No doubt the sudden loss of almost half the priestly caste brought many difficulties in the work, but there was something even more important than the rituals of tabernacle worship, and that was the honor of the divine name. Thus the Lord said, "I will be sanctified in them that come nigh me" (Leviticus 10:3). In sanctifying His name He visited judgment on His enemies. This is an aspect of the petition "Hallowed be Thy name" that is seldom considered, but we should keep it in mind when we pray these words.

Today the cause of Christ is opposed not only from outside the professing church, but also—and perhaps more viciously—from inside it. Apostasy from biblical truth is rampant. Corruptions of the gospel have become so commonplace that when a preacher sets forth such truths as justification on the ground of the imputed righteousness of Christ and not because of any righteousness of character we may come to possess, he is looked on with suspicion. To many he appears to be promoting some new doctrine. Only God can deal with such culpable ignorance of His truth; He will do so by hallowing His name, and in the process He will judge the apostates who corrupt His truth. This is what we pray for when we pray, "Hallowed be thy name."

Of course not all opposition to the cause of Christ arises from apostates within the church. The world has never been a friend to grace or to God, and it constantly keeps up its bitter opposition to Christ and His gospel. But God will hallow His name even among the heathen, both by saving a people out of the systems of the world and by executing judgment on stubborn opponents. What He said of Zidon has a message for every enemy of His truth: "Thus saith the Lord God; Behold, I am against thee, O Zidon; and *I will be glorified in the midst of thee: and they shall know that I am the Lord, when I shall have executed judgments in her, and shall be sanctified in her*" (Ezekiel 28:22). Judging the enemies of His cause hallows the name of God. Describing His judgment of Gog He says,

"I shall be sanctified in thee, O Gog before [the heathens'] eyes.... I will plead against him with pestilence and with blood.... Thus will I magnify myself, and sanctify myself" (Ezekiel 38:16, 22–23). His words to Israel spell out the invariable rule: "The Lord of hosts shall be exalted in judgment, and God that is holy shall be sanctified in righteousness" (Isaiah 5:16). Thus when we pray, "Hallowed be thy name," we give voice to David's vehement cry, "Let God arise, let his enemies be scattered" (Psalm 68:1).

Restore and Revive Thy People in the Experience of Thy Greatness and Thy Power

Not only is the Lord's name sanctified in judging His enemies, but also, and perhaps even more so, it is sanctified in reviving His saints. There is a lovely promise in the book of Ezekiel. It first occurs in 20:41: "I will accept you with your sweet savour, when I bring you out from the people, and gather you out of the countries wherein ye have been scattered; and I will be sanctified in you before the heathen." Again in 36:21, 23–24 the promise is repeated: "*I had pity for mine holy name, which the house of Israel had profaned among the heathen*, whither they went. ... And *I will sanctify my great name, which was profaned among the heathen,* which ye have profaned in the midst of them; and the heathen shall know that I am the Lord, saith the Lord God, when *I shall be sanctified in you before their eyes. For I will take you from among the heathen, and gather you out of all countries, and will bring you into your own land.*" What a glorious promise!

This is how our God answers the prayer, "Hallowed be Thy name." He sees it as a heartfelt longing for a powerful spiritual revival, a mighty visitation of God to His people, and He answers it as such. What can demonstrate the glory and holy majesty of the name of the Lord more than an outpouring of His Spirit with power on His church, rendering her witness effective to the pulling down of Satan's strongholds? This is an aspect of the prayer for His name to be hallowed that our God loves to answer (2 Chronicles 7:14; Isaiah 41:17–18; 44:3).

"Hallowed be Thy name" is an extensive prayer. The words may be few but the thoughts included in them are many and deep. Here is a petition that is worthy of our purest and profoundest meditation—and, as we shall next see, of our complete submission to becoming a means whereby God will answer.

Willingness to Be Part of the Answer

Those who profess a concern for the hallowing of the Lord's name must be willing and ready to be a means of hallowing it. We cannot pray against the profanation of the Lord's name by others while we commit the same sin without compunction. If we honestly pray, "Hallowed be Thy name," we must be ready to live as those who know God's name, who accept all that He says about Himself, who live accordingly, and who are consistent witnesses to "that worthy name" (James 2:7). One of the Scripture's stated reasons for God's blessing of His people is that His salvation may be made known among the nations: "God be merciful unto us, and bless us; and cause his face to shine upon us; that thy way may be known upon earth, thy saving health among all nations" (Psalm 67:1–2). This shining of God's face is nothing more or less than His hallowing His name among His people, making Himself known to us in the full glory of His revelation. And He does so, not that we may confine the blessing to ourselves but "that [His] way may be known upon the earth, and [His] saving health among all nations."

Thus when we pray, "Hallowed be thy name," we not only profess our vexation at the profaning of His name, but we offer ourselves as His instruments in setting forth His glory to the world around us, both by our works and our witness. It is important to realize, however, that only those who have the experience of the shining of His face can share that glory with others. Let us learn to pray "Hallowed be thy name" in all the fullness of what this means, and let us offer ourselves to our Father as willing instruments through which He may answer our prayer.

12

The Kingdom of Grace and Glory

"Thy kingdom come."   _Matthew 6:10_

H aving focused on the holy greatness of our Father's name, it is natural that we should now proceed to the thought of His dominion, for that is really the meaning of the word _kingdom_. It expresses the idea of dominion, rule, or reign. The concept of the kingdom is one of the most complex and multifaceted themes in the Bible, but it is one with which we must become familiar if we are to obey our Saviour and pray, "Thy kingdom come."

Kingdom Defined

Kingdom is used in three ways. First, it may mean the kingdom of God's government. The Lord has an essential sovereignty over all His creatures. _Essential sovereignty_ is the right and power to rule that is inherent in the very essence of God. God is by definition the Being who necessarily exercises rule over all created beings because all creation depends completely on Him for its existence. "In him we live, and move, and have our being" (Acts 17:28), and by His eternal Son "all things consist [or cohere]" (Colossians 1:17). God is, and everything else exists at His will because of His creative fiat; it continues to exist because of His sustaining power. Thus everything that God has created is under His absolute, eternal sovereignty. David spoke of this: "The Lord hath prepared his throne in the heavens; and his kingdom ruleth over all" (Psalm 103:19). It is obvious that this kingdom of essential sovereignty is not the subject of the prayer that Jesus taught us to pray. That sovereignty is not a matter for prayer. We may as well pray that God may exist as to pray that this kingdom may come about. We may pray that men would recognize it and joyfully submit themselves to it, but we may not pray that this kingdom would come about. It does not need to be prayed for. It is—there is nothing in heaven, earth, or hell that can alter it.

The second use of *kingdom* is much more specialized: It designates the kingdom of grace. This is the use of the term that lies at the heart of the petition, "Thy kingdom come." This kingdom of grace is central to the four gospels and indeed to the whole revelation of God in His Son.

The third use of the term *kingdom* designates a future kingdom of glory; "kingdom of heaven" even seems to be used as a place name. For example, the Lord Jesus Christ said, "Many shall come from the east and west, and shall sit down with Abraham, and Isaac, and Jacob, in the kingdom of heaven. But the children of the kingdom shall be cast out into outer darkness: there shall be weeping and gnashing of teeth" (Matthew 8:11–12). Again He described the Day of Judgment in terms of entering into or being debarred from that kingdom: "Then shall the King say unto them on his right hand, Come, ye blessed of my Father, inherit the kingdom prepared for you from the foundation of the world.... Then shall he say also unto them on the left hand, depart from me, ye cursed, into everlasting fire, prepared for the devil and his angels" (Matthew 25:34, 41). Paul described the future kingdom of glory as the heavenly destination of God's people: "The Lord shall deliver me from every evil work, and will preserve me unto his heavenly kingdom: to whom be glory for ever and ever. Amen" (2 Timothy 4:18).

Given this wide usage of the word, it is not surprising that *kingdom* appears frequently in the New Testament, some fifty times in the book of Matthew alone. Yet there is not one single text or passage that actually defines it. Here then is a term that is so fundamental that it is employed with great frequency. But it is never defined; instead, the Lord Jesus describes it in parables and pictures. Again and again He says, "The kingdom of heaven is like unto" and proceeds to set before us a parabolic description of some aspect of it. For example, He describes it as being like a sower sowing seed or like a woman putting leaven in her dough. He says the kingdom is like treasure hidden in a field or like a pearl of great price, to purchase which a man sold all that he had. Given the lack of a definition of the term and the variety of descriptions given in the Gospels, how are we to understand the term? If we don't gain a scriptural understanding of it, we cannot intelligently pray, "Thy kingdom come."

A Significant Fact

In answering this question we must commence with a very significant fact. In Matthew 11:11 we read, "Among them that are born of women there hath not risen a greater than John the Baptist: notwithstanding he that is least in the kingdom of heaven is greater than he." The clear implication is that something very significant happened after the preparatory ministry of John the Baptist.

Christ draws a line between *before John* and *after John*. Up until that time there was no greater man of God than John. But on the other side of this timeline, something that our Lord calls "the kingdom" commenced, and such was its significance that "he that is least in the kingdom of heaven is greater than [John, the greatest of men until then]." What happened after John's ministry? Jesus Christ came preaching the kingdom. John had prophesied it. Jesus proclaimed it. The kingdom came with Christ. That is the all-important fact that we must grasp if we are to learn what the Bible means by the kingdom and particularly what we pray for in the petition "Thy kingdom come."

The kingdom that came with Christ was the kingdom of grace. Essentially, this kingdom is Christ's coming—His revealing Himself, working, saving, blessing, and ruling. Scripture shows us that God's grace was active among men before the time of Christ's birth, but that Christ was nevertheless the mediator of that grace. All grace is through Him: "The law was given by Moses, but grace and truth came by Jesus Christ" (John 1:17). Every sinner ever saved was saved by grace, which means that he was saved by Jesus Christ. Every soul who ever received grace from God received it through His merits and mediation.

A Spiritual Realm Occupied by Believers

The kingdom is the spiritual realm that believers occupy. Paul tells us that God "hath delivered us from the power of darkness, and hath translated us into the kingdom of his dear Son" (Colossians 1:13). Believers in Christ are no longer "under sin" or "under law" (Romans 3:9; 6:14). Grace reigns in them (Romans 5:21) because Christ reigns. They now occupy and are citizens of the kingdom.

The Kingdom of Heaven and the Visible Church

This kingdom is called "the kingdom of heaven" and is used as a near synonym of the visible church. This is apparent from Christ's parables in Matthew 13. There He speaks of the kingdom as follows: "The kingdom of heaven is likened unto a man which sowed good seed in his field: But while men slept, his enemy came and sowed tares among the wheat, and went his way. But when the blade was sprung up, and brought forth fruit, then appeared the tares also" (Matthew 13:24–26). This idea of the kingdom as a mixed community of true and false believers recurs in other parables, notably those of the leaven and of the net. This is the visible church.

The idea of the kingdom also describes the reign of the Lord Jesus Christ on earth following His Second Coming. The prophet Daniel foresaw that glorious day: "In the days of these kings shall the God of heaven set up a kingdom, which shall never be destroyed: and the kingdom shall not be left to other people, but it shall break in pieces and consume all these kingdoms, and it shall stand for ever" (Daniel 2:44). This describes the coming of Christ to smash the embodiment of Gentile power and to fill the earth with His kingdom. Does that kingdom include any reference to a millennial earth? Jeremiah's statement leaves us in no doubt that the future of the kingdom includes Christ's millennial reign on earth: "Behold, the days come, saith the Lord, that I will raise unto David a righteous Branch, and a King shall reign and prosper, and shall execute judgment and justice in the earth" (Jeremiah 23:5). This cannot refer to the eternal state. The reference to Christ's execution of judgment precludes that idea. By the time the new heaven and the new earth are created, all judgment will be past. We must conclude then that this reign of David's Righteous Branch will take place on this earth after the Lord's return but before the inauguration of the eternal state—it is a millennial kingdom that is in view.

The millennial kingdom is not the final expression of the kingdom theme, however. We have noted Paul's reference to God's everlasting kingdom. The kingdom of grace exists now in the lives of those who have been brought under the dominion of grace by saving faith in the Lord Jesus Christ. They have entered a community that we call the church, which for all its imperfections is the kingdom of heaven on earth. The next great stage of the kingdom following the coming of the Lord Jesus will be His personal, glorious reign on the earth. But even then grace will not have reached its consummation. "Then cometh the end, when he shall have delivered up the kingdom to God, even the Father; when he shall have put down all rule and all authority and power" (1 Corinthians 15:24). This is the kingdom of glory indeed.

Here then are three distinct but closely related aspects of the kingdom theme. The kingdom is one of government, of grace, and of glory. All of these have one thing in common. They all designate a place, realm, or people under God's dominion in a particular manner, either now or in the future. As far as the aspects of glory are concerned, the kingdom is yet incomplete and imperfect. But in its full and final revelation it will be absolutely complete and perfect. From all these data we may learn important truths about our Father's kingdom, for the "coming" of which Christ taught us to pray.

The Kingdom Is Personal

Jesus speaks of being in the kingdom as the equivalent of entering into eternal life. Consider the comments He made to His disciples about His conversation with the rich young ruler. That young man asked Him, "Good Master, what good thing shall I do, *that I may have eternal life*? And he said unto him,… *If thou wilt enter into life*, keep the commandments.… Then said Jesus unto his disciples, Verily I say unto you, That a rich man shall hardly [or, with difficulty] *enter into the kingdom of heaven*. And again I say unto you, It is easier for a camel to go through the eye of a needle, than for a rich man *to enter into the kingdom of God*" (Matthew 19:16–17, 23–24). Entering into the kingdom of heaven is to personally come out from darkness into light, from the power of Satan unto God, from death unto life eternal.

That is why Jesus started his ministry by emphasizing that the kingdom is entered by repentance, "From that time Jesus began to preach, and to say, Repent: for the kingdom of heaven is at hand" (Matthew 4:17). Repentance is personal and therefore so is our entrance into and experience of the kingdom. There is a difference between being a professed citizen of the kingdom and one who has a genuine experience of Christ's kingship. Those whom Christ describes as tares, whose end is to be burned, may occupy a place in the visible church and are therefore in the public realm of the kingdom, but they have no saving relationship with the king. Their having been baptized and received into the visible church cannot gain for them an entrance into life, into the kingdom of God. That is received solely by means of personal faith and repentance, as the Lord Jesus made clear in His first recorded message: "The kingdom of God is at hand: repent ye, and believe the gospel" (Mark 1:15).

Paul emphasized the distinction between external religious observance and the reality of being in the kingdom: "The kingdom of God is not meat and drink; but righteousness, and peace, and joy in the Holy Ghost" (Romans 14:17). The background to this statement was a dispute in the early church over whether believers were bound by Jewish dietary restrictions. Those who exercised their liberty looked on those who felt bound in conscience to live within the limitations of the Mosaic code as legalists, while the latter looked on the former as libertines. Each side missed the point and was in danger of defining the kingdom in merely material terms. This is always an error, for the kingdom must be understood in spiritual not material terms.

Having a place in this spiritual kingdom is vital. Each of us has an invitation to enter it. Jesus says, "Come; for all things are now ready" (Luke 14:17). This is the invitation of the king who at the highest cost has provided a place for us in His kingdom. It is worth any cost or effort to enter His kingdom, so much so that Jesus says, "If thy hand offend thee, cut it off: it is better for thee to enter into life maimed, than having two hands to go into hell" (Mark 9:43). In other words, the kingdom is personal and entering into it is the all-important issue that faces each of us. It is so important that it is worth any earthly loss to achieve it.

The Kingdom Is Present

In a sense it has already come; it is here and now. Jesus said, "Behold, the kingdom of God is within you" (Luke 17:21). Many glibly quote this text to prove that Jesus taught that the kingdom was a matter of the heart, it was *within*

His hearers. However, a moment's thought will show that this was not His meaning. He was speaking to the Pharisees, and He never for a moment gave that group the slightest reason to believe that the kingdom of God was in their hearts. Indeed, He usually berated them as the enemies of His kingdom. They were of the same ilk as the lawyers whom He castigated: "Ye have taken away the key of knowledge: ye entered not in yourselves, and them that were entering in ye hindered" (Luke 11:52). His saying, "The kingdom of God is within you," may be better translated, "The kingdom of God is in the midst of you." That is, it has already come. The Lord Jesus says, "If I cast out devils by the Spirit of God, then the kingdom of God is [has] come unto you" (Matthew 12:28).

The Kingdom Is Powerful

With the coming of the kingdom, God has manifested His power to break the dominion of the old serpent, the devil, and to liberate souls from his evil dominion. This was the purpose of Christ's coming into the world: "For this purpose the Son of God was manifested, that he might destroy the works of the devil" (1 John 3:8). The coming of the King in His kingdom thus heralded the defeat of Satan. This is not merely high-sounding religious jargon because "the kingdom of God is not in word, but in power" (1 Corinthians 4:20). Christ is a real, living sovereign — the Son of God who rules in grace with power that "breaks the power of cancelled sin [and] sets the prisoner free." He described this exercise of the power to liberate souls as the triumph of His kingdom over Satan. Consider again His statement to the Jews that with His ministry the kingdom was already present with them; note the proof He gave of His claim: "If I cast out devils by the Spirit of God, then the kingdom of God is come unto you. Or else how can one enter into a strong man's house, and spoil his goods, except he first bind the strong man? and then he will spoil his house" (Matthew 12:28–29). This is largely what the present exercise of the kingly power of Christ is about, the spoiling of Satan's goods and the release of his prisoners.

The Gospels give us many striking illustrations of this kingly power in operation but perhaps nowhere more dramatically than in Mark 5. Here there are three outstanding miracles of kingly grace: the deliverance of the demoniac of Gadara who was possessed with a legion of devils, the healing of the woman who had suffered for twelve years with an issue of blood, and the raising from the dead of a twelve-year-old girl.

The story of the demoniac is certainly one of the most powerful statements of Christ's dominion over Satan and his power. That man was demon possessed, driven to insanity, and endowed with the unrestrained physical strength of a madman. He was a wicked, vile, and wretched creature, who lived among the tombs, cutting himself and representing a threat to all around him. His was a hopeless case. Had he lived today, modern medicine could have done little or nothing for him. Doctors and police would combine to do what the authorities in his day tried to do, namely, to put him in chains. That is the best that society can do for such a person—try to restrain his excesses without ever effecting any real change of nature and character. But that is not Christ's way. With one authoritative word He cast out the legion of demons that tormented the man and instantaneously set him free. The result was amazing to the local people, who could hardly believe their eyes when they found the delivered demoniac "sitting, and clothed, and in his right mind" (Mark 5:15). Wherever the kingdom comes, Christ the king exercises this gracious and glorious power.

The Kingdom Is Prophetic

In one sense the kingdom has already come, but in another sense it has not. To some this appears a conundrum, but the fact we highlighted above will explain the difficulty. Remember, the kingdom comes with Christ. At His first coming, He inaugurated His kingdom. After His resurrection and acsension, He brings in His kingdom by His coming in saving grace into the lives of His people. And when He comes again in His second coming, He will give the fullest-ever manifestations of His kingly power. His kingdom has yet to come millennially and then eternally. The prophet Daniel looked forward to this kingdom yet to come: "I saw in the night visions, and, behold, one like the Son of man came with the clouds of heaven, and came to the Ancient of days, and they brought him near before him. And there was given him dominion, and glory, and a kingdom, that all people, nations, and languages, should serve him: his dominion is an everlasting dominion, which shall not pass away, and his kingdom that which shall not be destroyed" (Daniel 7:13–14).

Keeping in mind all we have learned about the kingdom, we are now in a position to grasp the scope and intention of the second petition in the Lord's Prayer. When we pray, "Thy kingdom come," we ask our Father in heaven to advance in us and in the whole world the reign of His grace through Jesus Christ our Lord and to hasten the full and final establishment of Christ's reign in glory. Recognizing this, we may now trace five important pleas we make to God our Father every time we pray, "Thy kingdom come."

Praying for the Kingdom to Come

A Prayer for Salvation

Since entering the kingdom means entering into eternal life (Matthew 19: 16, 24), it is clear that the first and most personally immediate plea included in "Thy kingdom come" is this: "Let me enter into life by Jesus Christ." Anyone who seeks life from Christ must be ready for His answer, for there is no other possible way than that which He sets forth. That answer always calls for personal repentance and faith as the condition of entering into the kingdom of God. In other words, to receive eternal life from Christ is to come under His gracious rule or lordship. This is what the rich young ruler failed to grasp. He sought eternal life, but he was unwilling to enter the kingdom by personal repentance. Another way of putting that is to say that he sought to have Christ as his Saviour but was unwilling to submit to His kingly rule. That is why, on hearing the Saviour's answer to his question as to how to enter into life, "he went away sorrowful" (Matthew 19:22).

His problem was one that many people still have, a willingness to have Christ as Saviour while deliberately refusing to acknowledge Him as Lord and Master. Indeed, in evangelicalism there is a significant body of opinion that denies what is often termed "Lordship Salvation." They hold that receiving Christ as Saviour does not necessarily involve accepting His lordship. Obviously, such people would have given the rich young ruler a very different answer from the one the Lord Jesus gave him. But our Saviour's answer is the only true one, and thus any man who seeks life from Him must accept Him in all His offices, which means receiving Him as king to rule, as well as prophet to instruct and priest to forgive. Without this submission to Christ's kingship no man can be His disciple, for it would be impossible for him even to pray the prayer that Christ commanded His disciples to pray, "Thy kingdom come." It would be the greatest hypocrisy to pray these words while deliberately refusing Christ's lordship over one's own life. Repentance is the way to reconciliation; submission, the entrance to salvation.

After suffering a crushing defeat at the hands of Lord Nelson, a French naval officer went aboard the great English admiral's ship and proudly extended his hand to him. Nelson stood to attention and said, "Sir, give me your sword and then I will take your hand." Such are Christ's terms for receiving sinners, and those who have been convicted and conquered by saving grace gladly yield up their swords, repudiating their rebellion against God, penitently coming under His kingly rule, and entering into eternal life.

A Prayer for Sanctification

The Lord's Prayer was not given to be prayed once for all at the beginning of the life of a disciple. It was meant to be the constant plea of God's people. Thus "Thy kingdom come" is our ceaseless petition for the exercise of our Father's gracious dominion. If we are not to be hypocritical in praying this, we must desire Him to exercise that dominion in us. Obviously then, to pray this on a daily basis means that we are saying, "Lord, let Thy kingdom come in me. Bring me more and more under Thy gracious dominion."

Properly understood, this is a plea for increasing likeness to Christ, who alone in the history of the world lived in perfect submission to the Father's rule. Thus, "Thy kingdom come" is a plea for sanctification, for our Father to make our life more and more like our Saviour's. God's kingdom is not an abstract concept but a personal experience of our Father's reign over us. For us to pray, "Thy kingdom come," is to embrace that reign and plead for the grace to live our lives under His control. We may paraphrase the petition like this: "Let me be ruled and not live out of control. Let me be ruled by our Father and not live for self or for the world as the unsaved do. Let me be ruled by our Father through the Lord Jesus Christ and therefore experience the dominion of grace. Advance Thy reign in every part of me and govern all my thoughts, words, and actions. Thou hast promised, 'Blessed are the poor in spirit: for theirs is the kingdom of heaven' (Matthew 5:3)—make me 'poor in spirit,' destitute of all selfishness. Sanctify me wholly in my spirit, soul, and body (1 Thessalonians 5:23) and bring me safely to Thine everlasting kingdom."

When we pray, "Thy kingdom come," we confess that our liberty is submission to our Father to fulfill His will. Living under divine rulership is the essence of true Christian experience. Christian liberty is not liberty to live according to the dictates of the flesh or license to be as wicked as the world without paying the consequences in hell. It is freedom from the dominion of sin and Satan so that we may live in holiness. It is not freedom from all rule, but freedom from all rule except our Father's. It is therefore a joyous heart reception of the government of God. This is Christian liberty, and this is what we pray for when we say, "Our Father,… Thy kingdom come."

Many professing Christians have strange views on this subject. They pray, "Thy kingdom come," but treat God as a constitutional monarch. Indeed, many years ago one man actually used this term. He said, "I have been a Christian for some time and I have always acknowledged Christ as my King, but I have to say that He was a sort of constitutional monarch. He was the head of state but I was prime minister"—which meant that he made his own decisions and expected God to rubber stamp them. Thankfully, that man went on to say that God had broken his proud heart and had brought him to the place where Christ was no longer just a constitutional monarch but was the absolute sovereign of his life. That is what we pray for when we pray, "Thy kingdom come"—"Lord, bring me more and more under Thy gracious dominion. Let me not be ruled by public opinion or governed by what is expedient."

A Prayer for Soulwinning

To pray, "Thy kingdom come," is to pray for God's kingdom to flower and flourish: "Lord, bring others under the reign of grace in Christ." The Lord Jesus likened the kingdom of heaven to mustard seed and to leaven, two symbols of powerful growth and influence. He has promised that though His kingdom was, in its first appearance, small and insignificant like a mustard seed, it would grow and become powerful. Though it was at first so hidden in the vast lump of humanity that its existence was hardly noticed, it would exert a transforming influence in the world. This is Christ's promise, and it provides us with the ground for our prayer "Thy kingdom come." In praying this we are in effect praying Christ's promise back to God. We know that it is His purpose that His kingdom flourish. He does not intend that it remain a seedling or a sapling, but that it become the greatest of trees. So we have good grounds for praying for the kingdom "to come," for others to be brought into it and to acknowledge and serve Christ as Lord and Saviour.

This then is the most evangelistic of petitions. It scans the nations of the world and refuses to leave the kingdoms of men in the darkness of their rebellion against God. It believes that there is nothing too hard for the Lord and therefore it believes that He is well able to go forth to conquer multitudes by the almighty power of His redeeming love in Christ. "Thy kingdom come" has in it the vision of reaching the unreached with the word of God's grace, invading "the habitations of cruelty" (Psalm 74:20) and proclaiming liberty to the captives (Isaiah 61:1), and hastening the day when "the kingdoms of this world are become the kingdoms of our Lord, and of his Christ" (Revelation 11:15).

When we pray this prayer, we plead with our Father to set out on a mighty soul-winning crusade, to give power to the preaching of the gospel, and to bless every evangelistic outreach. We especially declare our willingness, indeed our yearning, to be personally used by the Spirit in this great work. "Thy kingdom come" is not just a prayer that souls will be saved somehow or other, but an expression of personal consecration in which we offer ourselves to the Lord as His instruments in this great work. It is even more than an expression of willingness to be evangelistically useful; it is a burden that cannot be ignored. We *must* have a part in winning the lost for Christ. This is the fire that burns in the hearts of all who honestly and earnestly pray, "Thy kingdom come."

A Methodist minister who had a very prosperous church informed his congregation that he intended to resign. The people were amazed, especially when he gave them the reason for his decision. His reason was that the church was not seeing anybody saved. Members went to him to persuade him to change his mind. They admitted that people were not being saved through their church's labors, but they said, "Your ministry here is edifying us." Their complacency grieved the preacher's heart, and he challenged them with this question: "My ministry edifies you to do what?" That was a good question, and it found its mark. From being self-absorbed and self-satisfied, that congregation began earnestly to pray for the advance of the kingdom of God through the conversion of sinners. One man spoke to his employees about the gospel, brought them to church to hear it preached, and saw them saved. The church began to feel that it must see God's kingdom advanced. It was no longer good enough for them to feel comfortable; they had to experience the conquering power of grace in their midst. They realized that the kingdom of God and the kingdom of darkness were in collision, and they could no longer stand aloof from the conflict. They took the petition "Thy kingdom come" seriously and saw glorious answers to their prayers. So may we.

A Prayer for the Subjugation of Satan

When we pray, "Thy kingdom come," we confess that this world has not yet seen the coming of the kingdom of God in its fullness. What John wrote is still true: "The whole world lieth in wickedness" (1 John 5:19). Satan is still "the god of this world" (2 Corinthians 4:4). But we confess more than this, for we also plainly state that we serve the living and true God who has the power to overthrow the powers of darkness and to establish His kingdom. Our Father is not a puny idol, as the gods of the heathen are (see Psalm 115:4–6); He is the omnipotent monarch who rules in absolute sovereignty over heaven, earth, and hell.

When we pray, "Thy kingdom come," we are asking God to exercise His sovereignty and to defeat the powers of hell. We pray, as David did, "Let God arise, let his enemies be scattered: let them also that hate him flee before him" (Psalm 68:1). Paul asked the Thessalonian Christians to pray "that the word of the Lord may have free course, and be glorified" (2 Thessalonians 3:1). Literally, pray that God's word may *run,* that is, that it may proceed unhindered, something like the flow of a mighty river that sweeps aside every obstacle. This is the power of the kingdom in operation, the fulfillment of Christ's claim to be the conqueror of Satan (Luke 11:21–22). Thus when we pray, "Thy kingdom come," we acknowledge that only the coming of the kingdom of God in power can destroy the reign of sin and death. That is what we pray for.

A Prayer for the Second Coming

"Thy kingdom come" refers ultimately to Christ's return and its consequences. When we pray this petition we plead, "Hasten the return and the reign of our Redeemer." Both Testaments hold out the promise of the glorious return of our Saviour to set up His kingdom. In prophetic vision Daniel saw the coming of Christ's kingdom at the end of the age. He saw it as a stone cut without hands that smashed the image of worldly government and then grew to become a mighty mountain that filled the earth (Daniel 2:35, 44). Concerning that day, the Lord Jesus promised, "The Son of man shall send forth his angels, and they shall gather out of his kingdom all things that offend, and them which do iniquity.... Then shall the righteous shine forth as the sun in the kingdom of their Father. Who hath ears to hear, let him hear" (Matthew 13:41, 43). It is with this vision in our hearts that we pray, "Thy kingdom come." It echoes the prayer with which John responded to the promise of Christ's return: "Even so, come, Lord Jesus" (Revelation 22:20).

There is a distinct personal aspect to this prayer. We do not merely pray for the return of Christ in general terms, but we express our earnest expectation and pledge our labor to hasten its arrival. Peter says, "Seeing then that all these things shall be dissolved, what manner of persons ought ye to be in all holy conversation and godliness, looking for and hasting unto the coming of the day of God, wherein the heavens being on fire shall be dissolved, and the elements shall melt with fervent heat? Nevertheless we, according to his promise, look for new heavens and a new earth, wherein dwelleth righteousness. Wherefore, beloved, seeing that ye look for such things, be diligent that ye may be found of him in peace, without spot, and blameless" (2 Peter 3:11–14). Though the day of Christ's return has been settled by the sovereign purpose of God, there is a sense in which the labors of God's people hasten its arrival. When we pray, "Thy kingdom come," we have this in mind and commit ourselves to do the work of the kingdom with a burning desire to see the coming of the King.

"Thy kingdom come." This is a prayer that the Lord directs us to pray. Therefore it is a prayer He will answer. Indeed, He has already answered it. Pentecost was an answer to this prayer. It was the first installment of the powerful activity of the Holy Spirit to carry the gospel to every tribe and nation. Any time God's people have seriously prayed, "Thy kingdom come," our Father has answered. He has sent times of Reformation and of revival and has raised great missionary enterprises that have transformed communities and continents. That power is still at work today and will continue to bring sinners out of the kingdom of darkness into the kingdom of God's dear Son.

Despite all the evil that we see in the world, we know that our Father's kingdom must prevail. "Thy kingdom come" is therefore not a vain wish or an empty hope. When we pray this prayer, we may do so with confidence because we are praying for a certainty. God's kingdom has come, is coming, and will come in all the fullness of power and glory.

13

Submission and Obedience to God's Will

"Thy will be done."   *Matthew 6:10*

Commenting on the development of thought in the first three petitions of the Lord's Prayer, Thomas Manton said, "In the first petition we express our care for [God's] glory, in the second, our desires for his kingdom; and now we beg obedience to his will." He was right. We cannot divorce the idea of the kingdom from personal acceptance of and adherence to God's will. The theory that a person may enter the kingdom—obtain eternal life—by believing on Christ as Saviour while deliberately rejecting His lordship is all together unscriptural. What God has joined together, let not man put asunder, and it is indisputable that He has joined saving faith and evangelical repentance.

The faith that brings us into the kingdom always produces the fruit of honest obedience to the will of God. The Lord Jesus said, "Not every one that saith unto me, Lord, Lord, shall enter into the kingdom of heaven; but he that doeth the will of my Father which is in heaven" (Matthew 7:21). The Lord Jesus did not teach that we enter the kingdom by our works anymore than James did in his epistle. What He taught was that acceptance of and adherence to the will of God is the fruit that proves our professed faith to be genuine. Clearly, the essential mark of every subject of the kingdom of God's grace is a sincere desire for the will of God to be done, and that as perfectly as possible.

"Thy will be done." This is certainly a beautiful petition. There is something in the depths of every Christian that responds to it and acknowledges it as the epitome of the true Christian spirit. However, having said this, we must still ask, What does this petition really mean? There are two ways of answering this question, and they correspond to the two ideas included in the expression "the will of God." First, we may think of God's will as His sovereign purpose as set forth in His eternal decree and His acts of providence. When we pray, "Thy will be done," with reference to the divine purpose, we express our *submission to God's will*. Second, we may think of God's will as His specific precepts, and when we pray, "Thy will be done," with reference to this meaning of the term, we express our obedience to God's will.

God's Sovereign Purpose

The petition "Thy will be done" teaches us that we should submit ourselves to God's will as the wise and loving purpose of our heavenly Father. By its very nature, the secret decree of God is inscrutable. His execution of that decree is often beyond our understanding. The book of providence is usually difficult to read and concerning many of its pages we must confess our ignorance. The question "Why?" with reference to God's purposes usually baffles us. We know that our Father sovereignly ordains whatever comes to pass (Ephesians 1:11), but we cannot give the reason for any particular disposition of His providence other than to say that all that God does is worthy of Himself and is for His glory and our ultimate good. As to *how* any particular event produces these results we can rarely tell. We must confess, as a young missionary wrote to me many years ago as he faced the fact that the Lord had allowed him to contract tuberculosis from the needy people he was seeking to win for Christ, "I have learned not to ask why, but what is the Lord teaching me through this experience." We must remember that we see only a little fragment of reality; the Lord sees it all. We are bound by time and sense; He is not. When we are able to view things from the perspective of eternity we will view them differently. Meanwhile we simply cry, "Thy will be done."

Bitter Resentment

William Barclay draws attention to the fact that there are different ways of saying, "Thy will be done." A lot depends on the tone of voice in which we say it. We may say to God, "Thy will be done," in bitter resentment. Barclay gives the example of Beethoven. For a great musician could there be a more trying affliction than deafness? It is said that when Beethoven was found dead, his fists were clenched as if he would strike God, and his lips were drawn back in a snarl as if he would spit His defiance and his bitterness at God. We cannot read Beethoven's thoughts as he faced death, and the impressions of those who saw the corpse may have done him a disservice. However, we can say with certainty that many people rage impotently against God's will. Others accept it in bitterness of soul. They cannot honestly pray, "Thy will be done." What they really mean is "Thy will be *changed*."

Hopeless Defeat

We may say, "Thy will be done," in hopeless defeat. Julian the Apostate earned his title because, having professed Christianity, he went back into heathenism. When he became emperor, he sought to bring the Roman Empire back under paganism by reversing the decisions of his predecessor Constantine. When Julian lay bleeding to death on the battlefield, it is said that he reached into a pool of his own blood and tossed it to heaven saying, "You have conquered, O Man of Galilee." He accepted the inevitable; there was nothing else he could do. In a sense he said, "Thy will be done," but not in the spirit the Lord intended when He gave us this petition. Such an acceptance of God's will as Julian's is a cold, lifeless, hopeless, joyless surrender that leaves life pointless, aimless, and useless.

Loveless Acquiescence

A third way in which we may say, "Thy will be done," is in loveless acquiescence. We have all known cases where people go along with the will of another just because they feel they cannot fight it. The philosopher Reinhold Niebuhr prevailed on his young daughter to take a walk with him. The weather was inviting, the temperature was pleasant, and the fresh air beckoned. So he decided to take a walk and naturally wanted his daughter to accompany him. The trouble was that she really had no interest in going for a walk, despite all the good reasons he set before her. Finally, under his constant pressure she gave in and went with him. He felt that they had an enjoyable time and so when they arrived back home, he said to the little girl, "Now aren't you glad that you decided to come?" Her answer was disturbing and profound: "I didn't decide. You were just bigger." Isn't that precisely how many professing Christians react to the sovereign dispositions of God in their lives and affairs? They believe that God is all powerful and that therefore they can do nothing other than to accept His will. It is tragic that these people rarely rise above the level of loveless acquiescence to God's will—a far cry from what our Lord had in mind when He taught us to pray, "Thy will be done."

Trusting Submission

The only proper way to pray this prayer is in trusting submission. Perhaps Job furnishes us with the Bible's most famous example of this virtue. Was any man more tried and afflicted than Job? In a single day he lost his fortune and children and must have felt utterly devastated. When he also lost his own health and was reduced to a pitiable mass of sores and boils, he was naturally heartbroken. Though he was under a particularly vicious attack of Satan, Job knew that his suffering must ultimately be traced to God's sovereign will. Thus he comforted himself in the loss of his wealth and his children with his now famous statement, "Naked came I out of my mother's womb, naked shall I return thither: the Lord gave, and the Lord hath taken away; blessed be the name of the Lord" (Job 1:21). With his health ruined and his body wracked with pain, he answered his wife's petulant advice to curse God and die with this expression of trusting submission: "What? shall we receive good at the hand of God, and shall we not receive evil? In all this did not Job sin with his lips" (Job 2:10). It is true that at times during his grilling by his so-called friends, Job lost this sweet spirit and spoke in bitterness. But all in all he is an outstanding example of trusting submission to God's will.

This is what Jesus commands in the third petition of the Lord's Prayer. This is how He lived His own life. In the Garden of Gethsemane He prayed, "Not my will, but thine, be done" (Luke 22:42). What our Saviour said to His Father about His sovereign concealment of the mysteries of the kingdom from the wise and prudent while He revealed those mysteries to babes, is an example to all His people of a trusting submission to the divine will: "Even so, Father, for so it seemed good in thy sight" (Matthew 12:26). All the great saints have exhibited the same attitude. The Virgin Mary showed her trusting submission to God's will when she responded to the angel's message that she would bear a son: "Behold the handmaid of the Lord; be it unto me according to thy word" (Luke 1:38). Similarly, when the Christians at Tyre failed to dissuade Paul from going to Jerusalem they said, "The will of the Lord be done" (Acts 21:14). Every Christian should exhibit this attitude of trustful submission to God's will. It has three important effects.

Trustful submission concentrates our attention on the perfections of our Father. Praying, "Thy will be done," in a spirit of trustful submission acknowledges that He is all powerful, all wise, and all good. Whatever He does is *right* because He can do nothing other than what is right: "Righteous art thou, O Lord, and upright are thy judgments" (Psalm 119:137). Whatever the Lord does is *good* because He can do nothing other than what is good: "Thou art good, and doest good; teach me thy statutes" (Psalm 119:68).

Trustful submission creates real peace in our soul. When we see the perfections of our Father and trustfully pray, "Thy will be done," we will be blessed with a real peace of heart whatever the circumstances we may be called on to face. This is the peace that David rejoiced in: "As for God, his way is perfect: the word of the Lord is tried: he is a buckler to all those that trust in him. For who is God save the Lord? or who is a rock save our God? It is God that girdeth me with strength, and maketh my way perfect" (Psalm 18:30–32). He did not understand God's providential doings any more than we do, but he was at peace in the knowledge that God's way is always perfect. With that assurance we can say, "He hath done all things well" (Mark 7:37).

Knowing this lifts our eyes from our afflictions to our great God and Saviour, and as a result, we will experience the fulfillment of the promise of Isaiah 26: 3: "Thou wilt keep him in perfect peace, whose mind is stayed on thee: because he trusteth in thee." This *keeping in perfect peace* comes from the great God who fills our hearts and minds, arming us with His peace, so that it stands as a garrison at the door of our hearts: "Be careful [anxious] for nothing; but in every thing by prayer and supplication with thanksgiving let your requests be made known unto God. And the peace of God, which passeth all understanding, shall keep your hearts and minds through Christ Jesus" (Philippians 4:6–7).

Trustful submission imparts power to live and serve. When we can say in faith what Eli said in defeat, we will feel free to serve the Lord, whatever our circumstances: "[Eli] said, It is the Lord: let him do what seemeth him good" (1 Samuel 3:18). When Richard Cameron, the Lion of the Scottish Covenant, was slain at Ayrsmoss, his enemies severed the head from his corpse, and then, because his hands were always noted as peculiarly beautiful, they cut off the hands. They put the head on public display at the Netherbow in Edinburgh, but they brought his hands to his father, Allan Cameron, who was then in prison for aiding the Covenanting preachers. Mockingly they said to the old man, "Do you recognize these hands?" His reply forms one of the brightest pages in Scottish Covenanting history: "I know them! I know them! They are my son's, my dear son's. It is the Lord! Good is the will of the Lord, who cannot wrong me or mine, but has made goodness and mercy to follow us all our days." Far from being defeated, embittered, or intimidated into submission to tyranny, Allan Cameron's spirit was set free to serve his Saviour more fully and powerfully.

That is the spirit of the prayer, "Thy will be done." With that spirit we will not pine or sulk. With that spirit we will not give way in the face of reverses but will go on to serve our God according to His will. It is inevitable that troubles will come. We will be perplexed and will often be left without an answer to the question "Why?" In such circumstances how will we respond? How will we repeat the words of this third petition of the Lord's Prayer? Will it be with trusting love? The Lord Jesus teaches us to pray earnestly and honestly for submission to the all-wise and loving purpose of the eternal God who is our Father and who will never wrong us as He brings us on our way to glory.

God's Specific Precepts

"Thy will be done on earth as it is in heaven" is a prayer for obedience to the revealed will of our Father, that is, to His actual commandments. Thomas Manton rightly observed, "We may judge our respect to his name and his kingdom by our obedience to his will, without which we neither sanctify his name nor submit to his kingdom." We will consider four aspects of the obedience to the revealed will of our Father for which we pray when we say, "Thy will be done in earth, as it is in heaven."

Personal Obedience

We cannot pray for obedience to God's will on earth unless we are first willing to make the petition personal: "Thy will be done *in me*. I desire to render personal obedience to Thy will."

Personal obedience to God is the essence of all true religion. Christianity is not a philosophy or merely a system of belief. Rather, its doctrines demand the response of obedient action. Its theology is the basis of our conduct, which should be the outworking of our obedience to the revealed will of our God. The man who says, "I believe God," but who does not obey Him is as deficient in faith as he is in practice. True faith must produce true obedience. Thus it is impossible for us to have faith in God and His Christ as the governing principle of our lives and not have obedience to His will as the outstanding mark of our conduct. That is why James said, "Faith, if it hath not works, is dead, being alone. Yea, a man may say, Thou hast faith, and I have works: shew me thy faith without thy works, and I will shew thee my faith by my works.... For as the body without the spirit is dead, so faith without works is dead also" (James 2:17–18, 26).

The Lord looks for this living faith—this faith that produces the fruit of genuine obedience to His will—in all His people. When the Israelites vowed obedience to the Lord, He said to Moses, "O that there were such an heart in them, that they would fear me, and keep all my commandments always, that it might be well with them, and with their children for ever!" (Deuteronomy 5:29). Later He testified through Samuel to Saul, who was boasting of the steps he had taken to provide animals for sacrifice, "Hath the Lord as great delight in burnt offerings and sacrifices, as in obeying the voice of the Lord? Behold, to obey is better than sacrifice, and to hearken than the fat of rams" (1 Samuel 15:22).

Personal obedience is the truest expression of our filial relationship with our Father. In his first epistle John tells us, "Now are we the sons of God" (1 John 3: 1). It is significant that this statement appears in a book that pays a great deal of attention to distinguishing between genuine and counterfeit Christian profession. As John traces the marks of the true Christian, he emphasizes that sonship is proved by obedience to God. Peter urges the same point: "As obedient children, not fashioning yourselves according to the former lusts in your ignorance: but as he which hath called you is holy, so be ye holy in all manner of conversation" (1 Peter 1:14–15).

The Lord Jesus Christ is our great example of filial obedience. In undertaking the obligations of the covenant of redemption He vowed to His Father, "Lo, I come (in the volume of the book it is written of me,) to do thy will, O God" (Hebrews 10:7). His supreme purpose in coming into the world was to do the will of God. Theologians speak of His life as His active obedience and His death as His passive obedience. In this context *passive* denotes suffering and carries the thought that Christ endured His suffering not as a helpless victim, but willingly, as a means of obeying the will of His Father. This was His constant purpose. He said, "I seek not mine own will, but the will of my Father which is in heaven" (John 5:30). This knowledge was what satisfied and sustained Him in the midst of all His sufferings: "My mcat is to do the will of him that sent me" (John 4:34).

This is the kind of genuine obedience that the Father looks for in every child of God. When we pray, "Thy will be done," we are praying that the Lord will give us a heart to honor Him with the obedience He desires and deserves. What Epaphras prayed the Lord to produce in the Colossian Christians we pray Him to produce in us: "That ye may stand perfect and complete in all the will of God" (Colossians 4:12). *That we may stand perfect and complete in all the will of God* is the yearning of all who honestly pray, "Thy will be done." We long that our Father may be able to testify of us as He did of David: "I have found David the son of Jesse, a man after mine own heart, which shall fulfil all my will" (Acts 13:22).

Such a testimony is not reserved for super saints. It is one that each of us may have and should have. It is the testimony God's word constantly commands us to attain: "I beseech you therefore, brethren, by the mercies of God, that ye present your bodies a living sacrifice, holy, acceptable unto God, which is your reasonable service. And be not conformed to this world: but be ye transformed by the renewing of your mind, that ye may prove what is that good, and acceptable, and perfect, will of God" (Romans 12:1–2).

Practical Obedience

The word *done* in the petition "Thy will be done" tells us that this is a prayer that our Father's commands actually be accomplished or executed. In other words, we are not speaking of a mere dream. This petition is not a matter of pious words. In it we recognize that the will of God is not a matter for discussion but for action. When Field Marshal Lord Montgomery assumed command of the British army in North Africa, he set about laying the foundation for the great victories in the desert which marked the turning point in the Second World War. He described one of the first lessons he had to get across to his officers and men: "Orders no longer formed the basis for discussion but for action.... Previously orders had generally been queried by subordinates right down the line. I was determined to stop that state of affairs at once." He was teaching his army a lesson long acknowledged in the navy. To the serving man there are only two possibilities: duty or mutiny.

The same is true in the service of God. We are called to unquestioning obedience. Here we must be clear. This unquestioning obedience is owed to the commands of God, but not to the opinions of men. We do well to question and sift the interpretations that men place on God's word. God's word is what is inspired and infallible, not the constructions that men place on it. These constructions may or may not be scriptural, and we can determine this only by questioning or examining them in the light of Scripture. But the Scripture itself must be studied, not with a view to decide whether it is to be obeyed, but with the intention of completely obeying all its commands.

The Bible gives God's people a clear statement of His will. One of the great doctrinal foundations of the Protestant Reformation was the perspicuity, or the plainness, of Scripture. This does not mean that everything in the Bible is equally clear or that all is easy to understand. What it means is that the Bible is a book that God intends us to understand and that by prayerful reading we may grasp all that is essential for life and godliness.

Obedience to God starts with finding out from Scripture what His will is. "What saith the scripture?" must govern every part of a Christian's life. Paul told the Ephesians, "Be ye not unwise, but understanding what the will of the Lord is" (Ephesians 5:17). We must not determine our actions by what is easy or popular but by what our Father commands. Thus our prayer must always be, "Shew me thy ways, O Lord; teach me thy paths. Lead me in thy truth, and teach me: for thou art the God of my salvation; on thee do I wait all the day" (Psalm 25:4–5).

Christian obedience means that we consciously conform our lives to God's will as it is revealed in His word. This is implicit in the prayer, "Thy will be done." The psalmist's prayer expresses the desire of every regenerate heart: "O that my ways were directed to keep thy statutes!…I will praise thee with uprightness of heart, when I shall have learned thy righteous judgments.…Make me to go in the path of thy commandments; for therein do I delight" (Psalm 119:5, 7, and 35). When a child of God learns what his Father directs him to do, he longs to respond with a conscious, deliberate, honest, thoroughgoing, and faithful conforming of his life to his Father's commandment.

"Thy will be done on earth" means we render this obedience to God in a hostile environment. In this petition we state our desire to obey God "on earth," that is, in the world that is at enmity with God and that opposes His people with every kind of temptation and discouragement. With the full arsenal of the world, the flesh, and the devil turned against us, we vow our defiance of Satan and sin

and raise our cry to heaven, "Teach me thy way, O Lord, and lead me in a plain path, because of mine enemies" (Psalm 27:11).

Practical obedience is therefore separation from the world. The Lord Jesus Christ warned His disciples, "If ye were of the world, the world would love his own: but because ye are not of the world, but I have chosen you out of the world, therefore the world hateth you" (John 15:19). Every attempt to bridge this gulf between Christ and the world, or between doing God's will and the applause of the world, is bound to fail. "Know ye not that the friendship of the world is enmity with God? whosoever therefore will be a friend of the world is the enemy of God" (James 4:4)—and the converse is equally true: Whoever will be a friend of the Lord will be looked on as the enemy of the world. Thus separation must be the watchword of God's people. The apostle John wrote, "Love not the world, neither the things that are in the world. If any man love the world, the love of the Father is not in him. For all that is in the world, the lust of the flesh, and the lust of the eyes, and the pride of life, is not of the Father, but is of the world. And the world passeth away, and the lust thereof: but he that doeth the will of God abideth for ever (1 John 2:15–17).

Perfect Obedience

"Thy will be done on earth as it is in heaven" sets a standard that seems impossible to attain. But this prayer is not expressing a dream or dealing with impossibilities. *As* means "in like manner." Thomas Manton stated the point of the petition succinctly: "Though we cannot do [God's will] in the same *measure*, yet we should do it in the same *manner*." The question is, How do they do the will of God in heaven? Think of the angels. They do God's will fully and joyfully. David wrote, "Bless the Lord, ye his angels, that excel in strength, that do his commandments, hearkening unto the voice of his word" (Psalm 103:20). What is true of the angels' service is equally true of the service of the glorified saints.

John has recorded the lovely vision he received of the joyful service of all creatures—both unfallen angels and redeemed saints—in heaven: "I beheld, and I heard the voice of many angels round about the throne and the beasts and the elders: and the number of them was ten thousand times ten thousand, and thousands of thousands; saying with a loud voice, Worthy is the Lamb that was slain to receive power, and riches, and wisdom, and strength, and honour, and glory, and blessing. And every creature which is in heaven, and on the earth, and under the earth, and such as are in the sea, and all that are in them, heard I saying, Blessing, and honour, and glory, and power, be unto him that sitteth upon the throne, and unto the Lamb for ever and ever" (Revelation 5:11–13).

All in heaven do God's will consistently, unitedly, and with perseverance. The angel who spoke to Daniel said as much when he described his mission and the opposition he encountered: "From the first day that thou didst set thine heart to understand, and to chasten thyself before thy God, thy words were heard, and I am come for thy words. But the prince of the kingdom of Persia withstood me one and twenty days: but, lo, Michael, one of the chief princes, came to help me; and I remained there with the kings of Persia" (Daniel 10:12–13). From this passage we gather that there is a spiritual warfare going on that we know very little about. As soon as Daniel prayed, the Lord sent His angel with His response, but the angel was hindered by the evil powers that held spiritual sway in Persia. Nevertheless the angel continued with his task and received help from Michael the archangel and so prevailed. The three weeks of warfare were testing ones for Daniel, to whom it must have appeared that the Lord had made no move to give him an answer. However, that three-week period of angelic persistence gives us a clear grasp of how God's will is done in heaven. The words of Revelation 7:15 aptly summarize how those in heaven serve the Lord: "Therefore are they before the throne of God, and serve him day and night in his temple."

When we pray, "Thy will be done in earth as it is in heaven," we are asking the Lord to enable us to obey Him fully not partially, joyfully not grudgingly, and consistently not sporadically, and furthermore to keep us from the ego mania that all too often keeps God's people from harnessing their efforts in united service. These truths are none the less important for being obvious. In addition there are implications in our reference to how God's will is done in heaven that are not so obvious and that are yet essential to a true understanding of this great petition. Consider especially the references we have noted to the glorified saints in heaven and then think of the significance of the request that we may serve and obey the Lord as they do. Four ideas suggest themselves as loose paraphrases of this petition.

Lord, give me obedience that flows from the full joy of thy salvation. The redeemed in glory sing, "Worthy is the Lamb that was slain." They rejoice that He has made them kings and priests unto God (Revelation 5:9–12). They serve God in the full joy of salvation, and we can emulate their service only when we enter into their joy in Christ. Has He not redeemed us? Has He not made us kings and priests unto God? We do not need to wait until we enter heaven for these things to become true of us; they are as true now as they will be when we are glorified. We have a great Saviour who has wrought for us a great salvation. As we draw water from the wells of salvation (Isaiah 12:3)—that is, as we drink deeply of all Christ has done for us—we will be free to serve Him on earth with heaven-like obedience.

Lord, give me obedience that flows from a deep fellowship with Thee around Thy throne. The glorified redeemed have entered the nearer presence of the Lord. They serve around the throne of God. So may we, even before we quit this life. We are not yet glorified or made perfect (Philippians 3:12), but we have access to the throne of God and are privileged to have real fellowship with Him. John testifies, "Truly our fellowship is with the Father, and with his Son Jesus Christ" (1 John 1:3). We have "throne union" with Christ (as Ephesians 2:6 says, we now "sit together in heavenly places in Christ Jesus") and through Him a "throne fellowship" with the Father. It is out of this that we may serve Him with heaven-like obedience. True obedience can never be far removed from intimate fellowship around the throne of grace. As we noted in chapter 10, the old canard that spiritually minded Christians are so heavenly minded that they are of no earthly use is a lie. Those who spend much time with God in the secret place will be the best doers of His will and work, for obedient action arises from genuine fellowship with Him.

Lord, give me obedience that flows from a sight of the glorified Christ. In heaven the saints have an unimpeded view of Christ, and they serve Him in direct proportion to the clarity of their vision of Him. The same rule holds good for us here on earth. This is where almost every branch of modern Christendom has gone wrong. Most preachers try to motivate Christians to obedient service by making them feel the guilt of not doing what they should or by showing them the dire need of the world.

Now these things may succeed in making us see what we ought to do, but they cannot give us the spiritual grace of obedient service. Only a clear sight of Christ can impart this grace. When He fills our vision, we can do anything He asks us to do; but when we lose sight of Him, the smallest spiritual labor is too much for us. Let us pray therefore for a clear sight of Christ in all His fullness and that will do more than anything else to lead us to serve God in the manner in which He is served in heaven.

Lord, give me obedience that flows from the conviction that Thou art working out Thy grand design in the world, even through the struggles of Thy people on earth. The book of Revelation records the ultimate victory of gospel grace over satanic wickedness. However, the steps toward the accomplishment of that victory involve many distressing events. The Lord warns, "Woe to the inhabiters of the earth and of the sea! for the devil is come down unto you, having great wrath, because he knoweth that he hath but a short time" (Revelation 12:12).

The record of satanic fury against the saints of the Most High does not gloss over the sufferings of the saints: "I saw under the altar the souls of them that were slain for the word of God, and for the testimony which they held: and they cried with a loud voice, saying, How long, O Lord, holy and true, dost thou not judge and avenge our blood on them that dwell on the earth? And white robes were given unto every one of them; and it was said unto them, that they should rest yet for a little season, until their fellow servants also and their brethren, that should be killed as they were, should be fulfilled" (Revelation 6:9–11). Looking at such things—to say nothing of plagues, earthquakes, and a host of other "natural disasters," as they are usually but inaccurately described—from a merely human standpoint, we may be tempted to think that God has either abdicated or given up any interest in the world. Nothing could be further from the truth, for the book of Revelation shows us that despite—or rather *through*—the darkest days of antichristian persecution, our Father will bring His glorious purpose to its full fruition.

The sufferings of His people are never pointless or useless. This conviction is what enabled Paul to rejoice, "We know that all things work together for good to them that love God, to them who are the called according to his purpose. For whom he did foreknow, he also did predestinate to be conformed to the image of his Son, that he might be the firstborn among many brethren. Moreover whom he did predestinate, them he also called: and whom he called, them he also justified: and whom he justified, them he also glorified" (Romans 8:28–30). This is our assurance and it is one that will keep us consistently faithful, even when times are difficult. It is then that we will learn the great lesson that Isaiah taught: "Who is among you that feareth the Lord, that obeyeth the voice of his servant, that walketh in darkness, and hath no light? let him trust in the name of the Lord, and stay upon his God" (Isaiah 50:10).

The saints in heaven see that it is the Lamb who is opening the book and is scrolling through the roll of God's purpose. He is the one who is directing every detail, not only of world events, but of each individual life. With this vision the saints in heaven serve God in the happy assurance that God is on the throne and that He will do His perfect will and accomplish His perfect purpose.

This is the vision we need and for which we pray when we ask, "Thy will be done in earth as it is in heaven." With this conviction of the absolute sovereignty of our Father and of the absolute certainty of the victory of His purpose, we will be able, as Dr. Bob Jones, Sr., used to say, to do right though the heavens fall. That is the kind of obedience they render to God in heaven and that we seek to render to Him on earth.

Progressive, Plenary, and Perpetual Obedience

"Thy will be done in earth as it is in heaven" is a prayer about the present and the future. It is a prayer for the success of the gospel and is based on the belief that the statement that God "will have all men to be saved, and to come unto the knowledge of the truth" (1 Timothy 2:4) is true. In praying it, therefore, we pray that the gospel of Christ will be carried to the ends of the earth and will succeed in bringing in the full complement of His redeemed out of every nation.

Ultimately, "Thy will be done in earth as it is in heaven" is a prayer that looks forward to the return and reign of Christ and to the new heavens and the new earth in which righteousness dwells (2 Peter 3:13). Those who honestly make this petition the prayer of their hearts wait in submission to God's purpose and work in obedience to His command until His kingdom comes in its fullness and His will is done in earth as it is in heaven.

Three Essential Elements in Prayer

"Hallowed be thy name. Thy kingdom come. Thy will be done in earth, as it is in heaven." Matthew 6:9–10

There is an obvious unity in the first three petitions of the Lord's Prayer. While all of them are addressed to God the Father, the form in which the Lord Jesus casts them naturally directs our thoughts to the three persons of the Trinity. The first petition, "Our Father which art in heaven, Hallowed be thy name," teaches us that "God will be known as a holy Father throughout the world" (C. H. Waller). The second petition, "Thy kingdom come," teaches us that we must remember that in reality, the kingdom is Christ's kingdom, consummated and delivered up to the Father. Thus, it reminds us of the Son. The third petition, "Thy will be done," reminds us of the Holy Spirit, who appears throughout Scripture as the great executor of the Trinity, the one whose power gives effect to the eternal will and purpose of God. So at the commencement of the Lord's Prayer there is a valuable reminder of the trinitarian nature of the God whom we approach.

Many commentators take the words *in earth as in heaven* to modify not only the third petition, but all three. Thus they understand the opening section of the Lord's Prayer to mean "Hallowed be Thy name in earth, as it is in heaven. Let Thy kingdom come in earth, as it is in heaven. Thy will be done in earth, as it is in heaven." In other words, "Glorify Your name on earth as You glorify it in heaven. Reign on the earth as You reign in heaven. Do Your will on earth as You do it in heaven." Considered in this way, these three petitions force us in prayer to take an *upward* look to heaven, an *outward* look at what is happening and at what we desire to happen in earth, an *inward* look at ourselves, and a *forward* look, because their ultimate focus is on the future.

The petitions do something else. They set before us three essential elements in prayer, things that are necessary if we are to pray effectively. The first essential element in prayer that the opening petitions of the Lord's Prayer set before us is a vision of our God. The second is a vision of our need. The third is a vision of our hope and our future.

A Vision of Our God

The vision of God with which these three petitions present us is necessary to all genuine praying, yet it is probably the most obviously absent element in most people's prayers. Perhaps the most glaring weakness in the prayer lives of God's people is that they give little real thought to the God to whom they come. They are often consumed with thoughts of themselves and of their needs and personal circumstances. They are so overwhelmed by these thoughts that they barely think at all of the One to whom they pray. What the Lord Jesus plainly teaches is that the fundamental necessity in prayer is a vision of our God. We have already noted the words of Thomas Manton—"We should begin prayer with awful thoughts of God"—the word *awful* being used in its proper sense of "full of awe or godly fear." In other words, we should approach God with great and deep thoughts of God. To pray, we need a vision of our God.

A Vision of the Glory of God

We need to see the glory of God. This is our first and most important need in prayer. Nothing humbles the flesh, frees us from the cares of the world, delivers us from the fear of man, and lifts us above the tyranny of circumstances more than a vision of the glory of God. When Moses was leading a nation of millions through the wilderness, faced with a multitude of needs and with the clamor of a volatile people constantly harassing him, he prayed, "I beseech thee, show me thy glory" (Exodus 33:18). Similarly, the psalmist cried to the Lord from the depths of his afflictions, "Make thy face to shine upon thy servant" (Psalm 119: 135). What those men prayed was in effect, "Lord, take us beyond the clouds of unbelief, worry, and confusion, and let us behold the glory of our God." Some of us may need to ask the Lord to take us out of the darkness caused by disobedience, worldliness, and backsliding and to focus our souls again on the glory of our God.

At this point an important question arises: What does it mean to behold the glory of the Lord? Does it describe something mystical or visionary? Is it therefore a merely subjective or trance-like experience? Is this what beholding the glory of the Lord means? Not at all. What it is may be understood from some unmistakably clear Scripture statements. Replying to Moses' plea, the Lord said, "Thou canst not see my face: for there shall no man see me and live" (Exodus 33:20). Just as the human eye cannot fix itself, even at a distance of ninety-three million miles, on the blazing brightness of the sun in the heavens, so no man can look on the holy majesty of God and live. He "only hath immortality, dwelling in the light which no man can approach unto" (1 Timothy 6:16).

So how may we see His glory? The Bible gives us a clear answer: God has revealed His glory in His Son the Lord Jesus Christ. In the gospel of John we read, "No man hath seen God at any time; the only begotten Son, which is in the bosom of the Father, he hath declared him" (John 1:18). The Lord Jesus claimed, "He that hath seen me hath seen the Father" (John 14:9). Paul expounded the meaning of such statements: "God, who commanded the light to shine out of darkness, hath shined in our hearts, to give the light of the knowledge of the glory of God in the face of Jesus Christ" (2 Corinthians 4:6). *The light of the knowledge of the glory of God in the face of Jesus Christ.* In other words, it is in the revelation of His redeeming love in Jesus Christ that God shows us His glory.

Christ as He is revealed in the gospel is the full shining of God's glory to fallen humanity. What the psalmist said is true: "The heavens declare the glory of God; and the firmament sheweth his handywork" (Psalm 19:1). However, in all the history of the world no child of Adam has ever grasped the truth of God's glory by studying the heavens in such a way as to lead him to a personal, saving knowledge of Him. This is not because the revelation of God in creation is dim or uncertain but because we are blinded by sin and stupefied by the depravity of our hearts. It is only when we receive the redemption that is in Christ Jesus that we regain our spiritual eyesight and are capable of beholding the glory of God.

Thus, to see God's glory we must study the gospel. We must read the book of Scripture—and indeed the book of nature—in the light of the gospel. To understand either, we must study Christ. The way to see God's glory, then, is to meditate prayerfully and believingly on the gospel. The vision of God thus gained will have a powerful effect, as Paul teaches in 2 Corinthians 3:18: "We all, with open face beholding as in a glass the glory of the Lord, are changed into the same image from glory to glory, even as by the Spirit of the Lord." This glass or mirror is the word of God (James 1:23–25), so the message is that as we meditate on Christ as He is revealed in Scripture, we become more like Him.

The vision of God will give us faith and boldness in prayer and service. The knowledge that we "have a great high priest, that is passed into the heavens, Jesus the Son of God" enables us to "hold fast our profession" and to "come boldly to the throne of grace" (Hebrews 4:14, 16). We will be like Moses who "endured, as seeing him who is invisible" (Hebrews 11:27). That is always the secret of a believer's endurance. Nehemiah understood this and advised those who were rebuilding the walls of Jerusalem amid vicious and sustained opposition not to be "afraid of them: remember the Lord, which is great and terrible, and fight for your brethren, your sons, and your daughters, your wives, and your houses" (Nehemiah 4:14).

Remembering the Lord is the antidote to fear and the secret of courage. That is why Paul instructs us to "run with patience the race that is set before us, looking unto Jesus the author and finisher of our faith" and to "consider him that endured such contradiction of sinners against himself, lest ye be wearied and faint in your minds" (Hebrews 12:1, 3). Looking unto Jesus gives us the patient endurance and strength of mind to keep going despite every difficulty. In Psalm 48 the psalmist David expresses the same confidence: "For this God is our God for ever and ever: he will be our guide even unto death" (verse 14). "This God" is Jehovah who is great (verse 1), the great King (verse 2) who is known by His people (verse 3), and whose lovingkindness is the subject of their contemplation (verse 9). Gripped by such a realization of the nature of the Lord, we enjoy confidence whether we are confronted by the power of the enemy (verses 4–7) or of death (verse 14). Our first need in prayer, then, is to see the glory of God.

A Vision of the Grace of God

Our second need in prayer is to see the grace of God. When we pray, "Thy kingdom come," we are seeking the coming of the kingdom of grace, for what is the coming of the kingdom but the progress of grace? Therefore we need to understand something about grace. To pray with confidence, we must grasp *the sovereignty of God's grace*. We are praying to the King about His kingdom. The gospel does not envisage a constitutional monarchy or a republican presidency. Rather it presents the idea of an absolute monarchy under which we as the subjects of the great King render to Him absolute surrender and submission. Our God is King, and His sovereignty is seen in the free exercise of His grace. This is a wonderful truth witnessed throughout the scriptures: "Where the word of a king is, there is power: and who may say unto him, What doest thou?" (Ecclesiastes 8:4).

Consider the history of the kingdom. No power of Satan has ever been able to defeat the power of sovereign grace. The testimony of every believer bears witness to this fact, as does the history of the church. Despite every satanic plan and action, God's truth goes marching on and He continues to bring in the full number of His elect. His grace is the action of the King of glory bestowing His favor according to His own will. His regenerating grace is irresistible: All those whom He effectually calls, He actually justifies and glorifies (Romans 8:29–30). The progress of the gospel is the progress of His kingdom, and it has behind it all the unassailable authority of His eternal throne.

To grasp this truth is essential to effective praying. When we pray for the salvation of the lost, we are praying about hopeless cases, people who are "dead in trespasses and sins" (Ephesians 2:1) and are incapable of even cooperating with God in their regeneration. Apart from the sovereign grace of God to draw them, they cannot even come to Christ (John 6:44). The Greek term translated "draw" in this verse has the idea of dragging or pulling forcefully and effectively: Peter *drew* his sword (John 18:10); Christ's disciples *drew* their net full of fish to the land (John 21:6, 21); the masters of the demonized girl in Philippi *drew* Paul and Silas before the magistrates (Acts 16:19); the incensed Jews *drew* Paul out of the temple and tried to kill him (Acts 21:30–31); rich men oppressed God's people and *drew* them before the courts (James 2:6). The force of the verb is not lost in the two places where it is used metaphorically, John 6:44 and 12:32. It still carries the idea of the powerful and effective pulling of a sinner to Christ against the natural desire of his own will.

Grace makes unwilling sinners willing and thus, to use Isaac Watts' expression in his great hymn "How Sweet and Awful Is the Place," it "sweetly forces" them into God's kingdom. The strong conviction that the grace of God is bestowed by the irresistible word of the King gives great boldness and confidence in prayer. As Creator He commanded the light to shine (Genesis 1:3); as Redeemer he speaks with equal sovereignty to command spiritual light to arise in those darkened by sin. Paul tells us, "God, who commanded the light to shine out of darkness, hath shined in our hearts, to give the light of the knowledge of the glory of God in the face of Jesus Christ" (2 Corinthians 4:6). This assurance gives us boldness to plead with God for even the most apparently immovable of sinners. None is beyond His sovereign, saving word; therefore, none is beyond the power of prevailing prayer.

Furthermore, to pray scripturally and effectively we must grasp the truth of *the scope of God's grace*. The biblical descriptions of grace set it forth in all its immensity. God has from the beginning chosen His people unto salvation (2 Thessalonians 2:13), and when Christ died, He made a particular redemption that had the definite aim of saving those people. This is the clear teaching of God's word. But we must never deduce from this truth that God's grace is stunted or constricted. The apostle Paul certainly did not view it in such a way. He said, "The grace of God that bringeth salvation hath appeared to all men" (Titus 2:11). Grace breaks through national and denominational barriers. It transcends color, creed, and culture. It reaches to men of every tribe and nation with the message that Christ "the Saviour of the world" (John 4:42) has come.

The realization of the scope of divine grace is a powerful stimulus to prayer. It gives us a vision in prayer that encompasses the whole world. With this vision we can never fall into the arrogant folly of those church leaders who greeted William Carey's proposals to preach Christ in India with the complacent remark that if the Almighty desired to convert the heathen, He was quite able to do so without Carey's help! On the contrary, we pray with the assurance that God has called us to be His witnesses and that no matter how dark and depraved the people to whom He sends us, His gospel "is the power of God unto salvation to every one that believeth; to the Jew first, and also to the Greek" (Romans 1:16).

The scope of grace encourages us to pray in confidence, not only because the gospel is the message for all men, but also because it is God's answer to every need of the soul. God's grace superabounds over our sin (Romans 5:20). It carries the Lord's provision for every aspect of our lives. Peter says, "His divine power hath given unto us all things that pertain unto life and godliness, through the knowledge of him that hath called us to glory and virtue" (2 Peter 1: 3). This means that we may pray effectively about everything that has to do with living in the power of vital godliness in this present evil world. There is grace to cover every situation. That is a conviction that will energize our praying.

To pray scripturally and effectively we must also grasp the truth of *the success of God's grace*. God is moving. He is doing all He purposed to do. He is right on schedule. Sometimes we get the impression that God's mighty acts of grace are merely the stuff of history, that somehow He has either forgotten to be gracious, as Asaph feared (Psalm 77:9), or that He no longer works as He once did. Nothing could be further from the truth.

One of the last things the Lord Jesus told His disciples before His ascension was that the Father has reserved the times and seasons in His own power (Acts 1:7). He chooses when, where, and how He will work. But He has never ceased carrying forward the great work of the gospel. It may well be that when the history of the twentieth century is fully understood, the numbers won for Christ in that century will exceed those of any century thus far. In the West we have had only brief glimpses into what He has been doing in places such as China, but it is a fair estimate that since the Communists took over that vast land, scores of millions have been saved, despite all the atheistic propaganda of the government. In South America millions more have come to Christ and have proved the reality of their profession in their constancy in the work and witness of Protestant churches and in their evangelistic efforts to bring others to Christ.

God is working. The success of grace is never in question. Wherever we are called on to serve Christ, we need not lose hope of seeing the Lord work powerfully through the preaching of the gospel. The grace of God is always successful. The gospel of the kingdom will be preached in every nation (Matthew 24: 14) and will produce a glorious harvest before Christ returns (Revelation 7: 9–10, 14). That is the confidence that energizes our praying. When we pray we need a vision of the grace of God.

A Vision of the Greatness of God

The third petition of the Lord's Prayer, "Thy will be done," teaches us that if we are to pray effectively, we need also a vision of the greatness of God. This petition reminds us of the invincible power of the Holy Spirit to effect the Father's eternal purpose. The Lord declares, "My counsel shall stand, and I will do all my pleasure" (Isaiah 46:10). God accomplishes His pleasure by the powerful activity of the Holy Spirit. This is how He has always worked.

When the Son of God came to earth and became incarnate, we might have expected Him to act purely in virtue of His own eternal deity. However, we would have been wrong. He acted in the power of the Holy Spirit. At the very beginning of His public ministry He said, "The Spirit of the Lord is upon me, because he hath anointed me to preach the gospel to the poor; he hath sent me to heal the brokenhearted, to preach deliverance to the captives, and recovering of sight to the blind, to set at liberty them that are bruised" (Luke 4:18). Peter testified in the house of Cornelius, "God anointed Jesus of Nazareth with the Holy Ghost and with power: who went about doing good, and healing all that were oppressed of the devil; for God was with him" (Acts 10:38).

Everything the Lord Jesus did, He did by the power of the Spirit of God, including His offering up of Himself on the cross: "Through the eternal Spirit [Christ] offered himself without spot to God" (Hebrews 9:14). In His resurrection, He was "quickened by the Spirit" (1 Peter 3:18).

The Holy Spirit is the great executor of the purpose of God. The apostles carried on their work in His power. We are told that on the day of Pentecost "they were all filled with the Holy Ghost" (Acts 2:4) and that Paul exercised his great missionary ministry "through mighty signs and wonders, by the power of the Spirit of God" (Romans 15:19).

We urgently need to catch the vision of God working through His church by the mighty power of His Spirit. The work of God needs organization, as is evident from the fact that parts of the New Testament give us detailed instructions as to how to organize the ministry of the church. However, the work of God cannot prosper on the strength of organization alone. All the organization in the world cannot bring in a spiritual revival or win the lost for Christ. The work of God goes forward by the power of the Holy Spirit and by no other power. Any "success" achieved by any other means will be part of the wood, hay, and stubble that, as Paul warned ministers, will be burned up in the day of judgment (1 Corinthians 3:12–13). Thus when we pray, we must have a genuine longing for a scriptural experience of the power of the Holy Spirit. The vision of the glory and grace of God will inevitably lead us to see that the greatness of His power alone is sufficient to carry on His work. It will make us dissatisfied with anything less than "the demonstration of the Spirit and of power" (1 Corinthians 2:4), and it will keep us praying earnestly until we can say with Peter that we "have preached the gospel ... with the Holy Ghost sent down from heaven" (1 Peter 1:12).

This matter of praying for the demonstration of the Holy Spirit, for the fullness of His power, is a part of prayer that we cannot afford to neglect. But it is sadly neglected in many churches and by vast numbers of believers. Some have been scared off the whole subject by the wild excesses of some Charismatics. Others have reduced the work of the ministry to a mere mechanical process. Still others have fallen into the error of attributing the flow of grace to some mystical virtue inherent in the sacraments.

Jesus commanded us to pray for the Holy Spirit. Elaborating on His teaching in the Lord's Prayer, He went on to tell us that we are like a householder confronted with the problem of feeding a hungry man who arrives at the door at midnight when there is no food in the house. Such a householder would go urgently to his friend and rouse him out of bed to obtain what he needed to feed his guest. Similarly, we must urgently apply to our heavenly Father for the means of feeding the hungry souls of men. If we ask for bread, He will not give us a stone. If we ask for a fish, He will not give us a serpent. He will give us what we need to live for Him and to serve Him. What is it that we need to do these things? The power of the Holy Spirit. What does our Father give us to enable us to do them? The power of the Holy Spirit. Nothing else will do. Thus Jesus promised, "If ye then, being evil, know how to give good gifts unto your children: how much more shall your heavenly Father give the Holy Spirit to them that ask him?" (Luke 11:13). This is a promise that we must ever keep before us in prayer. It is a vital part of the vision of God upon which all true prayer is based.

A Vision of Our Need

When He taught us to pray, "Hallowed be thy name. Thy Kingdom come. Thy will be done," the Lord Jesus added the words *in earth as it is in heaven*. While there is no doubt a prophetic element in this part of the petition, it expresses our urgent need for a true experience of heaven here and now on the earth. This may sound somewhat utopian, but it is not. Moses spoke of God's people enjoying "days of heaven upon the earth" (Deuteronomy 11:21). Christians are not meant to limp through life. They may be called on to face affliction and hardship, according to the all-wise purpose of their Father, but they are not meant to live in defeat, depression, or despair. They are not intended to be victims of circumstances but to live as God's kings and priests, enjoying a taste of heaven before they actually get there. Already they "sit together in heavenly places in Christ Jesus" (Ephesians 2:6). Already their citizenship is in heaven, as Paul told the Philippians (3:20), who would not have missed his message: Just as Philippi is a distant colony of Rome, the Christian life is a colony of heaven right here on earth. When we pray, the vision or heart conviction of this need for an experience of heaven on earth must grip our hearts. There are three aspects of this need that are suggested by the three opening petitions of the Lord's Prayer.

We need the communion of heaven on earth. As Christians, we should live on earth in the light and sight of our Father's glory. The Bible promises, "If we walk in the light, as he is in the light, we have fellowship one with another, and the blood of Jesus Christ his Son cleanseth us from all sin" (1 John 1:7). Walking in God's light—having fellowship with Him and knowing the constant application of the merits of the blood of Christ—describes an earthly communion that is like the communion of heaven. Is not this a worthy objective to have before us when we pray? This is not something reserved for some particularly eminent saints. It is the will of God for all of His people. It is possible for each of us, whatever our station in life. We have often sung, "Where Jesus is, 'tis heaven there," and it is true. It is not the gold of the streets of the New Jerusalem that is the essence of heaven, but the immediate presence of our Saviour. It is this very presence that every Christian is promised for his journey through life. Jesus said, "I am with you alway, even unto the end of the world" (Matthew 28:20). Paul assures us that "Christ in you [is] the hope of glory" (Colossians 1:27). The Greek word for "hope" carries the idea of a joyful expectation. With that hope burning brightly in our souls, we have a foretaste of heaven's communion even while we walk the dark places of the earth. By the very act of praying, we are confessing to our Father our need and are yearning for deep, daily, personal communion with Him. That is one aspect of the experience of heaven on earth.

We also need the conquest of heaven on earth. When we pray, "Thy kingdom come," we are asking that on a personal level we may experience the grace of our King both to conquer sin and to overcome Satan. This is what the apostles of Christ experienced after Pentecost and what they commended to the church at large as their rightful experience. Faced with enormous opposition, the early church prayed for boldness (Acts 4:29). The Lord answered in a powerful way: "And when they had prayed, the place was shaken where they were assembled together; and they were all filled with the Holy Ghost, and they spake the word of God with boldness.... And with great power gave the apostles witness of the resurrection of the Lord Jesus: and great grace was upon them all" (verses 31, 33). Paul assured the believers in Rome, "The God of peace shall bruise Satan under your feet shortly" (Romans 16:20). The book of Revelation describes Christians as overcomers (2:7, 11, etc.) and reveals both the secret and the extent of their victory over Satan: "They overcame him by the blood of the Lamb, and by the word of their testimony; and they loved not their lives unto the death" (Revelation 12:11). This is the kind of power we need if we are to serve the Lord effectively. This is the second aspect of the need to experience heaven on earth.

We also need the commitment of heaven while we are on earth: "Thy will be done in earth, as it is done in heaven." Here is the key to enjoying days of heaven on earth: We must be yielded to the control of the Holy Spirit and to the government of God over every part of our lives. As Christians we have a sincere desire to surrender ourselves to our Saviour and to do His will in a way that reflects the way those in heaven do it. How is God's will done in heaven? Surely it is done perfectly, not half-heartedly, and joyfully, not grudgingly. We are not sinless and cannot be while we are in the flesh, but we can have what the old writers used to call a universal holiness. They meant a holiness that touches every part of our lives. We cannot pray for God's will to be done without asking that it be done in us in a comprehensive manner. This is the kind of commitment we need to have. The urgency of this need must never leave us, and we must give ourselves to prayer that our Father may graciously give us a genuine experience of heaven while we live for Him on earth.

If we are to learn to pray, we must have a vision of our God and a vision of our need. That much is clear from the opening petitions of the Lord's Prayer. There is one final truth that is also clear and we must not miss it, for without it faith will falter.

A Vision of Our Future and Our Hope

Each of these three petitions has its ultimate focus on a point in the future. The point at which each of these three petitions will be dramatically and gloriously realized is the coming again of the Lord Jesus Christ. He will come in the brightness of His glory and "shall be revealed from heaven … in flaming fire" (2 Thessalonians 1:7–8). At that time every knee will bow to him and every tongue will confess that He is Lord to the glory of God the Father (Philippians 2:10–11). Returning as the King of kings and Lord of lords, He will reign on the earth, and so God's will shall be done on earth as it is in heaven. This is what the prophets saw in their visions. "The Spirit of Christ that was in them … testified beforehand the sufferings of Christ, and the glory that should follow" (1 Peter 1:11).

This "blessed hope" of Christ's "glorious appearing" (Titus 2:13) is a vital part of the secret of the early church's boldness and confidence. It had the vision that had so enthralled the Old Testament prophets, the glory that would surely follow the sufferings of Christ. As long as the early church retained that hope, she was an unstoppable church. Threats did not deter her. Her martyrs went to the stake with the joyous assurance of everlasting glory and the certain hope of a glorious resurrection. The vision of glory sustained them in every situation and breathed hope into the darkest trial. This is how young men and women could face the ordeal of the Roman arena and sing the praises of their Saviour as the wild beasts leapt upon them. They had the vision of a glorious hope and a certain future. May God give us that vision. May all our praying be in the light of the hope, that joyful expectation, that Christ has given us. May we never lose the vision of His return.

The more *this worldly* we become—that is, the more tied to the things of this present age—the less useful we will be in the world. The more *next worldly* we become—that is, the more we let our future hope govern our present conduct—the more useful we will be in furthering the cause of Christ in the world. We must live and pray with our eyes on the prize and our hearts alight with the certainty of Christ's return. We are praying for what God has assured us will come to pass. His name will be hallowed. His kingdom will come. His will shall be done in earth as it is in heaven. Praying as the Lord Jesus tells us to pray lifts us on to the chariot of the King of glory as He rides forth in certain and eternal success.

At the beginning of this study we noted that these opening petitions of the Lord's Prayer force us to take four looks—upward, outward, inward, and forward. With the vision of our God, our need, and our hope that we have been studying, we will be able to look upward with confidence, outward with courage, inward with commitment, and forward with certainty.

15

Holy and Happy Christians

"Give us this day our daily bread. And forgive us our debts, as we forgive our debtors. And lead us not into temptation, but deliver us from evil."
Matthew 6:11–13

G ive us this day our daily bread" commences the second main division in the petitions of the Lord's Prayer. The first three are concerned with the Lord's glory, kingdom, and will. Though we include serious prayer for others in these petitions, we do not pray directly for ourselves. We enter the picture only as we may be instruments for accomplishing what we request. Now in the second group of petitions we start praying directly for ourselves and our needs. The needs we pray about are temporal, material, and spiritual: "Give us this day our daily bread. And forgive us our debts, as we forgive our debtors. And lead us not into temptation, but deliver us from evil."

Commentators dispute whether there are three or four petitions in this section. The point of contention is whether we should consider "Lead us not into temptation, but deliver us from evil" as one petition or two. Do the two parts of the sentence suggest two aspects of a single idea or two related but distinct ideas? While many writers treat them as a single petition, we will not do so because the differences in concept between "Lead us not into temptation" and "Deliver us from evil" (or "from the evil one," as the Greek phrase may be translated) seem to demand that we treat each clause as a separate petition.

At first sight it may appear that there is a sudden drop in the spiritual level of these petitions. Concerns about our food, our temptations, and our struggles with evil appear of small significance compared to the majestic sweep of the first three petitions. However, they are not. It is in answering these petitions about mundane matters that the Father glorifies His name, advances His kingdom, and accomplishes His will on earth. There is no greater testimony in the world to the glory and grace of God than Christians leading clean and contented lives in an immoral and avaricious world. That is what these petitions are all about. Viewing them as a group, we see that the Lord Jesus is teaching us to pray for ourselves to be happy and holy Christians. As we consider His instructions we shall see that these petitions show us three simple but far-reaching truths to humble, challenge, and encourage us.

To Humble Us, They Show Us Ourselves

God works on the principle that He gives grace to the humble (1 Peter 5:5). Since humility is an essential condition of answered prayer, each petition reveals a humbling truth about us.

"Give us this day our daily bread" shows us our *poverty*. To be able to pray, Christians must overcome pride, the most basic element in fallen human nature. The very essence of the sin that led our first parents into rebellion against God was the proud notion of self-sufficiency and the delusion of personal ability. These arrogant assumptions still control the heart of man. Thus the first thing our Saviour instructs us to pray about in reference to ourselves emphasizes our poverty. We depend on our Father in heaven for even our daily bread. We have a responsibility to labor to earn our food: "This we commanded you, that if any would not work, neither should he eat" (2 Thessalonians 3:10). When we have done all, however, we are still dependent on the Lord to give us our food.

In this age of superior technology, when both European and North American farming yield enough surplus food to feed the world, making our first personal petition a plea for daily bread may appear strange or even ludicrous. Hasn't modern science done away with the need to depend on God for our daily bread? Rebellious men may like to think so, but the truth is far different. If it were not for the grace of God, both Europe and America would be reduced to the poverty and famine of an Ethiopia. It is God on whom we depend for our daily bread. What Paul stated as a spiritual principle holds true in the natural world: Men may sow seed and water the ground, but it is God who gives the increase (1 Corinthians 3:6–7). Nothing more clearly shows our utter poverty.

For Christians there is also a powerful lesson about prayer in general: God's blessing is for the poor in spirit. The Lord Jesus said, "Blessed are the poor in spirit: for theirs is the kingdom of heaven.... Blessed are they which do hunger and thirst after righteousness: for they shall be filled" (Matthew 5:3, 6). When we pray, "Give us this day our daily bread," we admit our poverty. But poor people are in a good position to appeal to the beneficence of our Father in heaven. Admitting our poverty and dependence on Him places us on good praying ground. God's promise is "When the poor and needy seek water, and there is none, and their tongue faileth for thirst, I the Lord will hear them, I the God of Israel will not forsake them" (Isaiah 41:17). Thus when we feel our need, we may pray with confidence as David did, "Bow down thine ear, O Lord, hear me: for I am poor and needy" (Psalm 86:1).

"Forgive us our debts" shows us our *depravity*. If we are to pray effectively, we must never take a light view of sin. We must not fall into the relativism that has so undermined the moral fiber of both the nation and the church. We must take a biblical view, not only of sin in general, but of our own sin in particular. We must neither deny nor overlook our sin, but rather confront it and confess it. We are in a constant battle with what the Bible calls "the flesh" or our "old man." While we remain in unglorified bodies we must confess with Paul, "I know that in me (that is, in my flesh,) dwelleth no good thing: for to will is present with me; but how to perform that which is good I find not.... O wretched man that I am! who shall deliver me from the body of this death?" (Romans 7:18, 24).

This kind of self-analysis does not appeal to those who have adopted the worldly concept of self-esteem. But a moment's thought should convince us that as Christians we cannot try to feel good about ourselves on the basis of anything but what God says about us. Our self-acceptance must be founded on the fact of our justification. Since God accepts us on the merit of Christ's obedience and imputes to us all Christ's righteousness, we can accept ourselves on the same basis. This acceptance on the merits of Christ does not breed moral and spiritual laxity in us, however; rather, it promotes a strong desire for a consistent experience of true holiness. Thus, rejoicing in our acceptance with God, we believers in Christ will maintain an acute sense of what grieves our Father. We will not be lulled into taking an optimistic view of our natural desires and abilities but will recognize our propensity to sin and make it a matter of constant and earnest prayer. We will be humbled by our continual battle with our own heart and will ever feel the need to plead, "Forgive us our debts."

"Lead us not into temptation" shows us our *folly*. We pray, "Lead us," because left to ourselves, we will always wander. It is our nature to go astray: "All we like sheep have gone astray; we have turned every one to his own way; and the Lord hath laid on him the iniquity of us all" (Isaiah 53:6). With the psalmist we must confess, "I have gone astray like a lost sheep; seek thy servant; for I do not forget thy commandments" (Psalm 119:176). It may seem strange that "I have gone astray" and "I do not forget thy commandments" should describe the same man at the same point in his life, but every born-again believer knows exactly what the psalmist means.

We are God's servants and cannot forget His commandments or give up His word. Yet, left to ourselves, we are always prone to wander. Take the case of Hezekiah. He was the best of Judah's kings, a true man of God, but on one occasion "God left him, to try him, that he might know all that was in his heart" (2 Chronicles 32:31). The result was disastrous: Hezekiah went sadly astray and gave the emissaries of the king of Babylon a guided tour of his treasures. The Bible furnishes an almost endless list of similar follies. Abraham wandered from the way of faith by lying about Sarah, his wife, and by making Hagar his concubine. Isaac also lied about his wife out of fear for his own safety. Jacob fell into unbelief and resorted to carnal methods to obtain temporal and spiritual blessings. Moses, the meekest and greatest of men, sinned by falling away into bitterness and anger. Joshua, after having met with the captain of the Lord's hosts and winning the battle of Jericho, fell into complacency and failed to inquire of the Lord before fighting against Ai. The consequences were disastrous. David, the man after God's own heart, wandered into lust, adultery, and even connivance at murder. Peter, the bravest of men, fell into cowardice when he was challenged by a slip of a girl. Years later he showed the same natural tendency to wilt under pressure when he hypocritically sought to placate the Jews at Antioch. Even Paul and Barnabas, after being constituted as a missionary team by the express command of the Holy Spirit, fell into bitter division over whether to take John Mark on their second missionary journey—and the saddest feature of the whole squalid episode is that there is no mention of either man making the issue a matter of prayer. We are no different from these ancient saints. We confess in the words of a well known hymn, "Prone to wander, Lord, I feel it; / Prone to leave the God I love." With such an ever-present realization of our natural folly, we feel the need to pray, "Lead us not into temptation."

"Deliver us from evil" shows us our *frailty*. We are no match for Satan, sin, calamity, and trouble. With Jehoshaphat we must confess to the Lord, "We have no might against this great company that cometh against us; neither know we what to do: but our eyes are upon thee" (2 Chronicles 20:12). Whether we think of the forces of the world, the flesh, or the devil, we must admit that we have no might to stand against them. We need divine deliverance. Our safety does not lie in the strength of our will power but in an honest confession of our frailty and consequent dependence on the help that our Father alone can provide.

Thus the petitions that the Lord Jesus teaches us to pray in reference to ourselves and our needs are calculated to humble us because they force us to see ourselves as we really are. By removing every shred of self-confidence, they cast us entirely on our God. Feeling our poverty, depravity, folly, and frailty, we will be driven to the throne of grace where God will graciously hear us.

To Challenge Us, They Show Us Our Need

To challenge us, the petitions Christ instructs us to pray show us our need. We have two kinds of need, physical and spiritual. Both are important and both are legitimate items for prayer, but it is significant that three out of the four emphasize our spiritual need. That is not to undervalue the importance of praying about our physical needs, but it is a strong warning against indulging in carnal praying that is consumed with physical and material concerns and pays scant attention to spiritual matters. This is a warning that is urgently needed, as a visit to most church prayer meetings will confirm. In many places the prayer list is entirely given over to requests that have to do with health and wealth. Physical and material needs are legitimate matters to bring before the Lord in private and corporate prayer, but they must not be allowed to control our prayer times so that we lose sight of what is spiritual and eternal.

We must repeat, however, that the preeminence of the spiritual aspects of our personal needs in no way underestimates the importance of the physical. Indeed, the Lord Jesus mentions our physical needs first. He first instructs us to pray, "Give us this day our daily bread." He does so for two reasons. The first is that our physical and material needs are usually the most obvious. The other reason is that it is difficult to speak of spiritual things to a starving man. No one knew this better than the Saviour. That is why he fed the five thousand before He launched upon His wonderful exposition of the true meaning of the bread of life. Throughout church history many of the greatest soulwinners have followed His example. William Booth, the founder of the Salvation Army, was one. No man burned with a more intense passion for souls or committed himself more constantly to reaching the poor and needy with the gospel. Booth ministered at a time when poverty, drunkenness, and vice made England's great cities harsh and cruel places for the poor. For the most part, established churches had little to offer the poor, and even the fires of the great Methodist revival were no more than embers. Booth felt compelled to meet the situation head on, as did other men of God, such as Thomas Barnardo, George Müller, and C. H. Spurgeon. He believed that it was a cruel mockery to tell a man that God loved him and offered him full and free salvation if he was starving and without the means of obtaining food. Though he longed to see people saved, Booth paved the way for his evangelism by providing for the physical needs of the poor. That was wise evangelism.

What is wise in the area of evangelism is equally so within the fellowship of the church. In the early church, in a determined effort to insure that every believer's needs were met, God's people had all things in common. The apostles recognized that in encouraging this sort of sharing of earthly goods, they had a difficult and delicate balance to maintain. This is evident from their teachings on the subject. On the one hand, Paul commanded every Christian to be hard working and responsible, not a leech in the body of believers. He said, "When we were with you, this we commanded you, that if any would not work, neither should he eat" (2 Thessalonians 3:10). On the other hand, the same apostle taught, "As we have therefore opportunity, let us do good unto all men, especially unto them who are of the household of faith" (Galatians 6:10). John put our obligation to our brethren in the starkest terms, questioning the salvation of any who refuse to share their goods with their brethren: "Whoso hath this world's good, and seeth his brother have need, and shutteth up his bowels of compassion from him, how dwelleth the love of God in him?" (1 John 3:17). God's people are to be a caring people, praying and laboring for each other's physical and spiritual needs. These are our two great areas of need, as may be seen from a cursory glance at the detailed petitions the Lord Jesus instructs us to make.

We need food for our bodies: "Give us this day our daily bread." We should pray and be thankful for it. We should never take for granted the Lord's grace either in giving it to us or in giving us the capacity to enjoy and benefit from it.

We need cleansing for our sins: "Forgive us our debts, as we forgive our debtors." In prayer we must never forget that we approach a holy God and that we must seek cleansing from our sins. The command of Scripture is "Touch no unclean thing;... be ye clean, that bear the vessels of the Lord" (Isaiah 52:11). Unless we live in the present experience of the cleansing virtue of the blood of Christ (1 John 1:7) and the sanctifying power of His word (John 17:17), we will not be able to pray. On this point the word of God is unmistakably plain: "Who shall ascend into the hill of the Lord? or who shall stand in his holy place? He that hath clean hands, and a pure heart" (Psalm 24:3–4). Thus with David every Christian feels the need to cry, "Wash me throughly from mine iniquity, and cleanse me from my sin" (Psalm 51:2).

We need guidance: "Lead us not into temptation." Perhaps nowhere in Scripture are we introduced to the secret striving of godly souls in the place of prayer as in the book of Psalms. It is therefore worthy of notice that one of the most frequently repeated petitions in the book is "Lead me." The reasons for the repetition of this prayer are simple. The psalmist desired to escape iniquity, so he prayed, "Lead me, O Lord, in thy righteousness" (5:8). He wished to be kept from error, so he prayed, "Lead me in thy truth, and teach me" (25:5). He wanted to escape the snares laid for him by his enemies, so he prayed, "Teach me thy way, O Lord, and lead me in a plain path, because of mine enemies" (27:11). When he felt oppressed by the darkness that prevailed around him (43:3) or overwhelmed by the afflictions he bore (61:2), he cried, "Lead me." We need to make the words of Frank M. Davis's hymn the prayer of our hearts:

Saviour, lead me lest I stray,
Gently lead me all the way;
I am safe when by Thy side,
I would in Thy love abide.
Lead me, lead me,
Saviour lead me lest I stray;
Gently down the stream of time,
Lead me, Saviour, all the way.

We need protection: "Deliver us from evil." This includes deliverance from evil of every kind. Paul reminds us of our need to be delivered from the evil of sin. He warns us to "flee fornication" and to "flee from idolatry" (1 Corinthians 6:18; 10:14). Peter speaks of our need to be delivered from Satan: "Be sober, be vigilant; because your adversary the devil, as a roaring lion, walketh about, seeking whom he may devour" (1 Peter 5:8). David shows us that we need the Lord's deliverance from evil in the sense of trouble or calamity: "The Lord hear thee in the day of trouble; the name of the God of Jacob defend thee" (Psalm 20:1).

These various material and spiritual needs pose a challenge for us, but it is a challenge that will drive us to our knees. Facing it, we make the prayer of Psalm 25:20 our own: "O keep my soul, and deliver me: let me not be ashamed; for I put my trust in thee." The Lord will answer that prayer. He will not put us to shame. We share Paul's confidence: "The Lord shall deliver me from every evil work, and will preserve me unto his heavenly kingdom: to whom be glory for ever and ever. Amen" (2 Timothy 4:18).

To Encourage Us, They Show Us Our God

The four petitions we make for our needs encourage us by showing us our God. With those petitions, the Lord Jesus Christ paints a vivid picture of the God we approach in prayer.

He is our Father on whom we may call. He tells us to do so: "Call upon me in the day of trouble: I will deliver thee, and thou shalt glorify me" (Psalm 50:15). His promise regarding His child is "He shall call upon me, and I will answer him: I will be with him in trouble; I will deliver him, and honour him" (Psalm 91:15). "I will hearken unto you" (Jeremiah 29:12) is the constant assurance He gives to His people. Amid the difficulties of life there is no sweeter comfort than this: Our Father is in heaven, controlling all that happens on earth, and His "ears are open to [our] prayers" (1 Peter 3:12).

He takes a personal interest in us. By commanding us to ask our Father in heaven for our daily bread, the Lord Jesus makes it clear that even the most mundane need of the individual believer matters to God. When we consider the vastness of the universe and the majestic greatness of the purposes of God, we may be tempted to imagine that we are too small and insignificant to be of much account to the Lord of all. Nothing could be further from the truth. We have already noted the Saviour's assurance in the instructions with which He introduced the Lord's Prayer: "Your Father knoweth what things ye have need of" (verse 8). Every Christian can testify with David, "I am poor and needy; yet the Lord thinketh upon me" (Psalm 40:17). The Lord Jesus taught that our Father is concerned with the details of His creation, for not a sparrow falls to the ground without His knowledge (Matthew 10:29). God's children are of much more value to Him than sparrows, and they may rest assured that since they are precious in His sight (Isaiah 43:4), He takes a deep, constant, and personal interest in them.

He will have mercy on us when we fall. There is forgiveness with the Lord. His grace is greater than all our sin. So when we pray, "Forgive us our debts," He answers prayer. Micah the prophet rejoiced in this truth: "Who is a God like unto thee, that pardoneth iniquity, and passeth by the transgression of the remnant of his heritage? he retaineth not his anger for ever, because he delighteth in mercy" (Micah 7:18). What more encouraging word can we have in the midst of all our deeply felt failures than this: "If we confess our sins, he is faithful and just to forgive us our sins, and to cleanse us from all unrighteousness" (1 John 1:9)?

He is all-wise in the way He leads us. We may pray with confidence, "Lead us not into temptation" because, as David said, "His way is perfect" (Psalm 18: 30). At times we are tempted to say with Israel, "My way is hid from the Lord" (Isaiah 40:27), but it is not. The word of God assures us, "The Lord shall guide thee continually" (Isaiah 58:11). He knows our way (Job 23:10) and promises, "I will instruct thee and teach thee in the way which thou shalt go: I will guide thee with mine eye" (Psalm 32:8).

He can deliver us from every evil. As His children we are not meant to live as helpless victims of sin or Satan. Rather, we may live in the experience of the power of our Father that makes us "more than conquerors" (Romans 8:37).

In a word, *He has power to answer prayer.* This is the vision that these four petitions of the Lord's Prayer present of our God. We may pray with confidence because our Father can meet every need, forgive every sin, lead in every path of life, and deliver from every evil. As Jeremiah said to the Lord, "Behold, thou hast made the heaven and the earth by thy great power and stretched out arm, and there is nothing too hard for thee," to which the Lord replied, "Behold, I am the Lord, the God of all flesh: is there any thing too hard for me?" (Jeremiah 32: 17, 27). Nothing about our needs or circumstances perplexes the Lord. Nothing can tax His wisdom or power. He can do whatever He wills to do, so that we may take courage and cast all our cares on Him.

"Give us this day our daily bread. And forgive us our debts, as we forgive our debtors. And lead us not into temptation, but deliver us from evil." In making these four petitions, we will be humbled at the sight of ourselves, challenged at the sight of our need, and encouraged at the sight of our God. By answering them, our Father will make us happy Christians, who rest in the assurance that He can meet our needs, and holy Christians, who live in the experience of His pardon and power.

16

Daily Bread

"Give us this day our daily bread." Matthew 6:11

Nothing could be simpler than the prayer "Give us this day our daily bread." Yet in it the Lord Jesus Christ says a lot more than at first appears. Under the simplicity of His words lie some profound truths. Perhaps it was a conviction of this that very early in church history led some eminent teachers to adopt a tortuous manner of explaining this petition, a method of interpretation that for centuries robbed ordinary people of the blessing of its plain meaning. The trouble all began with the Greek word *epiousios,* translated "daily." It is a unique word, appearing only here and in the corresponding portion in Luke 11:3. Not only does it not appear anywhere else in the New Testament; it does not appear in secular Greek literature either. Scholars searched every extant Greek writer to try to discover the usage of this word but without success. It was not until the twentieth century that they finally found it, or something like it, in a papyrus fragment. The discovery did not throw much light on the true meaning of the word, however. The papyrus fragment, though written in Greek, was an Armenian text that set out a list of items for the marketplace. In addition, the ending of the word was missing, so that no one could be absolutely sure that it was actually the word *epiousios.* With all this difficulty in tracing the beginnings and usage of the word, it is not surprising that there should be much speculation as to its true meaning.

In cases in which we have no data to show the usage of a word, its etymology is our only clue to its meaning. It seems clear that *epiousios* is derived from the verb *epeimi.* The problem is that there are two verbs spelled that way, each with a distinctive meaning. Simply put, the root of the word in question is either the verb *to be* or the verb *to come/to go.* The latter is unquestionably the more obvious derivation, but that did not stop some early Christian writers from choosing to derive it from *to be* and terming the bread for which the Saviour taught us to pray as "the bread of being." From this they went on to say that this bread actually is Christ Himself as received in the feast of Holy Communion. Jerome adopted this sense of the word when he translated what became known as the Latin Vulgate version of the Bible. His phrase was "supersubstantial bread." In this view, the Lord's Prayer does not refer to ordinary bread eaten to satisfy the hunger of the body. This gave an appearance of plausibility to the notion that the bread of which the Lord Jesus spoke was the sacramental bread of Holy Communion which, on being consecrated, became His own body. Some, who did not go so far in misrepresenting the Saviour's meaning, said that the bread of which He spoke was *spiritual* bread. That is, He was commanding His disciples to pray each day for a portion of Himself, the bread of life.

In itself, instructing Christians to desire a fresh, daily portion of Christ is good. We should all long for an up-to-date experience of His grace. However, as the system of Roman Catholicism emerged, it equated this desire for a daily portion of Christ with the reception of the bread of the Eucharist. While some more biblically instructed people used the Lord's Prayer to mean no more than, "Let us partake each day of the bread of life, even of Christ Himself" (a yearning which, as we shall see, is a legitimate inference from the petition, though not its meaning), the inevitable drift was to make the simple petition for daily bread a basis for the monstrous theories with which Rome surrounded the Communion feast.

A moment's consideration should have convinced those early churchmen that they were misunderstanding the word and that it afforded no basis for the increasingly mystical significance they were giving to the bread used in Holy Communion. When the Lord Jesus taught His disciples to pray the Lord's Prayer, they knew nothing at all about the subject of the Communion feast. At that stage they had not even come to terms with the fact that Christ must die, and they certainly had no understanding of the sacrament of the Lord's Supper. The prayer the Lord gave them was in response to their request "Teach us to pray" (Luke 11:1). Evidently, "Give us this day our daily bread" was a petition they were meant to use right away. It clearly had no reference to "supersubstantial" bread or to sacramental bread that was transubstantiated into the body of Christ. To foist this interpretation on generations of unlearned people effectually robbed them of the comfort Christ's words were intended to bring them.

The word *epiousios* is derived from the verb *to come/to go.* In the book of Acts, *epiousa,* a closely related word, appears a number of times. This word is the feminine present participle of the verb *to come/to go.* Thus in Acts 7:26; 16:11; 20:15; and 21:18, the word describes the *next* or *following* day, while in 23:11 it refers to *the following* night. In all these cases the sense is clearly "the day or night which is to come." Here then we find the obvious derivation of the word in our text and the usage of a closely related word. Together they settle the meaning of the word that describes the bread for which Christ tells us to pray. It is the bread for the coming day. What the Lord Jesus commands us to pray is "Give us today [or *day by day*, as Luke 11:3 has it] the bread for the coming day." That is, "Day by day, give us enough bread for that day." Or, as some translators express the idea, "Give us today, or day by day, our needed bread," that is, the bread necessary for the day.

Our Lord is referring to ordinary bread, the staple food for the body. He makes no reference to Communion bread or to some Eucharistic sacrifice on which we may feast (an idea that is, of course, completely foreign to Scripture). Strictly speaking, He does not even make any reference to Himself as the bread of life. We must not lose the simplicity of our Saviour's meaning: As the children of Israel were dependent on the Lord to provide manna for them during their wilderness journeys and as they gathered that manna day by day, so believers wait on their heavenly Father for their daily provision. We may not live in a wilderness or in an area stricken by famine. We may be surrounded by shops with all the foodstuffs we desire, and we may have the money we need to purchase that food. At first glance it may appear that in such circumstances we hardly need to pray for our daily bread. Christ's words teach us to look beyond the mirage of our imagined independence of God and to see that we depend on Him for our daily food as much as the ancient Israelites did. Thus day by day we should cry to our Father, "Give us today our daily bread."

Give us what we need for the coming day. Some people have raised questions about how this relates to another part of Christ's teaching in the Sermon on the Mount. Does He not command, "Take no thought for the morrow" (Matthew 6:34)? Why then does He instruct us to pray about bread for tomorrow? How can we pray about tomorrow's needs without taking thought about tomorrow? The difficulty is more apparent than real. A closer examination will show that there is no tension between the two commands. In Matthew 6:34 the Greek verb translated "Take no thought" means "Do not be filled with anxiety." The Lord Jesus does not say, "Do not pray about tomorrow," but rather, "Do not worry about it." Thus it is entirely proper to pray, "Give us this day our daily bread." As a morning prayer this means, "Provide for us today." As an evening prayer it means, "While we sleep, provide what we need for the day that is about to dawn." That is what we are to pray.

In this study we will spend a little time considering this food for our bodily good of which the Lord Jesus speaks. He instructs us to pray that our Father in heaven will graciously give us what we need to sustain and enjoy life. As He does so, He teaches us some extremely important truths.

Mortality

The Lord Jesus stamps this first petition for ourselves with the searching thought of our mortality. In teaching us how to address God, He focused our attention on His eternal glory: "Our Father which art in heaven." As He set before us the thought of the hallowing of God's name, the coming of His kingdom, and the accomplishment of His will, He lifted our vision beyond our immediate circumstances to consider the transcendent greatness of our Father's person and purpose. These are the fundamental truths that must govern all our praying, and so the Saviour returns to them at the end of the Lord's Prayer: "Thine is the kingdom, and the power, and the glory for ever." In stark contrast, as soon as He begins to deal with our petitions for ourselves, He introduces the element of time—and a very brief span of time at that: "Give us today bread sufficient for the day ahead." The contrast between the eternity of God and the brevity of our time is intentional and has an obvious explanation.

Our Lord wants us always to remember that we are but children of a day. In comparison to the vastness of eternity, even the longest life span on earth is but a brief day. Moses felt this keenly as he witnessed the passing away of almost the entire adult generation of Israelites who had participated in the Exodus from Egypt. He described their life span as no more lasting than that of the grass of the field: "Thou carriest them away as with a flood; they are as a sleep; in the morning they are like grass which groweth up. In the morning it flourisheth, and groweth up; in the evening it is cut down, and withereth" (Psalm 90:5–6). The apostle Peter quoted Isaiah the prophet to the same effect: "All flesh is as grass, and all the glory of man as the flower of grass. The grass withereth, and the flower thereof falleth away" (1 Peter 1:24).

When we come to God in prayer, we should remember our mortality. Today we live and perhaps die. We have no guarantees about tomorrow. Thus the Scripture admonishes us, "Boast not thyself of to morrow; for thou knowest not what a day may bring forth" (Proverbs 27:1). James adds the caution, "Ye know not what shall be on the morrow. For what is your life? It is even a vapour, that appeareth for a little time, and then vanisheth away" (James 4:14). The truth underlying the petition for daily bread is that we live every day on the borderland of eternity and depend on our Father in heaven for the sustenance of our lives. But though the body is mortal, the Lord Jesus teaches us that we should pray for its nourishment.

A Sensible and Spiritual Attitude

In imparting this outlook, Christ teaches us a sensible and spiritual attitude to the needs of the body. "Give us this day our daily bread" means "Give us what we need for the health, strength, and usefulness of our body today." This expresses a proper attitude to the body, an attitude that will save us from both the vanity of worshiping it and the folly of neglecting or destroying it. The world tends to make too much of the beauty or appearance of the body and therefore to make it a vehicle for pride and lust. By contrast, the Lord Jesus Christ emphasizes the health and usefulness of the body. His message is clear: It is our duty to live each day to the best of our ability and therefore to seek to sustain our bodies in the strength needed to fulfill our Father's purposes.

Every Christian should strive to maintain this perspective. The body-worship that is so common today—the almost total absorption with it to the virtual exclusion of any scriptural care for the soul—is incompatible with the teaching of Christ, and the pride it breeds hardly comports with the humility of soul that He requires of His people. The opposite vice—neglecting or destroying the body—is equally condemned by Christ's teaching. If we are at all sincere in praying, "Hallowed be thy name, Thy kingdom come, and Thy will be done," then we must seek to have these purposes accomplished in us. Our bodies should therefore be treated as instruments through which we look for the Lord to answer these petitions. If this is so, obviously our prayer for daily bread to sustain the body includes the thought that we will avoid introducing into it anything that is calculated to destroy it, and we will not wantonly keep from it what God has provided for its health. For example, anyone who rots his system with alcohol, tobacco, or some other poisonous drug or who indulges self-destructive eating habits such as anorexia or bulimia[1] cannot honestly pray the Lord's Prayer. The same is true of those who indulge in sexual immorality, which according to Paul is, among other things, a sin against one's own body (1 Corinthians 6:18). We cannot ask God to sustain our bodies while we deliberately seek to destroy them.

Because our bodies are instruments for the Lord's service, we should look after them and therefore control them. There are at least three good reasons for doing so. First, a Christian's body is "the temple of the Holy Ghost" (1 Corinthians 6:19). Second, it is to be presented as "a living sacrifice, holy, acceptable unto God" (Romans 12:1). Third, it has been bought with the price of the Redeemer's blood to be a vehicle for the glory of God (1 Corinthians 6:20). If we keep these things in mind, we will be able to maintain a spiritual and scriptural attitude to the needs of the body.

---

[1] These are serious and complex conditions that cannot be discussed here in any detail. The point I am making is simply that at bottom they represent not merely psychological but spiritual problems. Anything that stops a Christian from praying what Christ commands His people to pray must be dealt with as sin, and this is as true of eating disorders as of anything else. This approach to the problem is actually good news for Christians ensnared in these disorders because the Bible clearly shows God's people how to deal with their sins and how to get the victory over them.

Humility

The third thing that the Lord Jesus impresses on us with the petition for daily bread is a due sense of humility. As we have indicated, this is a prayer not only for bread, but also for all we need for life. Thomas Boston, the great eighteenth-century Scottish preacher, said, "Men depend on God's bounty for all the means and comfort of life." This is true, right down to the bread we eat. We are entirely dependent on our Father in heaven, and the Lord Jesus chose these words to make every one of us know it. He owns everything we need to sustain us, for "the earth is the Lord's, and the fulness thereof; the world, and they that dwell therein" (Psalm 24:1). It is He who keeps each of us alive.

Even in this age of advanced technology, when man imagines that he has made himself independent of his Creator, we have only what He graciously gives us. Hear how Psalm 104 makes this very point: "Man goeth forth unto his work and to his labour until evening. O Lord, how manifold are thy works! in wisdom hast thou made them all: the earth is full of thy riches. So is this great and wide sea, wherein are things creeping innumerable, both small and great beasts. There go the ships: there is that leviathan, whom thou hast made to play therein. These wait all upon thee; that thou mayest give them their meat in due season. That thou givest them they gather: thou openest thine hand, they are filled with good. Thou hidest thy face, they are troubled: thou takest away their breath, they die, and return to their dust" (verses 23–29). When we pray for our daily bread, we recognize the truth of what Daniel told Belshazzar: The breath of every man's life is in God's hand (Daniel 5:23).

This is a humbling truth. It is also instructive, for it teaches us to keep in close touch with the Lord every day. When the children of Israel were in the wilderness the Lord provided them with fresh manna every day. Except for a double portion on the day before the Sabbath, He did not give them more than a daily supply, and what He gave them stayed fresh and usable for a single day only. Thus in learning their dependence on Him, the Israelites also learned the lesson of daily obedience and communion. These were necessary lessons for naturally proud people. Had the Lord given them all they needed in advance, they would soon have forgotten the giver and would have imagined themselves self-sufficient providers for their own needs. Thus the Lord kept them with a humble sense of their dependence on Him. He thereby taught them the truth that Agur spelled out many years later in his prayer to be kept from vanity: "Give me neither poverty nor riches; feed me with food convenient for me: lest I be full, and deny thee, and say, Who is the Lord? or lest I be poor, and steal, and take the name of my God in vain" (Proverbs 30:8–9). This is the spirit of our prayer for daily bread.

This petition encourages humility in other ways. We pray for bread, not because we will not work for it, but because we confess that our labour would be in vain without the blessing of the Lord. What Paul stated regarding his spiritual ministry is true of our daily labors: "I have planted, Apollos watered; but God gave the increase" (1 Corinthians 3:6). Paul put a humbling question to the Corinthians: "What hast thou that thou didst not receive?" (1 Corinthians 4:7). All our possessions are gifts of God. Recognizing this will lead us to a humble consecration of all we are and have in Him. As the Scripture says, "Therefore glorify God in your body, and in your spirit, which are God's" (1 Corinthians 6:20).

Comfort

The Lord Jesus introduces a note of special comfort into this prayer for daily bread. This petition does not seem to deal with matters of earth-shattering importance. It paints the picture of a number of individuals who are no doubt insignificant in the eyes of the world praying for something as mundane as bread to eat. Yet, according to our Saviour, the God of heaven — the one who holds the whole world in His hand, who maintains the heavenly spheres in their appointed places and regulates their ceaseless motion — is our Father who hears us when we cry to Him. We may bring to His throne things that appear so small that we would be ashamed to call them to the attention of others. As we saw in one of our early studies, He knows our needs and is personally interested in meeting even the smallest of them.

Here is the antidote to the depressing worry that dogs the steps of so many Christians. Our Father's eyes are on us, and His ears are open to our cry (1 Peter 3:12). He "shall supply all [our] need according to his riches in glory by Christ Jesus" (Philippians 4:19). Nothing is too small for His care, for as the Lord Jesus said, "The very hairs of your head are all numbered" (Matthew 10: 30). "Therefore take no thought, saying, What shall we eat? or, What shall we drink? or, Wherewithal shall we be clothed? (For after all these things do the Gentiles seek:) for your heavenly Father knoweth that ye have need of all these things. But seek ye first the kingdom of God, and his righteousness; and all these things shall be added unto you. Take therefore no thought for the morrow: for the morrow shall take thought for the things of itself. Sufficient unto the day is the evil thereof" (Matthew 6:31–34). Here is our comfort: Our Father will take care of tomorrow and will give us our needed bread. We should therefore leave tomorrow's cares with Him and live today in the enjoyment of His provision.[2]

---

[2] Making such statements forces us to consider the plight of Christians in regions torn by war or stricken by famine or poverty, where people frequently die of starvation. How does all this apply to them? The fact that David could testify, "I have been young, and now am old; yet have I not seen the righteous forsaken, nor his seed begging bread" (Psalm 37:25) does not mean that Christians are always exempt from the sufferings common to the people of the regions in which

Challenge

To the note of comfort in the petition for our daily bread the Lord Jesus adds one of challenge. He commands us to pray for bread—the most basic staple of our diet—not for luxuries. He exhorts us to ask for what we need for a day, not for great plenty or overabundance. In other words, this petition addresses our need, not our greed. The Lord may give us more than bread—indeed, He usually does—but Christ emphasizes the thought of obtaining our daily bread to teach us the necessary lesson of contentment. Paul taught Timothy this lesson: "Having food and raiment let us therewith be content" (1 Timothy 6:8). The apostle himself enjoyed this contentment. He testified, "Not that I speak in respect of want: for I have learned, in whatsoever state I am, therewith to be content. I know both how to be abased, and I know how to abound: every where and in all things I am instructed both to be full and to be hungry, both to abound and to suffer need" (Philippians 4:11–12).

Someone has said, "People are made happy less by reality than by comparison." In other words, what makes them happy is not what they possess but how their possessions stack up in comparison to what others have. Such people are driven by envy and greed. They should enjoy contentment from having their needs met, but they destroy it because they think that others have more than they do. To live like that is unworthy of a Christian. We are to look to our heavenly Father

---

they live. In many parts of the world Christians are going hungry and dying. Far more urgently than we in the affluent West can understand, they cry to God for their daily bread, but still they suffer hunger—despite the fact that the Lord has blessed both Europe and North America with enough food to feed the world.

In some places the Lord allows His people to join in the general suffering of their nation, suffering that is often the direct result of the deliberate policies of corrupt rulers. Ethiopia and Sudan are particularly painful but far from isolated examples of such corruption. If corrupt political and military rulers were removed from the picture, the worst instances of mass starvation would be avoided and the people's need for daily bread would be met, often through the instrumentality of Christian countries and charities. When corrupt rulers block the reception or distribution of food aid, God's people will be among those who suffer. Why our Father allows this to happen is as difficult to understand as why He allows some of His faithful witnesses to be martyred by His enemies. Yet He promises to be—and will be—present with His people in their sufferings and to uphold them by His grace.

I raise the question of the world's hungry not to suggest any facile answer to the problem but to force on our consciousness the bleak fact that some Christians who pray for their daily bread as we do are daily dying of starvation. According to James 2:15–16 we have fellow Christians who are "destitute of food," and we should seek to give them "those things which are needful to the body." We must remember that in prayer we address "*our* Father" and that in doing so we include all our brethren and sisters in Christ in our prayer. As with the opening petitions in the Lord's Prayer, when we pray, "Give us this day our daily bread," we offer what we are and have to the Lord's service for the fulfillment of what we request. In other words, our giving may be our Father's way of answering the prayers of many of His needy children for their daily bread.

for our daily bread—what we need for daily life—and live happily in His provision. That is why the apostle Paul exhorts us, "Let your conversation [that is, conduct] be without covetousness; and be content with such things as ye have: for he hath said, I will never leave thee, nor forsake thee" (Hebrews 13:5). In a materialistic society it is a challenge to live contentedly and without covetousness when we work harder than many around us and earn perhaps only half what they do. But this is a challenge the Lord enables His people to meet. He who says, "I will never leave thee, nor forsake thee," is our Father in heaven who will not fail to hear our cry for daily bread.

Needs of the Soul

We have already noted that the daily bread for which the Lord Jesus instructs us to pray does not refer to Communion bread or even to Christ who is the bread of life. This is true and any exposition of the text must reflect this truth. However, there is a difference between interpretation and application. It is well nigh impossible for a Christian to pray, "Give us this day our daily bread," without thinking of Christ's statement, "I am the bread of life" (John 6:35). Thus, the literal meaning of the text leads us quite naturally to a spiritual application of it. Nor are we without divine warrant in doing so. In Luke 11:11–13 the Lord Jesus specifically uses bread as the symbol of spiritual blessings: "If a son shall ask bread of any of you that is a father, will he give him a stone? or if he ask a fish, will he for a fish give him a serpent? Or if he shall ask an egg, will he offer him a scorpion? If ye then, being evil, know how to give good gifts unto your children: how much more shall your heavenly Father give the Holy Spirit to them that ask him?" If we must confess that we have needs of the body and cry to our Father to feed us, must we not also confess that we have needs of the soul and cry for Him to feed us on Christ as He is revealed in the gospel? Day by day we should be even more diligent in praying for our souls to be nurtured than we are in praying for our bodies to be fed.

Here then is a great petition. In effect we say to God: "Our life is but a brief day. Let us live, not just exist, in this world and enjoy the provisions of Thy grace. Make us happy and useful here and now and prepare us to live, not just exist, for all eternity. To exist eternally without Christ is everlasting death. To be with Christ is everlasting life. Therefore give us life and all we need to sustain it now and for eternity. Give us today the bread we need for our bodies and for our souls."

17

Give and Forgive

"Give us this day our daily bread. And forgive us our debts."
Matthew 9:11–12

I n his valuable treatment of the Lord's Prayer, Thomas Manton points out a peculiarity about the petition for the forgiveness of our sins: Unlike the opening petitions, it and the next one begin with the word *and*. The inclusion of the conjunction is both deliberate and significant. It is evident that the Lord Jesus Christ purposely links "Forgive us our debts" with what immediately precedes it, "Give us this day our daily bread." "Give us … and forgive us" are distinct but closely related prayers. There are four important lessons we may learn from their connection.

Lesson One

We learn first that unforgiven sin hinders prayer and robs us of the ability to get through to God on matters of great importance. When we pray, "Give us," we must add immediately, "Forgive us," because the Bible says, "If I regard iniquity in my heart, the Lord will not hear me" (Psalm 66:18). There is no greater or more immediate cause for unanswered prayer than unconfessed and unforgiven sin. Jeremiah bluntly asserts, "Your iniquities have turned away these things, and your sins have withholden good things from you" (Jeremiah 5:25). The same prophet records that the Lord commanded him not even to pray for the Jews of his day because of their stubborn impenitence. Ezekiel tells us that when the leaders of the nation approached him with a request to have prayer with him, the Lord forbade it. Why? Because their praying was always, "Give us," and they had no heart to pray, "Forgive us." They wanted the Lord's blessing, but like so many people they still loved their sin. It was impossible for them to be blessed because their unforgiven sin barred the way to God. The same holds true for us.

What the Lord said to Judah speaks to us as personally as to them: "Behold, the Lord's hand is not shortened, that it cannot save; neither his ear heavy, that it cannot hear: But your iniquities have separated between you and your God, and your sins have hid his face from you, that he will not hear" (Isaiah 59:1–2).

He will not hear you. Is there a more alarming prospect for any professing Christian? The case of King Saul furnishes one of the most dramatic examples of sin closing the eyes and ears of God to a man. We do well to heed its warning. Driven to the point of distraction, Saul finally felt forced to acknowledge, "I have played the fool, and have erred exceedingly" (1 Samuel 26:21). The result was inevitable: When he most needed to be able to get through to the Lord, he couldn't. He lamented, "I am sore distressed; for the Philistines make war against me, and God is departed from me, and answereth me no more" (1 Samuel 28:15). What a tragic end to a promising life! We should not miss the lesson: Sin will hinder our prayers. If we are going to be able to pray, "Give us," we must never forget to cry, "And forgive us our debts."

Lesson Two

We learn, secondly, that by joining these two petitions the Lord Jesus Christ emphasizes our unworthiness to receive the Lord's blessing and magnifies His great mercy in giving it. The plea for the forgiveness of our sins underlines the fact that we have not earned or merited the Lord's blessing. We are unworthy of His kindness even in regard to something as vital to life as our daily bread. In other words, we have no right to life. It is God's gift, given freely to those who have done nothing to deserve it. And how bountifully He has given! We must confess with Jacob, "I am not worthy of the least of all the mercies, and of all the truth, which thou hast shewed unto thy servant" (Genesis 32:10). Unworthy of the least of God's blessings, we have received the greatest, for in the gift of His Son He has given us His all. Paul felt this deeply. To the Romans he wrote, "He that spared not his own Son, but delivered him up for us all, how shall he not with him also freely give us all things?" (Romans 8:32). Writing to Timothy, Paul charged believers to trust "in the living God, who giveth us richly all things to enjoy" (1 Timothy 6:17).

Thus in dealing with the subjects of sin and pardon, the Lord Jesus at once establishes that the only basis on which we may obtain God's blessing is pure grace. This holds good for every kind of blessing, material or spiritual, temporal or eternal. Jesus said, "Your Father which is in heaven … maketh his sun to rise on the evil and on the good, and sendeth rain on the just and on the unjust" (Matthew 5:45). Theologians consider such gifts under the rubric of "common grace," which is, "every favour of whatsoever kind and degree, falling short of salvation, which this sin-cursed world enjoys at the hand of God" (John Murray,

Collected Writings, 2:96). We live amid the constant provisions of God's grace, and its overwhelming plenitude should not make us take it for granted. If it is obvious in the natural realm that all we have we have by the grace of God, how much more obvious is it in the spiritual? "Blessed be the God and Father of our Lord Jesus Christ, who hath blessed us with all spiritual blessings in heavenly places in Christ" (Ephesians 1:3).

Lesson Three

The third lesson we learn from Christ's joining of "Give us" and "Forgive us" is that without God's pardon, temporal blessings do us little good. The blessings of food, clothing, and health are necessary to our earthly well-being. They are important and we do well to make them matters for prayer. However, without the pardon of God for our sins, they are gifts lavished on condemned souls. We have all heard how in the final hours of his life a criminal awaiting execution is given his choice of food for his last meal. What a macabre spectacle that presents! The food may be of the best quality, but it is of small benefit in the light of the man's impending doom. Similarly, no matter how wonderful the blessings of common grace are—and they are many and great—they are of small benefit to people whose sins are unforgiven and whose souls are condemned to the everlasting punishment of outer darkness.

This thought in itself gives sufficient reason for Christ to join the petitions for food and forgiveness. We should all use it to take stock of our lives. If the Lord were to give us all the material blessings we desire in the present state of our lives, would we squander them on the further pursuit of sin? Would we use them to plunge even more recklessly into rebellion against God? Would we become so engrossed in the *things* the Lord has given us as to ignore the concerns of eternity and the destiny of our souls? The story that Christ told of the rich fool who was so thrilled with a sudden increase in worldly wealth that he ignored God and the needs of his own soul is a cautionary tale. The rich fool could think of nothing beyond the chance to indulge the appetites of his flesh and looked forward to years of ease and pleasure. He could not have been more wrong. The material blessings he gained were of little real benefit to him and certainly were power-less to bring him any comfort in the face of death and eternity. Just as he was planning a long life of pleasure, without a thought of the God who had given him the possessions he so much treasured, "God said unto him, Thou fool, this night thy soul shall be required of thee" (Luke 12:20). The rich fool learned the hard way the truth that "riches profit not in the day of wrath" (Proverbs 11:4). As Zephaniah says, "Neither their silver nor their gold shall be able to deliver them in the day of the Lord's wrath" (Zephaniah 1:18).

Silver and gold, abundant harvests and prosperous business, food and clothing, and shelter and safety are all rich blessings—if they are enjoyed as God's gifts and in conjunction with His greatest gift, namely His Son as the Saviour in whom we have the forgiveness of sin. Otherwise, they are misused blessings, gifts perverted to entrench us in our natural enmity to the great Giver. To receive His gifts and yet live and die unforgiven is the greatest tragedy that can befall any man.

Lesson Four

The final lesson we will draw from Christ's linking of the petitions for food and forgiveness in the Lord's Prayer is that God gives freely and forgives equally freely. He who feeds us will forgive us. He is not merely fattening us for judgment by the bounty of His material gifts. He waits to be gracious, to pardon us. This is one of the sweetest notes in the gospel. As Paul said in Antioch of Pisidia, "Be it known unto you therefore, men and brethren, that through this man [Jesus Christ] is preached unto you the forgiveness of sins: and by him all that believe are justified from all things, from which ye could not be justified by the law of Moses" (Acts 13:38–39). Everyone who feels his burden of sin may apply for pardon and receive it. He who assured the paralyzed man in Capernaum, "Son, thy sins be forgiven thee" (Mark 2:5) with the same promise encourages every other sinner who will come to Him.

This is the word that every lost soul who has come to the conviction of his spiritual state needs to hear. God is willing to hear his cry for pardon. Indeed, He invites men to sue for forgiveness and promises to give it freely: "Come now, and let us reason together, saith the Lord: though your sins be as scarlet, they shall be as white as snow; though they be red like crimson, they shall be as wool" (Isaiah 1:18).

The promise of pardon is something every backslider should attend to. There is a way back from spiritual failure. Our great Shepherd restores the souls of His people (Psalm 23:3) and He promises, "If we confess our sins, he is faithful and just to forgive us our sins, and to cleanse us from all unrighteousness" (1 John 1:9).

Not only the lost and backslidden need forgiveness. We all do. We should keep short accounts with God and daily cry not only for the food we need for our bodies but for the forgiveness we need for our souls. Our Father will give the one as freely as He gives the other.

18

Forgive Us Our Sins

"And forgive us our debts." Matthew 6:12

It is highly significant that in the Lord's Prayer the Lord Jesus Christ centers most of our praying for ourselves on the subject of sin and its consequences. "Forgive us our debt … and lead us not into temptation, but deliver us from evil." Here is a triple emphasis on sin as it affects believers. It is obvious the Lord Jesus Christ takes the matter of sin seriously, and He wants us to take it seriously. Only fools make a mock at sin (Proverbs 14:9) and Christians should never play the fool.

In placing this emphasis on sin as it affects believers, the Lord Jesus raises some very important issues. First, He addresses the problem of sin for believers. Second, He speaks of the pardon of sin for believers. Third, He deals with the prevention of sin in believers: "Lead us not into temptation." Finally, He teaches us to pray for divine protection from sin: "Deliver us from evil." For the moment we will concentrate on the ideas of sin's problem and pardon.

The Problem of Sin

Every time a Christian prays he must honestly face the problem of sin in his life. The problem is real, for though sin does not occupy the place in his heart that it once did, it is still a force to be reckoned with. Before we were saved, sin reigned in us. It was the governing principle in our souls. But that is no longer the case, for Christ has dethroned sin and now "grace reign[s] through righteousness unto eternal life" by Him (Romans 5:21). The problem we have with sin is not what it used to be. There is now a new monarch in our hearts. This is the defining mark of a Christian.

The Problem Is Real

Though sin no longer reigns, it remains in us and cannot be ignored. There are two important facts about the remaining problem of sin that we must never forget.

First, sin is ever with us: "I find then a law, that, when I would do good, evil is present with me. For I delight in the law of God after the inward man: but I see another law in my members, warring against the law of my mind, and bringing me into captivity to the law of sin which is in my members" (Romans 7:21–23).

Second, sin easily besets us: "Wherefore seeing we also are compassed about with so great a cloud of witnesses, let us lay aside every weight, and the sin which doth so easily beset us, and let us run with patience the race that is set before us" (Hebrews 12:1). We have all felt the force of these two facts of the Christian life. We can never in this world escape the presence of sin, and we are always vulnerable to its attack.

The Problem Is Universal

The problem of sin is not limited to weak Christians. In fact, the closer we get to the Lord—the clearer our vision of His glory—the more acute will be our sense of sin. We cannot come into the presence of our Father in heaven, whose name is Holy (Isaiah 57:15), without feeling the need to cry for the forgiveness of our sins.

Thus people who really pray will of necessity have an acute sense of sin. The Bible gives us many examples. As soon as Isaiah "saw … the Lord sitting upon a throne, high and lifted up" (Isaiah 6:1), he cried, "Woe is me! for I am undone; because I am a man of unclean lips, and I dwell in the midst of a people of unclean lips: for mine eyes have seen the King, the Lord of hosts" (verse 5). When the apostle John received his vision of the glorified Christ, he felt his unworthiness so deeply that he fell at His feet as one dead (Revelation 1:17). Paul also felt his sinfulness, especially when he strongly desired to do good. The more he learned of God's law and the more he sought to be conformed to His will, the more he had to confess, "In me (that is, in my flesh,) dwelleth no good thing" (Romans 7:18). These were eminent saints, men who breathed the atmosphere of heaven while they lived on earth, and the closer they got to the Lord the more they felt their own sinfulness and the need for God's forgiveness.

The Problem Is Clearly Defined

What is sin? We may answer this in various ways. The Shorter Catechism defines it as "any want of conformity unto, or transgression of, the law of God" (Question 14). This reflects John's plain statement, "Sin is the transgression of the law" (1 John 3:4). However, we will best understand what Christ meant by sin by noting the terms employed in the Lord's Prayer.

The Lord Jesus taught us to pray, "Forgive us our debts" (Matthew 6:12). In his parallel account, Luke represents Him as saying, "Forgive us our sins" (Luke 11:4). Our Lord spoke to His disciples in Aramaic, probably using the word *choba*. Matthew and Luke use Greek terms that give us different but equally accurate translations of the word. These Greek terms are instructive and together give us a full understanding of Christ's meaning.

Luke uses *hamartia,* the usual word for sin in the New Testament; it carries the basic idea of missing the mark. The Greeks used the verb *hamartano* when arrow-shots and spear-throws failed to hit a desired target. Metaphorically it meant "to fail to achieve a given purpose, to go wrong, to err." The famous statement of Romans 3:23 illustrates the force of the word: "For all have sinned [*hemarton*], and come short [literally, *are behind*] of the glory of God." This is the word Luke uses in the petition "Forgive us our sins."

Matthew uses *opheilema,* a word that carries the ideas of debt and duty, as a quick survey of the New Testament use of the noun and its corresponding verb will establish.

Opheilema *signifies debt.* Paul uses the word in Romans 4:4: "To him that worketh is the reward not reckoned of grace, but of debt." In Matthew 18 Jesus tells a parable about a servant who was a "debtor" (*opheiletes,* verse 24) to his king to the tune of ten thousand talents. He was utterly unable to pay, and when he pleaded for time to pay, the king, realizing that he could never hope to repay such an amount, forgave him his debt. Immediately this same servant found a fellow servant who "owed [*opheilen*] him an hundred pence." At once he demanded, "Pay me that thou owest [*opheileis*]" (verse 28). His fellow servant pleaded with him as he had with the king, but to no avail, for the pitiless servant threw him into prison "till he should pay the debt [*to opheilomenon,* that which was owing]" (verse 30; cf. verse 34). From all these references it is clear that the central idea in the noun *opheilema* and the verb *opheilo* is that of debt.

Opheilema *signifies duty.* It is natural that the word should also carry the idea of duty, for our duty is what we *ought* to do. In other words, we *owe it to someone* to do it. Having washed His disciples feet, Jesus said to them, "If I then, your Lord and Master, have washed your feet; ye also ought [*opheilete*] to wash one another's feet" (John 13:14) — literally, "You owe to wash one another's feet." A similar usage is found in John 19:7, which records the Jews' words to Pilate about the Lord Jesus: "We have a law, and by our law he ought [*opheilei*] to die, because he made himself the Son of God" — literally, "According to our law he owes to die." In all these references the idea of duty is clear.

Paul brings these two aspects of the word's meaning together in Romans 15: 27: "It hath pleased them verily; and their debtors [*opheiletai*] they are. For if the Gentiles have been made partakers of their spiritual things, their duty is [*opheilousin,* "they ought"] also to minister unto them in carnal things." So the ideas of debt and duty lie at the heart of the word used in Matthew 6:12: "Forgive us our debts [*opheilemata*]."

From the two words that Matthew and Luke used to convey the original meaning of Christ's language we can come to a clear view of what sin really is.

Sin is a deviation from God's standard. It is missing the mark that He set for us. We are not left to speculate about the standard He has set: "He hath shewed thee, O man, what is good; and what doth the Lord require of thee, but to do justly, and to love mercy, and to walk humbly with thy God?" (Micah 6:8). God's law is His revealed rule of righteousness. His revealed will is His standard for our lives. "All scripture is given by inspiration of God, and is profitable for doctrine, for reproof, for correction, for instruction in righteousness: that the man of God may be perfect, throughly furnished unto all good works" (2 Timothy 3:16–17).

Any deviation from God's revealed rule and standard is sin. He accepts no substitute for adherence to it: "To the law and to the testimony: if they speak not according to this word, it is because there is no light in them" (Isaiah 8:20). He denounces those who turn away from His law as "rebellious people, lying children, children that will not hear the law of the Lord" (Isaiah 30:9).

Sin is a dereliction of duty. We have not done what we ought to have done. Jesus said to His disciples, "When ye shall have done all those things which are commanded you, say, We are unprofitable servants: we have done that which was our duty to do" (Luke 17:10). When we have done all that we ought, we are yet unprofitable servants—and which of us can claim that we have done all that we ought? We fail in doing our duty. The first three petitions of the Lord's Prayer may be taken as a summary of our Christian duty. We should pray. We should hallow our Father's name—that is, glorify Him, confess Him before men, and honor Him by our obedience. We should seek the establishment of His kingdom. We should do His will. These aspects of our duty govern and control all that God expects us to do. Every failure to do our duty is sin.

Sin is a debt we have incurred. "We are debtors, not to the flesh, to live after the flesh" (Romans 8:12). We stand in debt to God, His law, and His grace. We owe it to Him to do His will and to leave no part of our duty undone. We owe it to Him to live a life of full and obedient surrender to His will. "And now, Israel, what doth the Lord thy God require of thee, but to fear the Lord thy God, to walk in all his ways, and to love him, and to serve the Lord thy God with all thy heart and with all thy soul, To keep the commandments of the Lord, and his statutes, which I command thee this day for thy good?" (Deuteronomy 10:12–13).

Take some specifics. We owe God godly worship (1 Corinthians 11:7, 10). We owe it to Him to grow into fully mature Christians (Hebrews 5:12) and to walk as Christ walked (1 John 2:6). Those who worship and walk like this will feel that the Lord has placed them in His debt to preach the gospel to the lost (Romans 1:14) and to show the love of Christ in the home (Ephesians 5:28) and in the church (1 John 3:16; Romans 15:1). Failure in any of these areas is sin.

The Problem Is Urgent

If it is not dealt with, sin will ruin our fellowship with the Father, hinder our prayers, and rob us of many of the blessings and gifts that the Lord gives to His children. It is the peculiar blessing of God's redeemed children to be able to get through to Him in prayer. Consider two urgent pleas that David made: "Unto thee will I cry, O Lord my rock; be not silent to me: lest, if thou be silent to me, I become like them that go down into the pit" (Psalm 28:1); "Hear me speedily, O Lord: my spirit faileth: hide not thy face from me, lest I be like unto them that go down into the pit" (Psalm 143:7). God hides His face from those who go down into the pit; it is the privilege of His children to gain His ear and to live in His fellowship. David feared to lose this intimacy. He knew that "if I regard iniquity in my heart, the Lord will not hear me" (Psalm 66:18). It is to make sure that we do not lose the blessings of the place of prayer that the Lord Jesus pays so much attention to the problem of sin in our lives. He instructs us to pray, "Forgive us our debts," to lead us to the joy of pardon and to an unimpeded fellowship with our Father in heaven.

Pardon for Sin

The Lord Jesus commands us to pray, "Forgive us our debts," not to burden us with guilt but to impress on us the truth that our Father is the great pardoner of sin. All Scripture witnesses to this truth. In answer to Moses' prayer that He would show him His glory (Exodus 33:18) the Lord "passed by before him, and proclaimed, The Lord, The Lord God, merciful and gracious, longsuffering, and abundant in goodness and truth, keeping mercy for thousands, forgiving iniquity and transgression and sin, and that will by no means clear the guilty" (Exodus 34:6–7). Through Isaiah, the Lord addressed the stubbornly rebellious people of Judah with a gracious offer of forgiveness: "Come now, and let us reason together, saith the Lord: though your sins be as scarlet, they shall be as white as snow; though they be red like crimson, they shall be as wool" (Isaiah 1:18). Isaiah's younger contemporary, the prophet Micah, also magnified the Lord's pardoning grace: "Who is a God like unto thee, that pardoneth iniquity, and passeth by the transgression of the remnant of his heritage? he retaineth not his anger for ever, because he delighteth in mercy" (Micah 7:18). David rejoiced that the Lord stands ready to pardon those who call on Him: "Thou, Lord, art good, and ready to forgive; and plenteous in mercy unto all them that call upon thee" (Psalm 86:5).

The Meaning of Pardon

No word is more frequently used and less understood than *pardon.* "Forgive us our debts." What precisely does the word *forgive* mean? It is the translation of the Greek verb *aphiemi,* which means to leave, let go, send away. For example, we read that after he had tempted the Lord Jesus Christ, "then the devil leaveth him" (Matthew 4:11). A few verses later in Matthew 4 we read that James and John "straightway left their nets" and followed Jesus (verse 20). After teaching the people by parables, "then Jesus sent the multitude away" (Matthew 13:36). Writing to the Corinthians, Paul commanded, "Let not the husband put away his wife" (1 Corinthians 7:11). In all these cases the verb is *aphiemi.* So it has the idea of removing or putting away. It may also mean to disregard, as in Matthew 15:14 where Jesus said of the Pharisees, "Let them alone: they be blind leaders of the blind." In other words, disregard them and their hypocritical teachings.

All this throws light on the meaning of *aphiemi* when it is used to signify forgiveness. When we pray, "Forgive us our debts," we ask the Father to put away our sins from us and to disregard them, that is, put them away from Him. Specifically, in this petition we ask for seven particular blessings.

First, blot out our sins from Thy memory. David prayed, "Have mercy upon me, O God, according to thy lovingkindness: according unto the multitude of thy tender mercies blot out my transgressions" (Psalm 51:1). This is a proper request, for the Lord has said, "I, even I, am he that blotteth out thy transgressions for mine own sake, and will not remember thy sins" (Isaiah 43:25).

Second, do not inflict the punishment that our sins merit. When we plead for pardon, we ask the Father to deal with us according to the merits of Christ and on the ground of His precious blood. God's pardon is always and only "for Christ's sake" (Ephesians 4:32). His blood is our only plea and it is a sufficient plea. Thus John writes, "My little children, these things write I unto you, that ye sin not. And if any man sin, we have an advocate with the Father, Jesus Christ the righteous: and he is the propitiation for our sins: and not for ours only, but also for the sins of the whole world" (1 John 2:1–2). Our sins deserve the wrath of God, but we point to the one who bore all that wrath for us and ask for pardon through Him.

Third, release us from debts we cannot discharge so that we may do our duty toward God and man. Sin is a debt we have incurred that we have no means of paying. Nothing we do now or in the future can pay a cent of what we owe. We need a free forgiveness such as Christ spoke of in His parable of the king who was moved with compassion toward his servant who owed him ten thousand talents; the king "forgave him the debt" (Matthew 18:27). When we pray for forgiveness, we do not ask to be released from our present duty but from the stain of our dereliction of duty, with the obvious implication that we intend by God's grace henceforth to do our duty as Christians.

Fourth, cleanse our conscience and deliver us from guilt. This was David's plea: "Wash me throughly from mine iniquity, and cleanse me from my sin.... Deliver me from bloodguiltiness, O God, thou God of my salvation" (Psalm 51:2, 14). This is one of the most important aspects of pardon and one of the most difficult for us to enjoy. Many of us live under the shadow of past sins. In the jargon of today, we believe God has forgiven us, but we find it hard to forgive ourselves. We find it difficult to forget. We feel hypocritical in acting as if our past sins had not happened. Sometimes we even feel that we need to do something to "make up" for those sins.

While the memory of our failures should humble us, it should also drive us constantly to the merits of Christ. It should lead us to plead for the full, free, and faithful pardon that our Father bestows. *Faithful* is an important term here. It is used in 1 John 1:9: "If we confess our sins, he is faithful and just to forgive us our sins, and to cleanse us from all unrighteousness" (1 John 1:9). It means that God will keep the covenant that Christ's blood has sealed and that on the basis of that blood He will give us a *just* or *righteous* pardon. The more we grasp the all-sufficiency of Christ's merits the more we will know deliverance from the accusations of a guilty conscience (Hebrews 9:14; 10:1–2, 12–14). So the plea for deliverance from guilt is a cry to have a clear view of the merits of Christ.

Fifth, remove from us everything that hinders our fellowship with Thee. We know that sin robs us of answers to our prayers (Psalm 66:18). We feel the force of Isaiah's words, "Your iniquities have separated between you and your God, and your sins have hid his face from you, that he will not hear" (Isaiah 59:2). We also feel that we share Asaph's testimony: "Whom have I in heaven but thee? and there is none upon earth that I desire beside thee" (Psalm 73:25). Thus, to lose the intimacy of fellowship with our Father is a bitter grief. Here is a vital difference between Christians and the unregenerate: We would rather be removed from our sins than from our Father's fellowship. We echo David's urgent cry, "Cast me not away from thy presence; and take not thy holy spirit from me" (Psalm 51:11). William Cowper's famous lines exactly capture our desire:

> O for a closer walk with God,
> A calm and heavenly frame,
> A light to shine upon the road
> That leads me to the Lamb.
> Return, O holy Dove! Return,
> Sweet messenger of rest!

I hate the sins that made Thee mourn,
And drove Thee from my breast.
The dearest idol I have known,
Whate'er that idol be,
Help me to tear it from Thy throne,
And worship only Thee.

Sixth, give us the conscious enjoyment of what Christ did for us and contin-ues to do for us. This is a vital aspect of the experience of pardon, a grasping by faith of all the fruits of Christ's mediation. We have already considered how an understanding of Christ's all-sufficient merits deals with feelings of guilt. But there is more to pardon than relief from guilt. God's pardon is like the asses Joseph sent to Jacob in famine-stricken Canaan (Genesis 45:23); it is laden with all sorts of rich provision for our souls. In Christ, God has blessed us with all spiritual blessings (Ephesians 1:3) and with "all things that pertain unto life and godliness" (2 Peter 1:3). Though these blessings belong to all Christians, many live as spiritual pau-pers. The key to "possessing [our] possessions" (Obadiah 17) is to live in the sunlight of the merits of Him for whose sake God has given us a perfect pardon.

Seventh, restore us to useful service for Thy glory. Forgiveness is not merely a blessing to bring a renewed sense of purity and peace to the heart. It is always ac-companied by a yearning to be able to serve and glorify Him who has pardoned us. Thus David prayed, "Restore unto me the joy of thy salvation; and uphold me with thy free spirit. Then will I teach transgressors thy ways; and sinners shall be converted unto thee" (Psalm 51:12–13). Pardon is the platform for service.

The Means of Obtaining Pardon

The Lord Jesus not only shows us the problem of sin in our lives and assures us of pardon; He also makes it clear how we are to go about obtaining this pardon. We will trace three vital ingredients in the ordained means the Lord has made available to us to receive His forgiveness.

Confession

The first step in dealing with the problem of sin is to acknowledge that it exists. Before we can enjoy pardon, we need to make an honest recognition of our personal deviations from God's law, our debts to God and our fellow men, and our derelictions of duty in every sphere. We cannot excuse our sins, or hide behind others, laying our guilt on them. Solomon was right: "He that covereth his sins shall not prosper: but whoso confesseth and forsaketh them shall have mercy" (Proverbs 28:13). Confession is necessary if we are to receive release and pardon.

Repentance

True confession is always accompanied by a sincere desire to be rid of our sins, not just of their consequences. We certainly desire to be rid of the consequences, but even more of the cause of our sins. As we have just seen, only he who confesses and forsakes his sins will receive mercy. Confession without a sincere purpose to turn from the sins confessed is a mockery. Thomas Manton wrote:

> There is required an unfeigned purpose to forsake sin. He that hath been released from his debt, must not run into new arrears. Christ never blotted out our debts that we might renew them, and go on a new course of offending God again; this is to dally with God, to run into the snare when He hath broken it for us and given us an escape, to plunge ourselves into new debts again. (*Works* 1:174)

This willingness to deal with all known sin is important. It is implicit in what Christ says at the end of this petition: "as we forgive our debtors." The message is that though we may confess and repent of certain sins, if we harbor the sin of a bitter, implacable spirit, we will not be forgiven. In other words, we cannot be selective in the sins we want God to forgive. We cannot enjoy pardon if, while we ask for it, we deliberately hold on to known sins.

Petition

Christ's word to us is, "When ye pray, say,… Forgive us our sins" (Luke 11: 2, 4). In other words, prayer plays a major role in our receiving forgiveness for our sins and in our victory in the ongoing struggle with indwelling sin. When we pray, we cast ourselves on God's mercy and on Christ's merit. We consciously repudiate all personal ability to pay for our sins or to overcome our old man. We come to our Father because He is the one we have sinned against and because He is the only one who can forgive us. We know that He stands ready and willing to forgive, so believing His promise, we apply to Him for pardon and we receive it.

While we are in the flesh we will never get beyond the need for constant cleansing from our sins. In this life we will never be relieved from the need for constant vigilance against and victory over our old man. But the Lord Jesus has shown us that the problem of sin can be effectively dealt with by confession, repentance, and prayer. He teaches us to pray, "Forgive us our debts," because it is our privilege as the children of God to live in the experience and joy of our Father's pardoning grace.

Forgiven and Forgiving

"Forgive us our debts, as we forgive our debtors."   Matthew 6:12

In considering this text we will seek to answer two questions that preachers are recommended to ask of every text. First, what is this text about? That is, what is its subject? Second, what does it say about what it is about? That is, what message does it establish from its subject? In answering these fundamental questions we discover that the subject of our text is the connection between divine and human forgiveness. The message it establishes is that our forgiving those who have sinned against us is necessary if we are to be able to pray effectively for God's forgiveness for our sins against Him.

We may put the matter this way: Christ has so intimately connected divine and human forgiveness that unless we are willing to forgive those who have wronged us, we will not receive God's forgiveness for our sins against Him. In developing this theme we will follow the simplest line of inquiry. We will consider the meaning of the text by examining the precise terms it employs, and then we will proceed to the message of the text by noting seven important lessons it teaches us about Christian living.

The Meaning of the Terms

We must answer a number of critical questions if we are to understand the text. Who are "our debtors"? What does it mean for us to "forgive our debtors"? What is the force of the adverb *as,* and what do we mean when we pray, "Forgive us our debts, as we forgive our debtors"?

Our Debtors

Who are our debtors? In developing the proposition that He lays down in our text, the Lord Jesus goes on to say, "For if ye forgive men their trespasses, your heavenly Father will also forgive you: but if ye forgive not men their trespasses, neither will your Father forgive your trespasses" (Matthew 6:14–15). The Greek word *paraptomata,* "trespasses," used in these verses means offences, transgressions, or faults and is obviously intended to define the sins of those whom Christ calls "our debtors." From this word we learn that He is not referring to monetary debts so much as to moral debts, things in which people have committed offences against us and have injured us by word or deed, thereby justly earning our displeasure. Such people are our debtors; they have failed in their obligations to us and owe us something. Where possible, they ought to give it to us. But in the nature of the case considered in our text, they cannot pay their debt. They may apologize, but an apology does not merit the removal of a debt. But while an apology in itself does not *merit* our forgiveness, it must have it. Our debtors must receive pardon from us because as recipients of God's mercy we must be willing to show mercy.

In chapter 18 we looked at the parable of the unmerciful servant. Let's look at it again. The Lord Jesus told of a servant who owed a great debt to his master and, facing a life sentence in prison, pleaded for time to pay. His master realized that the servant could never make repayment, no matter how much time he had. However, instead of sending him to prison he had mercy on him and gave him a free pardon. Almost at once that servant met a fellow-servant who owed him a paltry amount of money. Grabbing him by the throat, he demanded immediate payment. The poor man pleaded for more time, but his creditor would not hear of it. Instead he threw him into jail, despite the fact that he himself had received such mercy from his king. But that is not the end of the story. Other servants, incensed at his harshness, told their master of the imprisonment, with the result that the king rescinded his pardon and cast the unmerciful servant into prison. The point of the whole parable is this: "So likewise shall my heavenly Father do also unto you, if ye from your hearts forgive not every one his brother their trespasses" (Matthew 18:35).

As we consider this parable we must remember that it is just a parable, and we must always be careful not to use a parable to teach more than our Lord originally intended by it. Many of its details are only the window dressing of the story; they are not theologically significant and must not be pushed. We must remember this particularly when interpreting any human actions ascribed to man in the parable but to God in the interpretation. In the parable before us Christ does not intend to teach that God's pardon is retractable or reversible. That is not the point of the story. In context, Christ was answering Peter's question, "How oft shall my brother sin against me, and I forgive him?" The point is that those who receive God's forgiveness must be willing to forgive others. After all, God has forgiven us an enormous debt, in comparison with which anything men may owe us is a mere pittance. So, in effect Jesus says, "You ought to be willing to forgive. If you are not, you will not have God's forgiveness." We have received mercy, so we ought to give it. "Be ye kind one to another, tenderhearted, forgiving one another, even as God for Christ's sake hath forgiven you" (Ephesians 4: 32). That leads us to an important question.

We Forgive Our Debtors

In the last chapter we considered what it means for God to forgive, but what does it mean for us to forgive? We often say, "To err is human, to forgive is divine." This is not altogether true, for humans must forgive. The force of the adage is that human pardon must be fashioned after divine pardon. It must exhibit in some measure the elements of God's gracious treatment of us. Thus, to forgive means to cease from anger against those who have wronged us. It means to cease from inflicting punishment on the wrongdoer. It also means that we let go of or cease to regard the offences committed against us and that we treat our debtors as if they had not offended us at all. Thus forgiveness involves a restoration to fellowship. When we pray for the Lord to forgive us our sins, we ask Him to treat us in this way. When He commands us to forgive others, He requires us to deal with them as He has dealt with us.

It is obvious therefore that those who pray, "Forgive us our debts, as we forgive our debtors," are making quite a statement. The Lord's Prayer is the most frequently recited prayer in the Christian world. How many of those who say its words take the slightest thought of the solemn profession they are making before God? It is easy for us to recite this petition glibly with very little personal consideration of what we are saying. But we must realize that in asking for God's forgiveness we are pledging ourselves to act toward others as He has acted toward us. We are saying to God, "We forgive our debtors." God sees our hearts; He knows whether what we profess with our mouths is the truth or only empty words. To say truthfully that we forgive means that we are not implacable, vengeful, or spiteful: "We forgive our debtors, as Thou hast forgiven us."

At this point we must face some questions that usually arise in any discussion of forgiving others. Must we forgive all our debtors, even the obstinate who continue their offensive behavior toward us? Or do we forgive only those who repent? Must we never seek redress for wrongs done to us or pursue legal satisfaction in the church or in the courts? These are enormously important questions, the answers to which lie in understanding the meaning of *forgive*. As we have seen, our forgiveness should be modeled on God's. In other words, as far as possible we should have the Lord for our example and should follow the pattern He has laid down in His dealings with us. There are infinite differences in kind, degree, and power between divine and human pardon, but as much as in us lies we must seek to follow the Lord's procedures and precepts.

Since it is our duty to forgive, we never have the right to be vengeful. Thus Paul says, "Dearly beloved, avenge not yourselves, but rather give place unto wrath: for it is written, Vengeance is mine; I will repay, saith the Lord" (Romans 12:19). We are to love even our enemies. Thus in the sense of not retaining anger and bitterness and of refraining from inflicting punishment, we are to forgive all. We are to have Christ as our example: "Christ also suffered for us, leaving us an example, that ye should follow his steps: who did no sin, neither was guile found in his mouth: who, when he was reviled, reviled not again; when he suffered, he threatened not; but committed himself to him that judgeth righteously" (1 Peter 2:21–23). This is one aspect of forgiveness and we must extend this forgiveness to all men.

However, the aspect of forgiveness that reconciles an offender and restores him to the fellowship of the offended party is not always possible. God Himself does not receive the obstinate or bring into His fellowship those who refuse to repent. For the time being, He suspends vengeance. He does not drop every offender into hell at once but still gives the wicked time and opportunity to repent. But He does not restore to His fellowship or give a place in heaven to those who obstinately refuse to repent. There is an exact parallel in human—including church—relationships. It is not always possible to effect reconciliation. Sometimes one or both of the parties will prove obstinate and stubborn.

Sometimes an offender must give adequate evidence of genuine repentance and of a consistent walk with the Lord; otherwise it would be foolish to embrace him. Take the example of Abner. According to Scripture Abner died as a fool because he too readily accepted the apparent embrace of a man who was his sworn enemy. There had never been the slightest evidence of a change in the murderous heart of Joab, yet when he put out his hand to embrace him, Abner open-heartedly accepted him in good faith. He paid dearly for his action, for Joab "smote him there under the fifth rib, that he died" (2 Samuel 3:27). No wonder David lamented, "Died Abner as a fool dieth? Thy hands were not bound, nor thy feet put into fetters: as a man falleth before wicked men, so fellest thou" (verses 33–34). There are times when, having let go of our own bitterness and anger against a debtor, we must yet refuse fellowship with him until there is clear evidence of his repentance toward God and us.

This principle has a particular and sometimes difficult application to church life. Paul instructed the Thessalonians how to deal with an obstinate brother: "If any man obey not our word by this epistle, note that man, and have no company with him, that he may be ashamed. Yet count him not as an enemy, but admonish him as a brother" (2 Thessalonians 3:14–15). We must never lose sight of the fact that we are dealing with a brother. That means that we must not seek to demean or despise him. We are not to count him as an enemy—and yet we are not to include him in our fellowship as long as he continues in his sin. In a word, if we treat men as God treats us, our pardon will be given to those who confess their fault and seek forgiveness. However, since we cannot see the heart as God does, there are cases—usually involving public scandal or the danger of moral or physical danger—in which we must await fuller evidence of repentance before restoring the offender to fellowship.

As far as serious breaches of the legal code of either church or state are concerned, personal pardon does not necessarily preclude judicial action. David refused to execute personal vengeance on Shimei, who cursed him when he was fleeing from Absalom (2 Samuel 16:5–7; 19:16–23). Nevertheless, he later delivered him to Solomon's official judgment for his crime (1 Kings 2: 8–9). Paul shows that it is sometimes necessary to take legal steps against certain types of offenders. He speaks of some who have put away a good conscience and "concerning the faith have made shipwreck: of whom is Hymenaeus and Alexander; whom I have delivered unto Satan, that they may learn not to blaspheme" (1 Timothy 1:19–20). John, the great apostle of love, retained judgment against Diotrephes: "I wrote unto the church: but Diotrephes, who loveth to have the preeminence among them, receiveth us not. Wherefore, if I come, I will remember his deeds which he doeth, prating against us with malicious words: and not content therewith, neither doth he himself receive the brethren, and forbiddeth them that would, and casteth them out of the church" (3 John 9–10). These were judicial, not personal, actions. They did not express mere personal animosity on the part of the apostles.

As they proved many times, the apostles were willing to bear being wounded by foes and false friends—yes, and even by fellow-believers—with a sweet, forgiving spirit. Writing to the Corinthians, who had viciously maligned and attacked him, Paul said, "O ye Corinthians, our mouth is open unto you, our heart is enlarged" (2 Corinthians 6:11). That is, "I have opened my mouth to speak to you in truth and my heart to embrace you in love." But even though Paul and John personally had kind and forgiving spirits, both encountered circumstances in which they felt compelled to institute proceedings against offenders whose sins threatened the purity, welfare, and testimony of the church. In such circumstances they did not hesitate to act. Their action in those cases did not conflict with having a personally loving and forgiving character; rather, it beautifully expressed it. As Paul testified, when he set strict judgment to work against an offender, he did so "that our care for you [that is, the church as a whole] in the sight of God might appear unto you" (2 Corinthians 7:12).

These cases involve invoking church censures. But church action is not the only legal action we may be obliged to take against a person. At times we may have to use the courts of the land, even against a professing brother in Christ. Where a crime is involved, we may personally forgive the offender and yet have to hand him over to the judicial system. In other words, crime often includes more than a personal dimension—that is, it places the offender in debt to the law and no personal pardon from the offended party can relieve that debt. This is so in those cases in which we are obliged by law to turn known offenders over to the authorities and when our failure to do so is itself a crime punishable by law. A good example of this is the case of child molestation. Even if the parents of the molested child forgive the molester—even if they think he has reformed— they are obligated (at least during the years of the victim's minority) to turn him over to the law. The same holds good for every other third party who gains knowledge of the crime. A similar obligation exists in a number of other cases in which the law does not allow us to protect a criminal, even if we have personally forgiven him. Yet again, personal forgiveness does not preclude judicial action.

We have gone into all these details because there is a widespread misconception among Christians that Paul's teaching in 1 Corinthians 6:4–8 prohibits Christians ever going to law against another professing Christian. In this passage Paul is dealing with matters of dispute, things that need arbitration. This is clear from verse 5: "Is it so, that there is not a wise man among you? no, not one that shall be able to judge between his brethren?" Here *judge* is the translation for the Greek verb *diakrino,* which means to decide or to arbitrate. The apostle did not believe that cheaters should be accommodated in the church but that the church, not the heathen, should conduct the arbitration for its members. So, far from prohibiting one Christian from citing another before a judicial tribunal, he was in fact arguing that they should bring him before a church court. However, there are cases that are not merely matters of arbitration but are breaches of the criminal code. In all such cases, we may be free, or even obligated, to invoke the law of the land. And doing so does not conflict with Christ's teaching in the Lord's Prayer or hinder our prayer for God's forgiveness.

Forgive Us As We Forgive Our Debtors

To discover the meaning of this petition, we must keep in mind that Christ is not speaking of the pardon God gives us at our initial exercise of saving faith, when we receive justification. He is speaking of the continuing forgiveness we must have if we are to enjoy fellowship with our Father from day to day. One condition of this forgiveness that He insists on is our forgiving others—and again He is not speaking of an isolated act but an ongoing willingness to forgive, the "seventy times seven" that He commanded Peter to forgive his brother (Matthew 18:22).

One of the great hindrances to our enjoying forgiveness and fellowship with God is a bitter, unforgiving spirit toward others. Thus the Lord Jesus makes our receiving forgiveness conditional on our forgiving others as our Father forgives us. He does not teach that we receive forgiveness *because* we forgive others, in the sense that our forgiveness merits God's forgiveness. That is not the force of the adverb *as* in the final clause of the sentence. This adverb may be used to express when, how, or why an action takes place. Take a few New Testament examples.

In Galatians 6:10 Paul uses it to tell us *when* we are to do good to others: "As we have therefore opportunity, let us do good unto all men, especially unto them who are of the household of faith"—that is, as often as, or whenever, we have opportunity.

In Colossians 2:6 he uses *as* to instruct us *how* we are to behave: "As ye have therefore received Christ Jesus the Lord, so walk ye in him"—that is, behave in a manner that is in keeping with your having received Christ as your Lord.

Some cite 2 Timothy 1:3 as a place where Paul uses the same adverb to state *why* he is thankful for Timothy: "I thank God, whom I serve from my forefathers with pure conscience, that without ceasing I have remembrance of thee in my prayers night and day"—literally, "as unceasingly I have remembrance of you." However, it is difficult to make sense out of the statement, "I am thankful for you because I remember you in prayer." It is more likely that Paul is saying the very opposite, "I remember you in prayer because I am thankful for you." Thus, "as I have remembrance" does not give the reason but the result of "I am thankful to God."

This last usage of the adverbial clause throws the most light on Christ's words in the petition we are considering. The words *as we forgive our debtors* do not give the reason but the result of God's forgiving us our debts. He forgives us and as a result we forgive others. Thus there is a clear connection between being forgiven by God and forgiving others. One cannot exist without the other. God's pardon provides us with the pattern for forgiving others.

That Christ intended us to understand Him in this way is clear from how Luke words the petition: "Forgive us our sins; for we also forgive every one that is indebted to us" (Luke 11:4). Note the force of the *also:* It shows that God's pardon precedes ours. This *also* appears in the Greek text of Matthew 6:12, though our Authorized Version does not translate it. What the Lord said was "Forgive us our debts, as also we forgive our debtors." The deliberate inclusion of *also* indicates that our forgiving others is patterned after God's pardoning us. Thus, the existence of a willingness to forgive in us, fallen creatures as we are, argues an infinitely greater willingness in our heavenly Father. So when we pray,

"Forgive us our debts, as also we forgive our debtors," we are saying, "Lord, we forgive those who offend us, though we are but sinners. How much more then wilt Thou, who art perfect love, forgive us?" It is interesting that in His exposition of prayer following the giving of the Lord's Prayer, the Lord Jesus uses this very form of argument: "If ye then, being evil, know how to give good gifts unto your children: how much more shall your heavenly Father give the Holy Spirit to them that ask him?" (Luke 11:13). How much more shall your heavenly Father manifest every grace that finds even limited expression in His fallen creatures?

From what we have noted, the Lord Jesus makes our forgiving others the condition of receiving God's constant pardon because the existence of a forgiving spirit in us is an evidence of grace in us. We may say then that "Forgive us our debts, as also we forgive our debtors" is a plea for God to continue the work of grace that He has begun in us. We must say something more, however, if we are to be faithful to the plain meaning of the Saviour's words: A bitter, unforgiving spirit argues either that there is no grace of God in our hearts, or that we have backslidden to such an extent that we have lost the enjoyment of it. Christ's blood is sufficient for those who have sinned against us. He is willing to forgive them if they ask Him to. Thus, for us to refuse to forgive them is to reject God's grace and Christ's merit, even though we would never think of formally denying either. So a refusal to forgive is in reality a denial of the blessings of Christ's atonement to our brethren and also to ourselves. It is sin, and as long as we hold on to known sin we cannot truly confess it and receive God's pardon for it.

When we pray, "Forgive us our debts, as we forgive our debtors," we ask our Father to treat us in a manner similar to that in which we treat others. If we are unwilling to forgive, we are unwilling to be forgiven, at least on God's terms, which are of course the only terms available. To recite the Lord's Prayer while we harbor an unforgiving spirit is equivalent to saying, "Lord, do not forgive us our debts."

Here then is the meaning of the petition: "Father we have received Thy grace and the merits of Christ's atonement. We accept those merits for our own sins and for the sins of those who offend us. As those who stand in constant need of God's forgiveness we grant forgiveness to our debtors in imitation of Thy pardoning grace to us. Let no bitter or vengeful spirit—no spiteful attitude—hinder our reception of Thy free pardon and perfect cleansing. Forgive us our debts, as also we forgive our debtors."

The Message of the Text

When the Puritans preached on a text they usually expounded its meaning and then followed that exposition with sections with names such as *Uses* or *Observations*, what we would term application. We will follow their example and, having come to understand the meaning of the text, we will now consider the message it applies to our hearts. What is this petition of the Lord's Prayer saying to us by the terms it employs? We will note seven truths it implies, things that arise directly out of its meaning.

First, we should maintain the same standards for ourselves that we do for others. We must not seek to deal with our sins differently from how we would deal with the sins of others. In the parable on forgiveness in Matthew 18 the unmerciful servant looked on his own debt differently from that of others. He cried for mercy, though the amount he owed would have taken a laboring man perhaps 150,000 years to earn. Yet he denied mercy to the man who owed him a comparative pittance, an amount equivalent to about three months of a laborer's pay. The unmerciful servant's sin is common to most of us. We tend to look more leniently on our sins and faults than we do on those of other people. But this is wrong and will hinder our praying. When we pray, "Forgive us our debts, as we forgive our debtors," we profess to take our sins against God at least as seriously as we do others' offences against us.

Second, we must avoid hypocritical babbling in prayer. It is easy to assume a pious attitude and glibly repeat the words "Forgive us our debts, as we forgive our debtors" while entertaining an unforgiving spirit. To do this is to insult God with vain words. It is sheer hypocrisy, which will make the very prayer an additional sin and bring upon the hypocrite the condemnation described in Psalm 109:7: "When he shall be judged, let him be condemned: and let his prayer become sin."

Third, we must never forget that our relationship with men affects our fellowship with God. If we are bitter and implacable, we will not be able to get through to God for the forgiveness of our sins. This means, in effect, that we cannot live in fellowship with Him at all, for Psalm 66:18 makes it clear that if we regard iniquity in our heart, the Lord will not hear us. The Bible warns us of the danger of sour human relationships hindering our fellowship with God, making special mention of our family and church relationships. Paul warns husbands not to harbor bitterness against their wives (Colossians 3:19), and Peter adds, "Likewise, ye husbands, dwell with them according to knowledge, giving honour unto the wife, as unto the weaker vessel, and as being heirs together of the grace of life; that your prayers be not hindered" (1 Peter 3:7). Many a person loses out with God because of an unforgiving spirit against his spouse. The same is true of church relationships. Christ's disciples are to love one another (John 13:34–35) and to be "kind one to another, tenderhearted, forgiving one another" (Ephesians 4:32). Too often, however, churches are weakened by division because their members will not practice the grace of forgiveness. James lamented the "wars and fightings" that devoured God's people (James 4:1), the result of which was that when they prayed, their motives were selfish and sinful and they received no answer. Human relationships matter and should always be maintained in a manner that will enhance our walk with the Lord, not hinder it.

Fourth, we should treat others as the Lord has treated us. Human nature tends to dictate that we treat others as they have treated us, but the Lord calls us to a higher standard. The Bible commands, "Say not, I will do so to him [my neighbor] as he hath done to me: I will render to the man according to his work" (Proverbs 24:29). The Christian standard is, "I will treat others as the Lord has treated me." "Let all bitterness, and wrath, and anger, and clamour, and evil speaking, be put away from you, with all malice: and be ye kind one to another, tenderhearted, forgiving one another, even as God for Christ's sake hath forgiven you" (Ephesians 4:31–32). Writing to the Colossians Paul said, "Even as Christ forgave you, so also do ye" (Colossians 3:13). The great sin of the unmerciful servant in Christ's parable was that he refused to treat others with the kindness and mercy with which his king had treated him. This is, alas, the great sin of many professing Christians and it must be dealt with if they are to have any effective access to God in prayer.

Fifth, we should govern our dealings with others according to the clear teachings of the gospel. When we pray, "Forgive us our debts, as we forgive our debtors," we confess that we need God's mercy on us in our sin and failure. To obtain that forgiveness we rely on the merits of Christ. Therefore, having come to experience the power of gospel grace and pardon we wish to introduce others to its enjoyment. With Christ's merits clearly in view we will not wish to do anything to obscure others' vision of Him by being unforgiving and unmerciful. We will want to lead them directly to Him—and how better to do that than by accepting their confession and repentance and forgiving them and exhorting them to seek God's mercy in His Son?

Sixth, we must exercise faith in the justice and rightness of God's decisions, especially when we pray. In making the plea, "Forgive us our debts, as we forgive our debtors," we declare to God that we have abandoned all thought of personal vengeance against those who have sinned against us. In the assurance that He will do right, we leave it to Him to judge or chastise. The flesh craves vindication and vengeance, but we pray as our Lord instructed us regarding forgiveness because we have a view to the glory of His name rather than the satisfaction of our flesh.

Seventh, we must not allow anything to come between us and our Father in heaven. We must not let our own sins or those of others come between us or obscure our understanding and enjoyment of the gospel. People may offend and hurt us. We may feel so deeply the wounds they inflict that it is difficult to accept any apology and forgive them. It is at this point that we need to be particularly careful; otherwise we will inflict more damage on our souls than they could ever do. If we allow ourselves to be consumed with bitterness and a desire for revenge, or if we sink in an ocean of self-pity and mope over the injury we have suffered, we will lose out with God. Our prayer life will become futile and frustrating, almost non-existent. Why would a Christian allow anything to rob him of what he acknowledges to be the most important thing in the world to him, his ability to commune with his heavenly Father? Charles A. Tindley expresses the yearning of all true Christians in his great hymn "Nothing Between." When we pray, "Forgive us our debts, as we forgive our debtors," we make his words our prayer:

> Nothing between my soul and the Saviour,
> So that His blessed face may be seen;
> Nothing preventing the least of His favor,
> Keep the way clear! Let nothing between.

A Prayer for the Prevention of Sin

"Lead us not into temptation." Matthew 6:13

This petition, like the one before it, sounds simple and straightforward. It seems the most natural thing in the world for us to pray, "Lead us not into temptation," but as soon as we do, we are forced to ask ourselves the question, "What precisely do we mean by asking God to do this?" The answer is not easy to arrive at, as commentators from the earliest times have had to confess. Think for a moment of some of the problems raised by this petition. Does God ever lead His people into temptation? Can we ever in this world expect to be free from temptation? How can this request be reconciled with those Scriptures that pronounce temptation a good thing, not something to be avoided?

The difficulty in answering such questions arises from the confusion about the various meanings of the word *temptation*. Consider the following apparent paradoxes:

James tells us that God does not tempt any man: "Let no man say when he is tempted, I am tempted of God: for God cannot be tempted with evil, neither tempteth he any man" (James 1:13). Yet we read "It came to pass after these things, that God did tempt Abraham" (Genesis 22:1).

Jesus teaches us to pray, "Lead us not into temptation," yet the Holy Spirit led Him to be tempted: "Then was Jesus led up of the Spirit into the wilderness to be tempted of the devil" (Matthew 4:1).

Again, while the Lord Jesus instructs us to pray, "Lead us not into temptation," his brother James says we should "rejoice" when we are tempted (James 1:2), because "blessed is the man that endureth temptation: for when he is tried, he shall receive the crown of life, which the Lord hath promised to them that love him" (James 1:12).

Obviously the words *tempt* and *temptation* have a variety of meanings. This variety is not a fault of our English translation. Rather it reflects the many-sided meanings of the Greek word *peirasmos*. Temptation may mean a seduction to sin, as when the serpent tempted Eve to disobey God or when he tempted the Lord Jesus Christ to commit sin (Genesis 3; Matthew 4). It may also signify a deliberate attempt to lead a victim to ruin, as when the Pharisees questioned Christ, "tempting" Him (Matthew 19:3). Temptation may also indicate a trial, which we may define as an investigation of what is in a person by subjecting him to searching experiences—a test that has the purpose of proving or purifying him. This last sense of the word is the equivalent of what Peter describes as "the trial (Greek, *dokimion,* 'proving') of your faith" (1 Peter 1:7). That this is a common use of *tempt* and *temptation* is clear from Revelation 3:10: "Because thou hast kept the word of my patience, I also will keep thee from the hour of temptation, which shall come upon all the world, to try them that dwell upon the earth." Moses relates how the Lord brought the Israelites through many trying circumstances in the wilderness to put them to the test: "The Lord thy God led thee these forty years in the wilderness, to humble thee, and to prove thee, to know what was in thine heart, whether thou wouldest keep his commandments, or no" (Deuteronomy 8:2). It was in the sense of testing and no other that "God did tempt Abraham." He did not induce him to sin or seek to bring him to ruin. He introduced him to testing experiences to prove the reality and extent of his dedication to Him.

What we find most perplexing is not that a single word can have such a variety of meanings but that in almost every case something of each meaning is discernible. Enticement to sin always has a vicious purpose, yet it also provides a test and a trial. A test or trial may have a laudable purpose, but the possibility of the tested person falling into sinful failure is always present. While all this sounds confusing, it actually removes confusion. The variety of meanings of the word *temptation* helps us narrow down what it is we ask of the Lord when we pray, "Lead us not into temptation."

There are three things that it cannot mean. First, it cannot mean, "Do not entice us to sin, or lead us into sinful enticements." As James says, "God cannot be tempted with evil, neither tempteth he any man" (James 1:13). Second, it cannot mean, "Never allow us to be tried or tested." Peter tells us, "The trial of your faith [is] much more precious than of gold that perisheth" (1 Peter 1:7). Third, it cannot mean, "Never allow us to be tempted to sin." To be beyond temptation we would have to be taken out of the world, but Jesus said that that was not God's purpose: "I pray not that thou shouldest take them out of the world, but that thou shouldest keep them from the evil" (John 17:15).

A view that dates back to the time of the early church fathers, reflecting what some take as a translation and some as a paraphrase of the Greek text, interprets the meaning of the petition as follows: "Lead us not into the hands, or power, of temptation." That is, "Do not allow us to be brought under the control of anything that would ensnare us or seduce us into sin." Or we may say that when we pray, "Lead us not into temptation," we ask our Father, "Providentially lead us so as to make us holy and watchful; let us not be taken unawares by temptation. Keep us humble and alert and do not allow the fact that we receive pardon from Thee make us less careful to avoid sin."

As Thomas Manton observed, we cannot be tempted without the will of God, that is, unless He wills it. We cannot resist temptation without the power of God. Therefore we should earnestly pray to our Father in heaven about our trials and temptations. This is the spirit in which we are to pray, "Lead us not into temptation." It is a prayer for the prevention of sin in our lives. In studying it we will note four things that this petition does.

It Stresses a Furious Warfare

Holiness is a battle. We are opposed by three interactive forces that are constantly working to draw us away from God. *First there is Satan, who is called our "adversary the devil."* He is a deceiver, tempter, and seducer. He is not a mythical creature with horns and hooves, as he is often portrayed. Nor is he the figure of fun or derision that third-rate comedians make him out to be. He is a real enemy, a creature of great power and undiluted malignity who is unceasing in his opposition to every aspect of the work of grace in our lives. The Lord Jesus warned Peter about the reality and imminence of the devil's attack: "The Lord said, Simon, Simon, behold, Satan hath desired to have you, that he may sift you as wheat" (Luke 22:31). Peter in turn passed the same warning on to us: "Be sober, be vigilant; because your adversary the devil, as a roaring lion, walketh about, seeking whom he may devour" (1 Peter 5:8).

The second force arrayed against us is the world, which keeps up a sustained attack on all our senses to draw us away from our God. That is why John warns us to maintain a strict separation from the world: "Love not the world, neither the things that are in the world. If any man love the world, the love of the Father is not in him. For all that is in the world, the lust of the flesh, and the lust of the eyes, and the pride of life, is not of the Father, but is of the world" (1 John 2: 15–16). What John means by "the world" is not the world that God created and pronounced "very good" but the corrupt system that produces sinful lust and the proud pursuit of selfish aims in defiance of God and His law. Such a system of corruption exists, and the Scriptures urgently warn us of its assault on all true godliness. Paul speaks of "the course of this world" (Ephesians 2:2), which is a course of rebellion against God. Thus Peter warns of the "corruption that is in the world through lust" (2 Peter 1:4) and the "pollutions of the world (2 Peter 2:20), while James reminds us that to keep ourselves "unspotted" from the world in this sense is the essence of true religion (James 1:27). This is the world that is crucified to us and to which we are crucified by the cross of Christ (Galatians 6:14).

This evil world system with its antagonism to God and His people is energized by Satan and run by men. Indeed, the masses of fallen humanity are willing instruments of the system. It was of the worldly crowd pursuing the policies of "the prince of this world" (John 12:31), that is Satan, that Jesus spoke when He said to His brothers, "The world cannot hate you; but me it hateth, because I testify of it, that the works thereof are evil" (John 7:7). He warned His disciples that the same crowd would direct its hatred against them (John 15:18–19). Here is a truth we should never forget: There is a system of corruption and pollution that is acceptable to the great majority of people in "this present evil age" (Galatians 1:4, Greek text). This system and those who live by it are opposed to all true godliness and those who practice it. All Christians are therefore at war with this corrupt world. It seeks to overcome us and we must seek to overcome it. It is the birthright of all God's children to do so: "Whatsoever is born of God overcometh the world: and this is the victory that overcometh the world, even our faith. Who is he that overcometh the world, but he that believeth that Jesus is the Son of God? (1 John 5:4–5). This victory presupposes a war, one that is waged against Satan and those who serve him in his rebellion against God and His people.

We also come under attack from a third enemy of godliness, our own flesh. The flesh is a Trojan horse that would throw open the gates of Mansoul to the enemy and betray us and our Saviour. Paul felt the danger and constant threat of the flesh: "I delight in the law of God after the inward man: but I see another law in my members, warring against the law of my mind, and bringing me into captivity to the law of sin which is in my members" (Romans 7:22–23). Because this other law—as he termed the principle of inbred sin that remains in us after our conversion to Christ—leads to disobedience toward God and His law, Paul felt the necessity to keep a strict watch over his body, which of course included his brain. He said, "I keep under my body, and bring it into subjection: lest that by any means, when I have preached to others, I myself should be a castaway" (1 Corinthians 9:27).

On all three fronts we are engaged in a furious war against forces that are just as determined to lead us into sin as Satan was to compel Job to repudiate his faith in God. This is what we recognize when we pray, "Lead us not into temptation." It is a prayer born out of the soul's agony as it strives against sin, a cry for victory in the battle that rages between us on the one side and the world, the flesh, and the devil on the other. Thus our text stresses a furious battle. But it does more.

It Confesses a Felt Weakness

The petition "Lead us not into temptation" also confesses a felt weakness and wickedness. Those who make this their prayer confess that they have no confidence in the flesh. By praying, "Forgive us our debts," we confess, "We have sinned." Similarly, when we pray, "Lead us not into temptation," we confess that our flesh is sold out to sin and has no inherent ability to withstand the assault of the world, the flesh, and the devil. We know all too well the truth of Paul's words, "I know that in me (that is, in my flesh,) dwelleth no good thing: for to will is present with me; but how to perform that which is good I find not" (Romans 7:18). Confronting the enemies of our soul—whether our fleshly lusts or our human or satanic foes—we must say what Jehoshaphat said when he was faced with a grand alliance of heathen armies determined to destroy Judah: "O our God, wilt thou not judge them? for we have no might against this great company that cometh against us; neither know we what to do: but our eyes are upon thee" (2 Chronicles 20:12).

None of us can afford to be complacent in our battle with temptation and sin. We need to be ever on guard and to remain aware of our natural weakness and of the wickedness of our flesh. Perhaps this is never more true than when we think we are doing well in the battle. Paul warns, "Let him that thinketh he standeth take heed lest he fall" (1 Corinthians 10:12). David confessed that he had foolishly ignored such advice: "In my prosperity I said, I shall never be moved" (Psalm 30:6). The history of God's people bears tragic testimony that such complacency always leads to failure. That is why the giant saints of Scripture so often failed the Lord at their strongest point. Abraham, the man of faith, failed through unbelief. Moses, the meekest of men, failed through violent anger. David, the man after God's own heart, failed through lust. Peter, a man of indomitable courage, failed through cowardly fear. And so it goes on. We are afflicted with natural weakness and inherent wickedness and can have no confidence in the flesh. "Our help is in the name of the Lord, who made heaven and earth" (Psalm 124:8), and therefore we must never fail to cry, "Lead us not into temptation."

In addition to stressing our warfare and confessing our weakness this petition describes the yearning of every Christian heart for true holiness.

It Expresses a Fervent Wish

The desire of our hearts is first, to be kept from sin and from whatever would incline us to sin. When we pray, "Lead us not into temptation," we ask the Lord not only to keep us from sin but from everything that would make it easy for us to sin and difficult for us to be holy. We ask Him to raise barriers before us that we may not fall into sin. We plead to be prevented from going where we will be liable to fall. We express not only our desire to escape sin's consequences but our willingness to be separated from its causes. Thus, "Lead us not into temptation" is a cry to be kept from everything that will sap our dedication to Christ, weaken our spiritual affections, blur our vision of God's glory, or stir up the lusts of the flesh.

Second, our fervent desire is to be delivered from making God's willingness to forgive an excuse for sin. The petition not to be led into temptation commences with the word *and*, which joins it closely with "Forgive us our debts." We pray, "Forgive us for sins we have committed and lead us so that we will not fall into them again." God's pardon is a rich blessing freely given, but we should never on that account become presumptuous and sin because we think forgiveness is easily obtained. We do well to remember the psalmist's prayer: "Keep back thy servant also from presumptuous sins; let them not have dominion over me" (Psalm 19:13). A proper sense of God's pardon will lead us to fear Him: "There is forgiveness with thee, that thou mayest be feared" (Psalm 130:4). Thus the Lord joins the promise of His grace with a warning to avoid sin: "He will speak peace unto his people, and to his saints: but let them not turn again to folly" (Psalm 85:8).

Third, when we pray, "Lead us not into temptation," we plead that our Father will never leave us to face any temptation or trial alone and that He will never leave us to try us. That is what happened to Hezekiah, a godly man whose pride robbed him of much of the blessing of divine healing and extended life. "In the business of the ambassadors of the princes of Babylon, who sent unto him to enquire of the wonder that was done in the land, God left him, to try him, that he might know all that was in his heart" (2 Chronicles 32:31). Trials and temptations will come, but if we must face them let it never be without the realization of the Lord's presence. As Jesus tells us, "Without me ye can do nothing" (John 15:5). Thus we pray, "Never leave me, even for a moment, and especially not in times of trial or temptation."

Fourth, to pray, "Lead us not into temptation," means, "Never let me be exposed to the full fury of Satan's power." The Lord Jesus faced this. When He was led up of the Spirit into the wilderness to be tempted of the devil, He felt the full blast of Satan's personal attack. Concentrated into the temptations He endured were all the malignancy, hatred, and seductiveness of which the devil was capable. The Lord Jesus met Satan face to face and endured the full fury and subtlety of his malevolence. Then "when the devil had ended all the temptation, he departed from him for a season" (Luke 4:13).

Satan departed "for a season" but soon returned to the fight and continued his violent and vicious opposition throughout our Lord's ministry. What were all the recorded attempts on Christ's life but Satan's hatred of Him? What were the attempts to entrap Him in His words but Satan's temptations? The same may be said of the lying attacks upon His reputation. All this was a renewal of Satan's assault following his tactical withdrawal after Christ had repelled his temptations in the wilderness. Then came Gethsemane. There Satan launched an even more violent attack than before. Having failed to slay Christ at His birth and when He entered on His public ministry—and at various stages during it—Satan determined to succeed in Gethsemane. Paul refers to this life-and-death conflict in Hebrews 5:7, speaking of Jesus, "who in the days of his flesh, when he had offered up prayers and supplications with strong crying and tears unto him that was able to save him from death,… was heard in that he feared." By all known standards Satan's assault should have been fatal. The blood oozing from Christ's skin should have signaled His death, but it did not. He not only endured Satan's attack, He defeated it. There is a beautiful thought here. Faced with temptation we must confess our weakness, but we also confess Christ's strength. He fought the full power of Satan's temptation and overcame it all. The first Adam fell before Satan's power, but the last Adam stood unmoved and made Satan fall before His power. In Him human nature overcame the tempter.

This mighty conqueror dwells in every believer. We know that we could not withstand Satan, but He who dwells within us has vanquished him for ever. There is no need for a further trial of strength with Satan because our Head endured all that Satan could hurl against Him and conquered. By comprehensively defeating the tempter, Christ has provided protection for every believer in every trial and temptation. Therefore we pray to our Father in heaven, "Lead us not into temptation." That is, "Keep us in the victory of Christ. Christ has drawn the full fury of the devil, never let us face it. And never let us face the tempter in our own strength."

Fifth, in this petition we pray that God will keep us alert that we may not be surprised into sinning. We all need to pray this prayer. How often we are taken unawares and fall suddenly to some temptation. That is why Jesus warns us, "Watch and pray, that ye enter not into temptation: the spirit indeed is willing, but the flesh is weak" (Matthew 26:41). Slothfulness, carelessness, and pride are dangerous to a Christian. We should never forget the story of Achan's dreadful fall into sin at the very moment of Israel's great victory over Jericho: "I saw among the spoils a goodly Babylonish garment, and two hundred shekels of silver, and a wedge of gold of fifty shekels weight, then I coveted them, and took them; and, behold, they are hid in the earth in the midst of my tent, and the silver under it" (Joshua 7:21). He "saw," then "coveted," and finally "took" what was forbidden. Alone for a moment in the ruins of the city, he carelessly forgot the warning not to plunder and was betrayed by a look. A similar thing happened to David. He also was betrayed by a look, but only after he had laid himself open by slothfulness—for when he should have been at war, he remained lazily at home and left the work of God to others. Neither of these men remained alert and watchful. They exhibited the same kind of folly that afflicted Peter before his denial of the Lord Jesus, namely carnal confidence. In Peter's case, this took the form of complete self-assurance. He was certain that while the other disciples were perhaps not courageous enough to die for their Lord, he was. "Though all men shall be offended because of thee, yet will I never be offended" (Matthew 26:33). Such carnal confidence is deaf to all warnings, as Peter soon proved when he could not stand even before the challenge of a little girl who identified him as one of Christ's disciples. We need to be watchful, distrustful of our own weakness, and ever mindful of the danger of falling, "lest Satan should get an advantage of us: for we are not ignorant of his devices" (2 Corinthians 2:11). "Lead us not into temptation"—keep us from being surprised into sudden failure.

Finally, this petition asks the Father to enable us to use the resources that He has made available to us. By answering this prayer the Lord will not necessarily let us avoid the conflict with trial or temptation. He does not promise that we will be lifted out of the battle or that we will not bear the burden of testing. Paul explained this to the Corinthian Christians: "There hath no temptation taken you but such as is common to man: but God is faithful, who will not suffer you to be tempted above that ye are able; but will with the temptation also make a way to escape, that ye may be able to bear it" (1 Corinthians 10:13). We think of escape as deliverance from the experience of a given trial or temptation, but that is not how Paul defines it. Paul says God always provides a way of escape "that ye may be able to bear it." In other words, the victory of grace is just as real when God strengthens us to endure the assault against us as when He lifts us right out of it. In either case, He has provided in Christ all the resources we need for a victorious Christian life. When we pray, "Lead us not into temptation," we ask Him for grace to lay hold of all His rich provision in Christ and thus always to be "more than conquerors through him that loved us" (Romans 8:37).

We have seen that the petition "Lead us not into temptation" stresses a furious warfare, confesses a felt weakness, and expresses a fervent wish. There is one final truth we must consider.

It Professes a Faithful Walk

"Lead us" is the prayer of those who are following the Lord. It says to the Lord, "Go before us and we will follow. Let us know Thy will and we will do it. Show us Thy way and we will walk in it." This then is a prayer of resignation, discipleship, and obedience. It is vain and hypocritical to pray such words while walking according to the flesh, while willfully disobeying God, or while foolishly exposing ourselves to temptation. Anyone who prays not to get run over by a train should not lie down on the tracks. To do so while praying for safety is to tempt God. Similarly, to pray, "Lead us not into temptation," while carelessly placing ourselves in the way of temptation is an exercise in folly, not faith. But as we follow Christ we may pray this prayer with confidence. The Lord promises to guide us: "I will instruct thee and teach thee in the way which thou shalt go: I will guide thee with mine eye" (Psalm 32:8).

Temptations will come. The Lord will try us. His promises—or perhaps the delay in fulfilling them, as in the case of Joseph (Psalm 105:19)—will test us. Satan will tempt us. The world and the flesh will seek to seduce us. But our Saviour goes before us and calls us to "follow his steps" (1 Peter 2:21). As we do so we may cry to our Father in heaven, "Lead us not into temptation." He will answer that prayer, for though He delights to pardon His people's sin, He delights even more to prevent it.

21

The Great Escape

"Deliver us from evil." Matthew 6:13

This text, "Deliver us from evil," has a glorious subject. It is one that grips the attention of every Christian, especially in the context in which the Lord Jesus Christ sets it in the Lord's Prayer. He has been instructing us how to pray about sin. We must confess the problem of sin, cry for the pardon of sin, and seek the prevention of sin. It is the prevention of sin that the last two petitions address. In the last chapter when we looked at the petition "Lead us not into temptation," we noted the early church fathers' interpretation of it: "Lead us not into the hands, or power, of temptation." In other words, "Do not allow us to be brought under the control of anything that would ensnare us or seduce us into sin." This view is particularly significant in light of what follows: "But deliver us from evil." This final petition of the Lord's Prayer continues on the theme of the prevention of sin, with particular emphasis on freedom from the control of evil. "Lead us not into temptation" addresses the prevention of sin negatively; "but deliver us from evil" addresses it positively.

Thus the final petition of the Lord's Prayer introduces us to the glorious subject of power over sin. Indeed, as we shall see, it goes further and deals with power over Satan. This subject is of great personal interest to every Christian, giving us our Lord's teaching on how to pray for deliverance from the power of Satan and sin. In instructing us to pray for this deliverance the Lord Jesus speaks of three important matters.

A Pervasive Evil

The Greek text has the definite article before *evil:* "Deliver us from the evil." *The evil* may mean "the evil thing" or "the evil one." Since there is nothing in the words themselves that demands either translation, we should give the term the full scope of its meaning. To do this we will briefly survey the New Testament usage of the Greek word *poneros,* "evil."

The word "evil" usually means "wicked." It speaks of moral or spiritual evil. Evil spirits are "wicked spirits" (Luke 11:26). "Evil men" (2 Timothy 2:13) are wicked men who wax worse and worse. What in Luke 11:29 is translated "an evil generation," in Matthew 16:4 is translated "a wicked generation." *Wicked* is the fundamental force of the word translated "evil."

The word "evil" may mean grievous, hurtful, or painful. On the Isle of Patmos John received a vision of seven angels pouring out vials of wrath on the earth. He describes the effect of the first angel pouring his vial: "There fell a noisome and grievous [Greek, *evil*] sore upon the men which had the mark of the beast, and upon them which worshipped his image." The Lord Jesus uses the term in a similar way in the Sermon on the Mount: "Blessed are ye, when men shall revile you, and persecute you, and shall say all manner of evil against you falsely, for my sake" (Matthew 5:11). Here again *evil* refers to what is grievous or hurtful.

The phrase "the evil" in places means "the wicked one," namely Satan. In His parable of the seed falling into four types of ground, the Lord Jesus says, "When any one heareth the word of the kingdom, and understandeth it not, then cometh the wicked one, and catcheth away that which was sown in his heart" (Matthew 13:19). "The wicked one" is the same phrase that occurs in the petition we are considering. Our Lord uses it again in Matthew 13:38 in expounding the parable of the wheat and the tares. In each case He is speaking of "the evil one," Satan himself. When Paul wrote to the church in Ephesus, he spoke of the spiritual armor that the Lord provides for His servants. Having described the various parts of the armor he says, "Above all, taking the shield of faith, wherewith ye shall be able to quench all the fiery darts of the wicked," literally, "the wicked one." John also uses this title for Satan, addressing the young men of the church "because ye have overcome the wicked one" (1 John 2:13–14). He notes that "Cain … was of that wicked one, and slew his brother" (3:12), but assures us that "the wicked one does not touch" one who has been born of God (5:18). So the phrase *the evil* may be a reference to Satan.

It may also signify "the evil thing," that is, wickedness. John uses it in this sense in 1 John 5:19: "And we know that we are of God, and the whole world lieth in wickedness" (1 John 5:19). Here *wickedness* is the translation of the same Greek phrase, "the evil," that we have in the Lord's Prayer. What John says is "the whole world lies in the wicked one" or "the whole world lies in the wicked thing." There is not a lot of practical difference between the translations. The world is not "in Satan" by means of a mystical, covenant, or spiritual union as the believer is "in Christ." We may say that the whole world lies in the devil's lap—which is the very truth conveyed by the Authorized Version's translation. The world lies "in the evil"—it lies in wickedness, walking "according to the prince of the power of the air, the spirit that now worketh in the children of disobedience" (Ephesians 2:2). So the phrase, "the evil" may mean wickedness, the principle of evil.

Here then is the scope of the words that Christ uses in teaching us what we should pray for deliverance from. Using the phrase "the evil" He paints a picture of pervasive wickedness with all the hurtful results it brings. If we were to take a concordance of the New Testament and trace the use of *evil* we would soon be convinced of just how pervasive wickedness is. We may summarize the results of such a search like this: "evil people," like "evil trees," bring forth "evil fruit"; out of the "evil treasure" of "evil hearts" they bring forth "evil deeds." We live in an "evil day" in which an "evil generation," the children of the "evil one," vilify Christ and his people with "evil [malicious, 3 John 10] words." What was said of the world in the days of Noah may be said of the world today: "God saw that the wickedness of man was great in the earth, and that every imagination of the thoughts of his heart was only evil continually" (Genesis 6:5). That is why the Bible says that the whole world lies in wickedness, despite all the warnings and temporal judgments with which God has visited the earth. Various passages of Scripture bear witness to this universal dominion of wickedness, for example, Isaiah 1:6–7; Romans 1:18; 3:20; and 2 Timothy 3:1–5.

This evil is not merely an impersonal principle. Behind it lies a sinister, diabolic figure, "the evil one." Paul makes this abundantly clear in his Ephesian epistle. In chapter 2 he tells us that unsaved people act "according to the prince of the power of the air" and that this evil spirit works in those who live in disobedience to God. Paul also gives the reason believers must put on the armor of God: "For we wrestle not against flesh and blood, but against principalities, against powers, against the rulers of the darkness of this world, against spiritual wickedness [or, *the spiritual powers of wickedness*] in high places" (Ephesians 6: 12). Evil men are responsible before God for their evil deeds (Jude 15), but behind them lurks the active presence of that evil spirit who blinds and darkens men, who incites them to viciousness and stirs up their wicked passions, who opposes truth, fosters the lie, and deceives men, often by coming to them as an angel of light.

This principle of wickedness energized by the wicked one is the pervasive evil that is in the world today. It threatens to ruin every sinner eternally (Matthew 13: 38–43). It also invades the church (1 Timothy 4:1–3). It confronts and challenges every Christian (Ephesians 6:12–17), seeking to compromise him and neutralize his testimony (Matthew 5:13; 2 Corinthians 2:11). This all-pervasive evil is what the Lord Jesus deals with in the final petition of the Lord's Prayer, insuring that we remain alert to its existence and instructing us how to confront and conquer it. Now let us look at the second major matter of which Christ speaks in the text.

An Urgent Entreaty

What are we to do about the pervasive evil of which our Lord speaks? The answer is that we must pray. However else we confront evil, the first thing we must do is to learn how to prevail in prayer. Only in a serious, ongoing fellowship with God will we find the answer to evil and to the evil one who promotes it. Only those who really pray will be able to stand for God in the midst of the all-pervasive wickedness of the days in which we live. That is why Jesus taught us to pray, "Deliver us from the evil."

It is impossible to over-emphasize the importance of prayer in the battle with sin and Satan. Paul sets out to instruct us how to "be strong in the Lord, and in the power of his might," how to "be able to stand against the wiles of the devil," and how to "be able to withstand in the evil day, and having done all, to stand" (Ephesians 6:10, 11, 13). He tells us of the full armor that God had provided for His people—the girdle of truth, the breastplate of righteousness, the shoes of the preparation of the gospel of peace, the shield of faith, the helmet of salvation, and the sword of the Spirit—and then emphasizes that its use depends on the ministry of prayer: "Take unto you the whole armour of God…. Stand therefore … praying always with all prayer and supplication in the Spirit, and watching thereunto with all perseverance and supplication for all saints" (verses 13–14, 18). The effective use of the armor depends on "praying always with all prayer and supplication in the Spirit." The Lord Jesus makes the same point with reference to the coming fall of Jerusalem. He says, "Watch ye therefore, and pray always, that ye may be accounted worthy to escape all these things that shall come to pass, and to stand before the Son of man" (Luke 21:36). Once again, the ability to escape from the predicted evils and to stand before the Lord depends on keeping a watchful guard on the place of prayer. The primary response to pervasive evil is to pray.

The prayer "Deliver us from evil" is much more than a form of words; it is a prayer marked by sincerity. Note its position in the Lord's Prayer, following immediately upon "Lead us not into temptation." It is a petition that only those who are willing to follow the Lord can honestly make. It has no place on the lips of hypocrites who seek to live as close to sin as possible, while yet avoiding its consequences. To be effective, prayer must always be sincere.

This prayer for deliverance is marked also by simple trust. The first part of Matthew 6:13, "Lead us not into temptation," confesses our weakness. The latter part of the verse, "But deliver us from evil," confesses the Lord's power. It recognizes our Father's complete sovereignty and sees that even Satan and all the evil he sponsors in the world are under His control. In this prayer, therefore, we have the same assurance that buoyed up the heart of the apostle Paul as he lay awaiting execution in a Roman prison: "The Lord shall deliver me from every evil work, and will preserve me unto his heavenly kingdom: to whom be glory for ever and ever. Amen" (2 Timothy 4:18).

This sincere and believing prayer is certain to be heard. The Greek verb translated "deliver" is *rhuomai* and it is interesting that its participle form is used in Romans 11:26 as a title of Christ: "All Israel shall be saved: as it is written, There shall come out of Sion the Deliverer [Greek, *ho rhuomenos*], and shall turn away ungodliness from Jacob." We pray to be delivered. It is the particular purpose and calling of the Lord Jesus Christ to deliver us. He makes our deliverance a prominent part of His high priestly ministry of intercession: "I pray … that thou shouldest keep them from the evil" (John 17:15). When we pray, "Deliver us from evil," we are invoking the intervention and the power of our intercessor, and we are pleading that God will deliver us through Him. Such a prayer cannot fail because Christ cannot fail, either through lack of power or love. His praying for us cannot be in vain, for as He said to His Father, "I know that thou hearest me always" (John 11:42). Thus when we pray, "Deliver us from evil," we are asking for something that our Father is pledged to grant through the person, work, intercession, and merit of Christ. We are certain to be heard.

There is a third important matter that the Lord Jesus Christ raises in the petition "Deliver us from evil" which we must now consider.

A Great Emancipation

The great entreaty expressed in the text must lead to a great emancipation. The word *deliver* means "rescue" or "save." Peter tells us that "the Lord delivered just Lot, vexed with the filthy conversation of the wicked" and that He "knoweth how to deliver the godly out of temptations" (2 Peter 2:7, 9). The Lord is able to deliver the godly out of temptation. When Paul was facing such ferocious trials that death appeared imminent, he looked to the Lord in faith. He described his trust and the reason for it in 2 Corinthians 1:9–10, making three references to the power and certainty of divine deliverance: "We had the sentence of death in ourselves, that we should not trust in ourselves, but in God which raiseth the dead: who delivered us from so great a death, and doth deliver: in whom we trust that he will yet deliver us." Here then is the teaching of the petition "Deliver us from evil": God our Father has provided for His people a sure way of escape from every device of the wicked one.

There is a sure deliverance for believers from Satan's attacks. The Bible terms Satan our "adversary" (1 Peter 5:8) and "the dragon" (Revelation 13:2). The attacks of such an evil enemy are never to be taken lightly for they are always dangerous. But in Christ our deliverer our Father has provided an escape from all Satan's attacks.

He has also provided an escape from Satan's slanders. The title "the devil" signifies the slanderer or false accuser. When Paul instructed the wives of deacons not to be slanderers, he said, literally, "Even so must their wives be grave, not devils [Greek, *diabolous*]" (1 Timothy 3:11). The devil is a slanderer, and slanderous accusations against God's people are his stock in trade. But our Father has made a way of deliverance from Satan's slanders.

He has also made a way of escape from Satan's evil religion. Satan is called "the god of this world" (2 Corinthians 4:4). He stands in the shadows of every false religion, the real object of the worship of all the rejecters of the one living and true God. By nature we were all subjects of his evil kingdom and worshipers at his sensuous shrine, but our Father has made a way of escape and has "delivered us from the power of darkness, and hath translated us into the kingdom of his dear Son" (Colossians 1:13).

He has made a way of deliverance from Satan's seduction. Satan is that "old serpent" (Revelation 12:9), the same one who led Eve into sin and deceived her with his enticements. He still seeks to deceive, so that we need to call on our Father to "deliver us from the evil one."

God has also made a way of deliverance from Satan's dominion. The evil one is "the prince of the power of the air, the spirit that now worketh in the children of disobedience," but by the regenerating grace of God we who believe on the Lord Jesus Christ have been delivered. We have been brought into the experience of heaven begun here and now and soon to be fully realized in the eternal ages (Ephesians 1:1–7).

Because of our Father's delivering grace and power, in a day of wickedness, we may live in holiness. In a day of darkness, we may walk in light. In a day of lies and deception, we may worship God in spirit and in truth. In a day of apostasy, we may stand for God in faithfulness. In the great spiritual warfare in which we are unavoidably engaged, we may serve the cause of Christ in the power of His Spirit.

There is another aspect of delivering grace. We have seen that *evil* sometimes signifies "grieving" or "hurtful." While the Lord never promises us escape from suffering in this world, *He enables us to live above the power of painful circumstances to lead us into sin and defeat.* In life we all have to face distressing situations, grieving hurts, and bitter disappointments. There are only two ways of meeting such "evils." Either we will live under the tyranny of our circumstances or we will live in the triumph of Christ despite our circumstances. Remember the prayer of Jabez, recorded in 1 Chronicles 4:10. We read, "Oh that thou wouldest bless me indeed, and enlarge my coast, and that thine hand might be with me, and that thou wouldest keep me from evil, that it may not grieve me! And God granted him that which he requested." This must be our prayer: "Keep me from evil, that it may not grieve me." It is a prayer that our Father delights to answer.

This is the heritage of God's people. To every Christian belongs the assurance of the psalmist: "Though I walk in the midst of trouble, thou wilt revive me: thou shalt stretch forth thine hand against the wrath of mine enemies, and thy right hand shall save me" (Psalm 138:7). When the Lord Jesus sent forth his disciples He assured them, "Behold, I give unto you power to tread on serpents and scorpions, and over all the power of the enemy: and nothing shall by any means hurt you" (Luke 10:19). *Nothing shall by any means hurt you.* What a promise! In due course some of these disciples were called to suffer intense opposition as they served Christ, but the promise held good. Everything that Satan meant for evil the Lord turned to their good, so that, whatever the circumstances, they could say, "We know that all things work together for good to them that love God, to them who are the called according to his purpose" (Romans 8:28).

We can say the same thing. We have the same promise of deliverance: "No weapon that is formed against thee shall prosper; and every tongue that shall rise against thee in judgment thou shalt condemn. This is the heritage of the servants of the Lord, and their righteousness is of me, saith the Lord" (Isaiah 54:17). Like the three Hebrew children (Daniel 3), we may be called to walk in the midst of a fiery furnace of affliction or trouble, but the presence of Christ will be with us.

Our Father does not promise that we will never pass through the deep waters of suffering or of problems that defy all human solutions. What He promises is that we will not be destroyed by our circumstances but will live in the joy of the gospel as we live in fellowship with Him: "When thou passest through the waters, I will be with thee; and through the rivers, they shall not overflow thee: when thou walkest through the fire, thou shalt not be burned; neither shall the flame kindle upon thee. For I am the Lord thy God, the Holy One of Israel, thy Saviour" (Isaiah 43:2–3).

Peter gives us a vivid example of this triumph of grace over distressing circumstances. In 1 Peter 1 he speaks of those who "are in heaviness through manifold temptations" (verse 6) or literally, were put to grief in various trials. The picture is of people under great stress, people who were really feeling the pressures of a hard station in life. Yet in the same sentence Peter says of these same people, "Ye greatly rejoice." How can those who are feeling the stress and strain of living under constant trials "greatly rejoice?" Peter gives us the answer by emphasizing what those tried believers rejoiced in: "Wherein ye greatly rejoice." The *wherein* points us to what is said in the earlier verses. There we read of the activity of the triune God for their salvation, the Father's electing grace, the Spirit's regenerating grace, Christ's redeeming grace. We read further, "Blessed be the God and Father of our Lord Jesus Christ, which according to his abundant mercy hath begotten us again unto a lively hope by the resurrection of Jesus Christ from the dead, to an inheritance incorruptible, and undefiled, and that fadeth not away, reserved in heaven for you, who are kept by the power of God through faith unto salvation ready to be revealed in the last time" (1 Peter 1:3–5). Here is the secret of enjoying deliverance from the tyranny of earthly circumstances: letting the truths of the gospel, which hold good no matter what is happening in the world, fill our hearts and minds with joyful praise and hopeful expectation.

As well as escaping the devices of the wicked one and the overwhelming power of adverse circumstances, *we have the greatest deliverance of all awaiting us: We will escape being damned with the devil and his angels.* We have already noted the assurance of Paul, "The Lord shall deliver me from every evil work, and will preserve me unto his heavenly kingdom" (2 Timothy 4:18). That is when we will enter into the full experience of our glorious emancipation. We shall be free from both sin and Satan, being made perfectly like Christ: "Beloved, now are we the sons of God, and it doth not yet appear what we shall be: but we know that, when he shall appear, we shall be like him; for we shall see him as he is" (1 John 3:2).

Here is the full story of the great deliverance of the people of God. Our Father has not left us as a powerless prey to Satan and sin. He has delivered us from the wrath to come (1 Thessalonians 1:10). He "knows how to deliver the godly out of temptations" (2 Peter 2:9). In the final petition of the Lord's Prayer, the Lord Jesus shows us that our Father will deliver those who pray. Victory is ours for the asking. If we ask in faith, nothing doubting, we shall receive and will enjoy the emancipation of those whom the Son sets free.

Thus we may pray constantly and with confidence, "Deliver us from evil." We will find, as Paul assured the Thessalonian believers, that "the Lord is faithful, who shall stablish you, and keep you from [the] evil" (2 Thessalonians 3:3).

22

Certain Victory over Sin and Satan

"Lead us not into temptation, but deliver us from evil: for thine is the kingdom, and the power, and the glory, for ever. Amen."   Matthew 6:13

T he Lord's Prayer ends with a doxology: "For thine is the kingdom and the power and the glory for ever. Amen." Most modern translations of the Bible omit or cast doubt on these words because they are not found in a small number of Greek manuscripts. Their absence from a few manuscripts may be adequately explained.[1] It is both arrogant and audacious for any man to omit from God's word what the Holy Spirit has carefully preserved in the overwhelming majority of the manuscripts of the New Testament. This sublime conclusion to the Lord's Prayer is not some late, uninspired addition that owes its acceptance to church usage. It is the way the Saviour chose to bring His model prayer to a fitting climax and conclusion.

For thine is the kingdom, and the power, and the glory, for ever. Amen. These words deserve our closest attention. They perform two functions. First, they relate closely to the words immediately preceding. That is, the doxology is an

---

[1] Over five hundred Greek manuscripts carry the text of Matthew's version of the Lord's Prayer. The absence of the doxology from a small number of them may have arisen from the attempt of some early editors to make Matthew's version conform to Luke's, who records the same prayer given under different circumstances and without the doxology. A probable reason for its absence from a few manuscripts is that in early liturgies the people said the prayer and the officiating minister spoke the doxology. Thus the doxology came to be separated from the body of the prayer and in some localities its wording suffered some alteration. It is easy to see how these words were dropped in a few instances, but it is difficult to account for their almost universal inclusion in the ancient manuscripts and versions unless they are authentic and original.

appropriate way of stating why we are confident in praying, "Lead us not into temptation, but deliver us from evil"; it is because "Thine is the kingdom and the power and the glory." Second, they have a relation to the prayer in its entirety. That is, as related to the prayer as a whole, the doxology shows us why we pray and why we expect God to hear us when we pray. We will consider these two functions separately, dealing with the first in this chapter and with the second in the next. Noting that the doxology flows directly out of the final petition of the prayer, we will suggest three reasons we may be certain that God will give us victory over sin and Satan.

Our Father's Sovereign Prerogative

The first reason for our confidence in praying for spiritual victory is that our Father rules all the things that tempt and try us. Everything, including all that can possibly draw us into committing sin, is under His control. As Solomon said, "The Lord hath made all things for himself: yea, even the wicked for the day of evil" (Proverbs 16:4). In our study of the petition "Deliver us from evil" we found that *evil* may denote evil spirits, Satan, sin, sinners, or situations of calamity and affliction. Any or all of these may tempt and try us. It is with this fact in mind that the Lord Jesus instructs us to pray this petition, acknowledging that to our Father belong "the kingdom, and the power, and the glory." In the midst of all the evils that beset us we should recall the words of the psalmist: "The Lord hath prepared his throne in the heavens; and his kingdom ruleth over all" (Psalm 103:19).

He rules over every expression of evil. He even makes evil serve His own holy purpose: "Surely the wrath of man shall praise thee: the remainder of wrath shalt thou restrain" (Psalm 76:10). This is a truth that perplexes our puny understanding. But God is greater than our conception of Him. We are finite and we cannot at all grasp His infinite fullness. He rules over everything, including every form and expression of evil.

Our Father rules over evil spirits. The Gospel accounts tell us of Christ's encounters with many of the "wicked spirits" that tormented people. On every occasion He exercised total power over them. He spoke and they left in peace those whom they had long possessed. At His command they had to yield obedience. Even the most violent and deeply entrenched of them could mount no opposition to the sovereign command of Him whom they confessed to be "the Holy One of God" (Mark 1:24). The legion of demons who inhabited the demoniac of Gadara came out of the man they had long demented and could not even enter a nearby herd of swine without Christ's permission (Mark 5:12–13). It is not much wonder that when our Lord entered their synagogue and cast an unclean spirit out of a man, the people of Capernaum "were all amazed, insomuch that they questioned among themselves, saying, What thing is this? what new doctrine is this? for with authority commandeth he even the unclean spirits, and they do obey him" (Mark 1:27). As the Lord Jesus Himself made clear, He cast out demons by the power and authority of the Father (Luke 11:20; John 5: 19). He rules over evil spirits.

He rules over Satan. Some people hold to the notion of dualism, positing two ultimate spiritual powers, God and Satan, who are engaged in a momentous struggle for supremacy. Nothing could be further from the truth. There is only one ultimate spiritual power, for there is only one God. He is the sole Supreme Being, the only controller of all His creatures. Satan is one of those creatures and he is as completely under the control of his creator as any other creature. According to the book of Job, Satan, though filled with unspeakable hatred of Job and burning with a desire to destroy him, could not even touch him, except by divine permission. As He says to the waves of the sea, so our Father says to Satan, "Hitherto shalt thou come, but no further: and here shall thy proud waves be stayed" (Job 38:11). Satan's doom and the time of his final descent into the bottomless pit are settled by divine decree. Our Father rules him totally.

He also rules over sin. Our Father hates sin and will judge men for their sin, but He maintains control over it. Joseph grasped this truth and taught it to his brothers who, blinded by hatred and envy, had sold him into slavery and had deceived their father into believing that he had been killed by a wild beast. Years later, with Joseph occupying a position of almost absolute power in Egypt and feeling that with the death of their father they were vulnerable to their brother's vengeance, they cowered before him in fear. That was when he taught them this sound theology: "As for you, ye thought evil against me; but God meant it unto good, to bring to pass, as it is this day, to save much people alive" (Genesis 50: 20). God controls and uses for His own ultimate purpose even the wickedness of sinful men. The greatest example of this is furnished by the death of Christ. Evil men put Him to death, but in doing so they fulfilled God's eternal purpose, though they were unaware of doing so. Peter plainly stated this to the Jews: "Him, being delivered by the determinate counsel and foreknowledge of God, ye have taken, and by wicked hands have crucified and slain" (Acts 2:23).

Our Father controls not only the actions of sinners but sinners themselves. It was to a heathen king that the Lord said, "I ... withheld thee from sinning against me" (Genesis 20:6). It is not only the heart of a godly king that is in the hand of the Lord (Proverbs 21:1), but the heart of every man: "The preparations of the heart in man, and the answer of the tongue, is from the Lord" (Proverbs 16:1).

Our Father controls every situation, including those that bring calamity. This is not an easy truth to grasp. God's purposes are often beyond our comprehension. We find it difficult to understand why, when our loving heavenly Father controls all that happens, we endure suffering and sorrow. Skeptical philosophers seek an explanation of "why bad things happen to good people," as they often put it, by limiting either God's goodness or His love. To a Christian such a "solution" to the problem is worse than the problem itself. We recognize the truth of Paul's statement that our God "worketh all things after the counsel of his own will" (Ephesians 1:11) and that His will, or purpose, is always good and will be seen to be so either here or hereafter.

This truth is a key to our being able to call the Lord into the storms we encounter in the voyage of life—and therefore a key to our living in peace in a troubled world. When Christ's disciples were caught in a dangerous storm on the Sea of Galilee and could find no way out of it, they urgently called on Him. Jesus rebuked the winds and waves and said, "Peace, be still." The elements instantly obeyed Him so that the disciples marveled, "What manner of man is this, that even the wind and the sea obey him?" (Mark 4:39, 41). We also stand in awe of the Lord's complete control over not only the elements of nature but over everything that happens. He rules every situation in life. Unbelief fails to grasp this truth and therefore flies in God's face or bitterly complains against His providence. However, once grasped, the truth of God's sovereignty will inspire us to pray with earnestness and confidence. We will not be impotent victims of our circumstances but faithful prayer warriors crying to our Father, "Lead us not into temptation, but deliver us from evil: for thine is the kingdom, and the power, and the glory, for ever."

The experience of the early church provides us with a vivid example of how the truth of God's sovereignty over situations inspires powerful praying: "When they heard [the Jewish leaders' threat against Peter and John], they lifted up their voice to God with one accord, and said, Lord, thou art God, which hast made heaven, and earth, and the sea, and all that in them is: who by the mouth of thy servant David hast said, Why did the heathen rage, and the people imagine vain things? The kings of the earth stood up, and the rulers were gathered together against the Lord, and against his Christ. For of a truth against thy holy child Jesus, whom thou hast anointed, both Herod, and Pontius Pilate, with the Gentiles, and the people of Israel, were gathered together, for to do whatsoever thy hand and thy counsel determined before to be done. And now, Lord, behold their threatenings: and grant unto thy servants, that with all boldness they may speak thy word, by stretching forth thine hand to heal; and that signs and wonders may be done by the name of thy holy child Jesus" (Acts 4:24–30). What gave those early believers confidence to pray? It was the knowledge that they served the

God who ruled the very forces that opposed them and controlled the situation that threatened them. They knew the truth of the words of a gospel song written almost two thousand years later: "He's got the whole world in His hand." Our Father has the whole world in His hand—every person, every circumstance, every event. Let the truth of God's sovereign prerogative grip our hearts and it will inspire us with confidence to pray for victory over sin and Satan.

Our Father's Sanctifying Power

The second reason we may pray with confidence for victory over sin and Satan is that our Father has the power to deliver us, and He delights to use that power for our sanctification. Not only does He have the *authority* to deliver us from evil, for His "is the kingdom," but He also has the *ability* to do it, for His "is the power." He not only has the *right*, He also has the *might* to answer our cry. Thus when we cry, "Lead us not into temptation, but deliver us from evil: for thine is the kingdom, and the power, and the glory, for ever," we actively fulfill His command through Isaiah the prophet: "Hear, ye that are far off, what I have done; and, ye that are near, acknowledge my might" (Isaiah 33:13).

The Lord delights to sanctify His people. He says, "I am the Lord which sanctify you" (Leviticus 20:8). There are formidable forces opposed to our growth in grace. But as John wrote to believers battling the world, the flesh, and the devil, "Ye are of God, little children, and have overcome them: because greater is he that is in you, than he that is in the world" (1 John 4:4). Hezekiah, the beleaguered king of Judah, when facing the overwhelmingly superior forces of Sennacherib, prayed, "With him is an arm of flesh; but with us is the Lord our God to help us, and to fight our battles" (2 Chronicles 32:8). He is able to give us victory over every foe of our advancement in grace, a fact that gives the assurance of faith that He will hear us when we pray for victory over sin and Satan.

We need this confidence when we struggle with our own corruptions and are threatened by the world and Satan. Our God will help us if we cry to Him. Paul had this confidence as he prayed for the Ephesians: "He [will] grant you, according to the riches of his glory, to be strengthened with might by his Spirit in the inner man; that Christ may dwell in your hearts by faith; that ye [may be] rooted and grounded in love" (Ephesians 3:16–17).

When we pray, "Deliver us from evil," whether it is from sin, Satan, or circumstances, the Lord may do one of two things. He may remove the burden from our back, or He may strengthen our back to bear the burden. Either way, He will further our sanctification. Hebrews chapter eleven gives us a host of illustrations of both methods of God's delivering and sanctifying power. It tells us of eminent men of faith who were delivered by miraculous intervention, and it tells of other equally eminent men of faith who received no such intervention but who were graciously strengthened to suffer for their faith. Some received grace to do the impossible, while others received grace to bear the unbearable, all to the glory of God and the sanctification of their own souls.

Our Father has the power to answer our cry for victory over sin and Satan; thinking on that truth gives us confidence to pray for such victory.

Our Father's Sacred Praise

The final reason for our praying with confidence for victory over sin and Satan is that our Father is greatly glorified by the triumph of sanctifying grace in the lives of His people: "Thine is ... the glory." Nothing more eloquently glorifies God than genuine holiness in those who, before He saved them, were slaves of sin. This is what makes a Christian's testimony such a wonderful thing. Of course, our testimony is the witness not just of our lips but of our lives. In this case, actions often speak more loudly than words. We were all once slaves to sin, and when a slave to sin starts walking in holiness it glorifies God in a unique way. The Lord Jesus said, "Let your light so shine before men, that they may see your good works, and glorify your Father which is in heaven" (Matthew 5:16). Paul instructed Titus to exhort the saints to show "all good fidelity; that they may adorn the doctrine of God our Saviour in all things" (Titus 2:10). He commanded the Corinthians, "Glorify God in your body, and in your spirit, which are God's" (1 Corinthians 6:20).

Thus by their good works, honesty, and moral purity—in spite of the pressures of contemporary society to depart from such standards—Christians bring glory to the Lord. Their separation from the world unto God in true holiness is the most powerful witness they can bear to those around them. Religious compromisers have foisted on the church the lie that to be effective in the world we must "relate" to it, which usually means that we must minimize the distinctiveness of Christian holiness and live in a worldly manner. But worldly Christians and churches are spiritually powerless. They may glorify themselves in the eyes of men but they do not glorify God. Holiness in sin's ex-slaves is what brings glory to the Lord before men in the most incontrovertible manner. Holiness proclaims the reality and power of saving grace.

Not only does the evidence of sanctification in our lives bring glory to God before men, it also causes the Lord Himself to celebrate the triumph of His grace in His people. He boasted of Job's holiness before heaven and hell. What a challenge that is to us! Can He boast of the holiness of our lives? He delights to do so. Indeed, when He shows the marvelous accomplishments of His wisdom to the angels, He does not point to the wonders of His creative power in the universe but to the glorious success of His grace in bringing sinners from the dunghill and setting them among heaven's princes (see 1 Samuel 2:8). Paul tells us, "Unto the principalities and powers in heavenly places [will] be known by the church the manifold wisdom of God" (Ephesians 3:10).

Because true holiness in us who were sin's slaves but who are now the children of God so greatly glorifies Him, our Father encourages us to pray for His delivering power in every time of trial. He says, "Call upon me in the day of trouble: I will deliver thee, and thou shalt glorify me" (Psalm 50:15). In other words, "Pray, 'Deliver us from evil,' because the triumph of grace in us over all trials and temptations to evil will bring glory to Thy name."

Here are three reasons we may be confident that God will hear us when we pray for victory over sin and Satan. He has the prerogative to help us — "Thine is the kingdom." He has the power to help us — "Thine is the power." He will receive great praise when He helps us — "Thine is the glory." So let us take the final petition of the Lord's Prayer and the doxology that follows it and make them the basis for persistent prayer, with confidence that we will receive the answer of our Father in heaven. "This is the will of God, even your sanctification" (1 Thessalonians 4:3). To those who pray for it, God gives the assurance of victory over sin and Satan.

23

The Essence and End of All True Prayer

"For thine is the kingdom, and the power, and the glory, for ever. Amen."
Matthew 6:13

The Lord Jesus Christ so positioned and worded the doxology in the Lord's Prayer that it is related intimately to the petition that immediately precedes it. He did this to teach us the lesson that we have powerful reasons to be confident that our Father will hear us when we pray, "Lead us not into temptation, but deliver us from evil." But our Lord also related the doxology to the prayer as a whole and thereby teaches us further important lessons about true prayer.

"For thine is the kingdom, and the power, and the glory, for ever. Amen." As we have noted, this is what is termed a doxology. A doxology is a word of praise to God. It is praise *uttered* that naturally bursts forth from a soul that has caught sight of the greatness, goodness, and grace of God. It is significant that the Lord's Prayer ends with a doxology. The Lord Jesus has been teaching us how to pray and what to say in prayer. He has covered the great areas that we need to address when we come into God's presence. He commenced by making us think of the transcendent greatness of our Father in heaven. He then led us step by step through the areas that most concern us as we speak to God. Now He concludes by bringing us back to the greatness of our Father, this time in a mighty expression of praise.

The doxology in the Lord's Prayer echoes the great burden of Scripture, or perhaps we should say the great burden of the prayer warriors whom the Bible celebrates.

- When David prayed, he cried: "Thine, O Lord, is the greatness, and the power, and the glory, and the victory, and the majesty: for all that is in the heaven and in the earth is thine; thine is the kingdom, O Lord, and thou art exalted as head above all" (1 Chronicles 29:11).

- When Sennacherib and his army seemed to have Jerusalem at their mercy, "Hezekiah prayed before the Lord, and said, O Lord God of Israel, which dwellest between the cherubims, thou art the God, even thou alone, of all the kingdoms of the earth; thou hast made heaven and earth" (2 Kings 19:15).

- Paul exclaimed, "Now unto the King eternal, immortal, invisible, the only wise God, be honour and glory for ever and ever. Amen" (1 Timothy 1:17).

- Jude climaxed his brief epistle by ascribing all honor to the Lord: "To the only wise God our Saviour, be glory and majesty, dominion and power, both now and ever. Amen" (Jude 25).

- The worshiping saints and angels who surround God's throne utter the sentiment, "Blessing, and honour, and glory, and power, be unto him that sitteth upon the throne, and unto the Lamb for ever and ever" (Revelation 5:13).

So the doxology of the Lord's Prayer echoes the sentiments expressed in some of the greatest prayers recorded in Scripture. It would revolutionize our prayer lives if we never left the secret place until we were so completely overwhelmed by the vision of God's greatness that we uttered the doxology of the Lord's Prayer with complete sincerity. All our praying—our approach to God and our asking of Him—must lead to this conclusion.

Thus the doxology teaches us the essence of all true prayer. It reveals what should ultimately concern us in the place of prayer. It teaches us why we pray; that is, it shows what motivates and energizes true praying. It discovers the ground of our confidence in prayer.

The doxology also establishes the end of all true prayer. By *end* I mean something more than the mere conclusion. It goes beyond that and teaches us the design or purpose of true prayer. In studying the doxology we will learn more of what prayer really is and what it is not.

Devotion, Not Desperation

In the doxology to the Lord's Prayer we learn that true prayer is not desperation, but devotion. We may be in desperate circumstances and be driven to pray. This is clear from the wording of the Lord's Prayer. Here the Lord Jesus addresses circumstances of urgent need—the needs of the body and of the soul, the need for forgiveness of sin, the need for grace to forgive those who have wronged us, the need for strength to overcome temptation and to stand fast in times of trial, and the need for power to live a victorious Christian life. These are great needs and often as we face them we feel desperate, especially in light of our own natural weakness and wickedness.

Prayer must ascend out of the pit of desperation, however, and mount to the peaks of devotion. Before ever mentioning any of our needs, the Lord Jesus focuses our minds on our Father in heaven, and settles it in our hearts that our greatest goal is to see His name hallowed, His kingdom established, and His will accomplished. This is the perspective that brings the soul out of desperation into devotion.

By definition, *desperation* means "hopelessness." But prayer is an exercise of faith, an expression of hope—and that hope is based on what we know of our God. In Scripture hope is not some vague optimism that somehow things will turn out well. Rather it is a confident waiting on God, an expectation that He will do what He has promised to do. Thus, whatever our situation, we must get our eyes on the Lord. When we do, our praying will rise up out of the pit of desperation and become true devotion. When we see how great our God is, we will always have reason to pray and to "rejoice in hope of the glory of God" as we do so (Romans 5:2). When Paul penned the words of Romans 5:2, he proceeded at once to mention trials and tribulations, things that would test the patience and weigh down the heart. He was not imagining some impossible utopian state when he spoke of rejoicing amid experiences that others would term desperate. Rather he was describing the reality of what is available to the people of God in a world that is drowning in its own tears. A living faith in a living Christ through whom we have a living relationship with the living God is the fundamental reality of life for a Christian. When by faith we contemplate our God, we will always have reason to pray and to rejoice in hope.

We have hope even when we have been overtaken by sin because we know that "if we confess our sins, he is faithful and just to forgive us our sins, and to cleanse us from all unrighteousness" (1 John 1:9). The Jews who returned from Babylon expressed this hope. They confessed, "We have trespassed against our God, and have taken strange wives of the people of the land: yet now there is hope in Israel concerning this thing" (Ezra 10:2).

We have hope when we are depressed and defeated. David expressed the hope that he felt when he was distressed and tempted to despair: "Why art thou cast down, O my soul? and why art thou disquieted in me? hope thou in God: for I shall yet praise him for the help of his countenance…. Why art thou cast down, O my soul? and why art thou disquieted within me? hope thou in God: for I shall yet praise him, who is the health of my countenance, and my God…. Why art thou cast down, O my soul? and why art thou disquieted within me? hope in

God: for I shall yet praise him, who is the health of my countenance, and my God. (Psalm 42:5, 11; 43:5). "The help of God's countenance" is a poetic way of describing God's unhindered favor and acceptance. It is the brightness that the realization of His perfections and grace brings into otherwise hopeless lives. Assuring us of His promises, He restores health to our countenance, meaning that He replaces our dark despair with glorious hope.

From this we should learn that our praying must concentrate more on our God than on our need. Our view of the one will affect our view of the other. Concentrating almost exclusively on our need will cause us to have a small view of God and a limited conception of His ability to help us in our time of need. It will destroy the exercise of faith and will render what we think is prayer a vain and depressing repetition of our woes. In contrast, concentrating on our God will change how we view our need and how we face it. It will enable us to confront our difficult situations with new strength and vigor and with an assured hope.

Hope exists because God exists. He is our Father and He is glorious beyond all human conception. He is "great ... and greatly to be praised" (Psalm 48:1). True prayer is based on this faith and is therefore an act of devotion, not desperation.

Submission, Not Self-will

The second lesson we learn about true prayer from the doxology is that it is not an expression of self-will but of submission. The Lord's Prayer deals with sincere and spiritual desires. Prayer by its very nature is the expression of deep personal longings. When we pray we are telling the Lord what we want. We are stating our wills to the Lord. The Lord Jesus teaches us to pray, "Thy will be done," but however much we say these words, the fact is that if we do not focus on the greatness of our God, our praying will degenerate into an expression of petty and petulant self-will. He who prays with little or no contemplation of his God, will spend his prayer time sinning, seeking to impose his will upon God. True prayer leads us to behold our God and to cry, "How great thou art!" It therefore leads us to resign our designs in favor of God's. Indeed it leads us to lay all our desires at His feet and to cry, "The Lord be magnified" (Psalm 40:16).

That the Lord would be magnified in dealing as He sees fit with the circumstances and petitions we bring before Him would be the supreme answer to every true prayer. This was Paul's feeling as he lay in prison and wondered whether he would live or die. During Paul's imprisonment Christ was being preached in Rome, by some in truth and by others in pretence, hoping to hurt Paul's cause in the eyes of the law. The apostle's response was: "I know that this shall turn to my salvation through your prayer, and the supply of the Spirit of Jesus Christ, according to my earnest expectation and my hope, that in nothing I shall be ashamed, but that with all boldness, as always, so now also Christ shall be magnified in my body, whether it be by life, or by death. For to me to live is Christ, and to die is gain" (Philippians 1:19–21).

Christ shall be magnified in my body, whether it be by life, or by death. This is the attitude that a true view of God begets in us. It crucifies self-will and makes our praying a spiritual exercise of hearty submission to the will, purpose, and honor of our Father in heaven.

Heavenly, Not Earthly

The final lesson we learn about true prayer from the doxology is that ultimately it is not earthly but heavenly. Prayer must deal with the things of earth, but as it does, it recognizes that the God of heaven governs all things on earth. True prayer refuses to make heaven the servant of earth, eternity the servant of time, or God the servant of man. It does the very opposite. It makes earth the servant of heaven, time the servant of eternity, and man the servant of God. So in the doxology to the Lord's Prayer the Lord Jesus shows us what we really do in prayer and why we pray.

"Thine Is the Kingdom": Celebrating God's Sovereignty

Without this recognition of the absolute sovereignty of God, prayer would be a farce. This is why it is grieving to hear Christians trying to remove this doctrine from the faith and to recast Scripture so as to evacuate it of its teaching on such matters as God's eternal purpose, His predestination of His people, His foreordination of whatever comes to pass, and His absolute power in disposing all things of earth. Having withered their conception of God to a shriveled caricature of the God of the Bible, what basis do they have for prayer?

Not only would prayer to a God who is not sovereign be a farce, it would be an exercise in frustration. Remember Rachel's plea to Jacob and his retort: "Give me children, or else I die. And Jacob's anger was kindled against Rachel: and he said, Am I in God's stead, who hath withheld from thee the fruit of the womb?" (Genesis 30:1–2). Imagine our predicament if we were condemned to pray to a God who had no more ultimate authority over our affairs than Jacob had over Rachel's fertility. Jacob had all the goodwill in the world toward Rachel. But benevolence was not enough. He did not have the authority or ability to fulfill her desire. Unless God is absolutely sovereign, He is similarly limited. If that were the case what a frustrating misery prayer would be!

Christians are condemned to no such farce or frustration, for our Father is utterly and entirely sovereign. The prophet Daniel records how Nebuchadnezzar the king of Babylon had to learn that lesson. It took his being deposed from his throne and left to live as a wild beast in the fields before he humbly accepted it. The once proud monarch recorded his experience: "At the end of the days I Nebuchadnezzar lifted up mine eyes unto heaven, and mine understanding returned unto me, and I blessed the most High, and I praised and honoured him that liveth for ever, whose dominion is an everlasting dominion, and his kingdom is from generation to generation: and all the inhabitants of the earth are reputed as nothing: and he doeth according to his will in the army of heaven, and among the inhabitants of the earth: and none can stay his hand, or say unto him, What doest thou?" (Daniel 4:34–35).

Our God is sovereign. That is the joyous message of all Scripture. "The Lord is king for ever and ever" (Psalm 10:16). He is not a constitutional monarch. He is not king by the will or votes of his subjects. His kingship is not limited or in any way modified by the acts of any parliament or congress. He needs no counselor. He is the absolute monarch of heaven, earth, and hell, the creator and sustainer of all, the one in whom we live and move and have our being (Acts 17:28). As Paul said to Timothy, our God "is the blessed and only Potentate, the King of kings and Lord of lords" (1 Timothy 6:15). We may confidently come to God with the assurance that He can do whatever He wills. The only limitation on what God does is what God wills.

This truth of God's absolute sovereignty is not a dry or barren dogma. It is not a doctrine that will destroy a Christian's prayer life or his love for souls, as is often alleged. Rather it is a truth that sets God's people ablaze with a passion to pray and gives us strong confidence when we pray. To every praying saint God's sovereignty is therefore a matter of jubilant celebration.

"Thine Is the Power": Acknowledging God's Power

The Lord commands us to acknowledge His power: "Hear, ye that are far off, what I have done; and, ye that are near, acknowledge my might" (Isaiah 33:13). He challenged Abraham and Sarah, "Is any thing too hard for the Lord?" (Genesis 18:14). He issued the same challenge to Jeremiah the prophet: "Behold, I am the Lord, the God of all flesh: is there any thing too hard for me?" (Jeremiah 32:27). Jeremiah had already confessed the answer—and it is one that everyone who knows what it is to pray with devotion and submission gladly endorses: "Ah Lord God! behold, thou hast made the heaven and the earth by thy great power and stretched out arm, and there is nothing too hard for thee" (Jeremiah 32:17). This is why we pray. This is what gives us confidence in prayer, what lifts us from frustration to faith and from defeat to deliverance. We come to the one who has unlimited power to answer us according to His will.

"Thine Is the Glory": Aiming at God's Glory

Prayer must always have an eternal dimension. It must always look beyond the immediate to the ultimate. We naturally desire what is sweet and comfortable, what we consider to be of immediate benefit to us. But when we pray and behold our God, we ascend to a higher plane. We recognize that there is a purpose higher than our comfort or even our present happiness. That purpose is the glory of God. Once we aim at God's glory in prayer, we will be happy with His answer, whatever it may be. Our praying will transcend the petty things that so often absorb us. While we will always rejoice that we can bring even the smallest of our concerns to our Father, we will joyfully grasp the great purpose of our being, which is beautifully stated by the church triumphant: "The four and twenty elders fall down before him that sat on the throne, and worship him that liveth for ever and ever, and cast their crowns before the throne, saying, Thou art worthy, O Lord, to receive glory and honour and power: for thou hast created all things, and for thy pleasure they are and were created" (Revelation 4:10–11).

The only reason for our existence is the glory of God. In heaven the church triumphant clearly sees and confesses this. Here on earth we who make up the church militant must learn that true prayer is all about casting every crown at Jesus' feet and confessing that the glory of God is the sole reason for our living. The mere duration of our life on earth is not what really matters—though all too often it becomes the only issue that people are concerned about. What matters is whether we have glorified our God. What is important is not whether we have lived in prosperity or penury, but whether we have brought glory to our God.

This is why we pray—that God may be glorified. This burning desire is what governs what we pray for and how we pray for it. And it is what ultimately assures our faith that God will answer prayer, for He will most certainly glorify His own name.

Jesus said, "Father, glorify thy name" (John 12:28), and we are therefore never more like Christ than when we pray for God to be glorified. And we are never more sure of the Father's answer, for as soon as our Saviour had offered that prayer, "then came there a voice from heaven, saying, I have both glorified it, and will glorify it again."

Prayer is devotion. Prayer is submission. Prayer celebrates God's sovereignty, acknowledges His power, and aims to promote His glory. These are the things that constitute the essence and end of all genuine prayer. Blessed is the man who can honestly pray, "Thine is the kingdom, and the power, and the glory, for ever. Amen."

24

For Ever

"Thine is the kingdom, and the power, and the glory, for ever."
Matthew 6:13

F or ever" is a small phrase with an impossibly large meaning for mortal men. We are creatures of time. It is true that by God's decree we will live for ever, but our entire earthly experience is stamped with change and temporariness. In the poem "Mutability," the atheistic, libertine poet Percy Bysshe Shelley likens men to clouds that for a brief time "speed, and gleam, and quiver, / Streaking the darkness radiantly," but that soon "are lost forever." In a conclusion that reveals the abyss of hopelessness to which his godless philosophy brought him, Shelley says, "Naught may endure but Mutability." The only thing that remains constant is the fact of change; the only thing certain is uncertainty. Such is the creed of a libertine atheist. The Christian hymnwriter Henry Francis Lyte faced the same evidence of mutability as Shelley, but with his focus on the eternal God:

> Swift to its close ebbs out life's little day;
> Earth's joys grow dim, its glories pass away;
> Change and decay in all around I see:
> O Thou who changest not, abide with me.

The apostle Peter wrote, "All flesh is as grass, and all the glory of man as the flower of grass. The grass withereth, and the flower thereof falleth away: But the word of the Lord endureth for ever. And this is the word which by the gospel is preached unto you" (1 Peter 1:24–25). Human mutability and mortality stand in stark contrast with the eternal God and His unchanging word and make the term *for ever* too large for us to comprehend but too important for us to disregard. These two little words bring us face to face with eternity and with the God of eternity. He is a fool who lives for the passing moment and ignores eternity, who lives for self and ignores God his judge, or who lives for momentary pleasure and ignores the pain of hell that lasts for ever. The urgent call implicit in the words *for ever* is for us to obey the message chiseled on the gravestone of a man who evidently wanted his death to carry a solemn message to all who passed by:

> Consider, man, as you pass by,
> As you are now, so once was I.
> As I am now, soon you will be.
> Consider, man, eternity.

Here is a solemn warning for every unconverted man and woman. Whatever we say or do in this world is in the light of eternity. Every word and deed has an eternal dimension. Such a thought is foreign to millions who have accepted the humanistic pragmatism and existentialism of today. These are philosophies that center attention on "living in the moment" and on doing whatever feels good now, without reference to God or eternity. But all the humanistic theorizing in the world cannot change the reality that "it is appointed unto men once to die, but after this the judgment" (Hebrews 9:27). It cannot change the fact that as the consequence of that judgment every one of us will live for eternity in heaven or in hell, with Christ or without Christ, saved or damned for ever. Eternity is real and we must consider urgently our eternal destiny in the light of God's infallible word. This is the solemn message of the phrase "for ever" to all who are yet in their sins.

The words also carry a message to God's people. We live in "this present evil world" (Galatians 1:4), but as we do, we must live for eternity. In His high priestly prayer our Lord said of His people: "They are not of the world, even as I am not of the world" (John 17:14). We are *in* the world, but not *of* it. That is, the values that govern our lives are not those of this world but those of the world to come. This perspective is what enabled Paul to live with such a spiritual vision and to endure unspeakable suffering with such courage: "Our light affliction, which is but for a moment, worketh for us a far more exceeding and eternal weight of glory; while we look not at the things which are seen, but at the things which are not seen: for the things which are seen are temporal; but the things which are not seen are eternal" (2 Corinthians 4:17–18).

Living and serving with a view to eternity is the best way for a Christian to live, for it produces eternally enduring results. It is the best investment of time we can make, for it produces a harvest that will endure for ever. As Christians we must not focus on the temporal to the detriment of the eternal but must use the temporal to serve the interests of the eternal. Whatever we do, we must live with eternity's values in view. That is the general message of the phrase "for ever."

But this phrase also carries a more specific message to every praying child of God. "Thine is the kingdom, and the power, and the glory, for ever"—this glorious climax to the Lord's Prayer reminds us that the eternity and immutability of God's perfections and praise are a source of comfort to us and give powerful direction and strong confidence to our praying. As we study this message we will note that the phrase "for ever" performs five functions as it teaches us far-reaching lessons from the eternity and immutability of God.

"For Ever" Impresses the Solemnity of Eternity on Our Praying

As we have already seen, praying by its very nature is an earthly activity. It necessarily takes note of earthly situations and needs. But it must never lose sight of the eternal dimension. What does this mean?

Praying Without Ceasing

Keeping an eternal dimension in our praying means first, we must never become so burdened with temporal matters, even legitimate ones, that we neglect the place of prayer. The Bible regularly makes this point. Paul commanded the Romans to continue "instant in prayer" (Romans 12:12) and instructed the Thessalonians, "Pray without ceasing" (1 Thessalonians 5:17), no matter what demands on their time their earthly affairs might make. The Lord Jesus "spake a parable unto [them] to this end, that men ought always to pray, and not to faint" (Luke 18:1), no matter what pressures to quit praying may exist. Paul described to the Ephesians the reality and nature of our warfare against Satan, adding this necessary instruction: "Put on the whole armour of God ... praying always with all prayer and supplication in the Spirit, and watching thereunto with all perseverance and supplication for all saints" (Ephesians 6:11, 18). In the words of George Duffield's hymn God commands us, "Put on the gospel armor, each piece put on with prayer."

Spiritual conflict and opposition, far from leading us to neglect the place of prayer, should drive us to our knees. No earthly concern or consideration should be allowed to impede our praying. In the midst of unimaginable stress, trying to regroup his forces after fleeing his capital in the face of the rebellion of his son and the betrayal of his best friend, King David prayed, "Evening, and morning, and at noon, will I pray, and cry aloud: and he shall hear my voice" (Psalm 55:17). Whatever our circumstances, it is always time to cry to the Lord. We must never allow the affairs of this world—even our busyness in Christian service—to crush the spirit of prayer in us.

Praying for What Really Matters

Keeping an eternal dimension to our praying means that we must pray for what really matters and never limit our prayers to matters of temporal concern. The Lord Jesus clearly teaches us this lesson by how He structures the Lord's Prayer, placing its major emphasis on God's name, kingdom, will, and glory. He reinforces the lesson by giving much more attention to our spiritual concerns than to our temporal needs. He does not countenance the almost total concentration on matters of health and wealth that marks the prayers of so many modern Christians and churches. These are legitimate matters for prayer, but they should not be the exclusive or even the predominant theme of our praying.

The Lord Jesus gives us His personal example of what it means to pray with eternity in view, to pray for what really matters. Not long before His arrest and crucifixion, He prayed what is usually called His "High Priestly Prayer." It is recorded in John 17 and in it, after asking that the Father would glorify Him as He had glorified the Father, He prays for all the spiritual concerns of His people as they seek to live for God in an unfriendly world. He prays for their safety, sanctity, and unity and climaxes His requests with a glorious petition for their eternal security: "Father, I will that they also, whom thou hast given me, be with me where I am; that they may behold my glory, which thou hast given me: for thou lovedst me before the foundation of the world" (John 17:24). Our Lord lays down our priorities in prayer and shows us what it means to have an eternal dimension to our praying.

So do His apostles. They had many temporal needs. They were short of money and lacked the necessities of life. This was why Paul labored as a tentmaker while he sought to fulfill his ministry as an apostle. In addition to material needs, the apostles had physical needs. Almost daily they stood in peril of losing either their freedom or their lives. No doubt they prayed about all these issues, but they did not make them the chief burden of their praying. As we check their recorded prayers we are left in no doubt that their great burden in prayer was about spiritual and eternal matters. Take Paul's prayers as typical of all apostolic praying. From them we will learn what we should be concentrating on when we pray.

The Spread of the Gospel

Paul prayed for the spread of the gospel and invited others to do the same: "[Pray] for me, that utterance may be given unto me, that I may open my mouth boldly, to make known the mystery of the gospel" (Ephesians 6:19). He repeated this request to the Colossians: "Withal praying also for us, that God would open unto us a door of utterance, to speak the mystery of Christ, for which I am also in bonds" (Colossians 4:3). He asked the Thessalonians to join in this prayer effort for the spread of the gospel: "Finally, brethren, pray for us, that the word of the Lord may have free course, and be glorified, even as it is with you" (2 Thessalonians 3:1). Literally, he asked them to pray that God's word might *run and be glorified*. Clearly, He had an abiding passion for spreading the gospel and believed that it could happen only as the result of prevailing prayer. We must have the same conviction and the same burden in prayer.

The Salvation of Souls

Paul prayed for souls to be saved and so should we. He gives us a glimpse of his burden for the lost: "I say the truth in Christ, I lie not, my conscience also bearing me witness in the Holy Ghost, that I have great heaviness and continual sorrow in my heart. For I could wish that myself were accursed from Christ for my brethren, my kinsmen according to the flesh" (Romans 9:1–3). That burden had to find expression in prayer: "Brethren, my heart's desire and prayer to God for Israel is, that they might be saved" (Romans 10:1).

It is interesting that these expressions of his love and prayers for the lost come in the part of the Epistle to the Romans that deals with the profound truths of God's sovereign predestination and election. Some people imagine that embracing such doctrines will deaden zeal and hinder prayer. It must be confessed that some who loudly defend these doctrines seem to show little or no zeal for prayer or fervor for evangelism. That is a wicked perversion of truths which, as Paul demonstrates, go hand in hand with a flaming passion and fervent prayer for the salvation of souls. We must never lose this burden in prayer.

The Establishment of Saints

Paul prayed for the establishment of the saints and so should we. The Epistle to the Ephesians gives us two outstanding examples of the apostle's burden for God's people, the first in chapter one and the other in chapter three.

Ephesians 1:15–23: "Wherefore I also, after I heard of your faith in the Lord Jesus, and love unto all the saints, cease not to give thanks for you, making mention of you in my prayers; that the God of our Lord Jesus Christ, the Father of glory, may give unto you the spirit of wisdom and revelation in the knowledge of him: the eyes of your understanding being enlightened; that ye may know what is the hope of his calling, and what the riches of the glory of his inheritance in the saints, and what is the exceeding greatness of his power to usward who believe, according to the working of his mighty power, which he wrought in Christ, when he raised him from the dead, and set him at his own right hand in the heavenly places, far above all principality, and power, and might, and dominion, and every name that is named, not only in this world, but also in that which is to come: and hath put all things under his feet, and gave him to be the head over all things to the church, which is his body, the fulness of him that filleth all in all."

Ephesians 3:14–19: "For this cause I bow my knees unto the Father of our Lord Jesus Christ, of whom the whole family in heaven and earth is named, that he would grant you, according to the riches of his glory, to be strengthened with might by his Spirit in the inner man; that Christ may dwell in your hearts by faith; that ye, being rooted and grounded in love, may be able to comprehend with all saints what is the breadth, and length, and depth, and height; and to know the love of Christ, which passeth knowledge, that ye might be filled with all the fulness of God."

Christians often say, sometimes glibly, "We will pray for you." However, how many of us do the kind of praying that these and other such passages call for? This is the most important ministry we can exercise before the Lord for ourselves and our brethren. We should pray:

- That we may be enlightened by the Holy Spirit to understand our exaltation in Christ and His exaltation for us;

- That we may be strengthened by the Holy Spirit so that we may be well grounded in the assurance of Christ's love;

- That we may be established by the experience of all God's full provision for us in Christ.

So far-reaching are these petitions that it is not too much to say that our spiritual health and usefulness depend on their being answered. If we prevail with the Lord for answers to these requests for His people, our churches will recapture the spirit of the early church and the world once again will witness the irresistible progress of the gospel.

Praying for God's Sake

To maintain an eternal dimension to our praying means that ultimately we pray for God's sake, not ours. We often end our prayer with the words *for Jesus' sake,* meaning that we ask on His merit, by His authority, and for His glory. However, the "for ever" of the doxology of the Lord's Prayer has a more specific meaning, as the following three remarks will show.

First, to pray for God's sake is to pray for the advance of His eternal purpose. Carnal reasoning may argue that God's purpose needs no support from our praying. However, the Lord Jesus instructs us to pray, "Thy will be done." Far from God's purpose removing from us the need for prayer, it supplies the assurance that God will hear us: "This is the confidence that we have in him, that, if we ask any thing according to his will, he heareth us: and if we know that he hear us, whatsoever we ask, we know that we have the petitions that we desired of him. (1 John 5:14–15).

Second, to pray for God's sake is to pray for the display of God's eternal perfections. We are not called to pray for the promotion of self, or even of any human agency, in the Lord's work. Our prayer must be that men may behold the perfections of our great God and Saviour. The Psalmist prayed, "God be merciful unto us, and bless us; and cause his face to shine upon us;... that thy way may be known upon earth, thy saving health among all nations" (Psalm 67:1–2). God's presence validating the actions of His people makes Him known among the heathen. This special nearness of God—when He powerfully impresses both saints and sinners with the majesty of His own eternal perfections—is what is properly called revival (as distinct from the misuse of the term in statements such as "We are having a revival" to describe a series of special evangelistic services). In a time of revival the marvelous actions of God's grace prove His nearness to His people and draw the lost to Him: "That thy name is near thy wondrous works declare" (Psalm 75:1). That is what happened in all the genuine revival movements of the past, and it is what we need to pray fervently for in our day. In a word, we look for God to answer us when we pray the prayer He answered for Moses: "I beseech thee, shew me thy glory" (Exodus 33:18).

Third, to pray for God's sake is to aim at God's eternal praise. The design of every true prayer is the glory of God: "Not unto us, O Lord, not unto us, but unto thy name give glory, for thy mercy, and for thy truth's sake" (Psalm 115:1). All that God does for us is for His own glory.

- *He predestinated and elected us for His glory:* "He hath chosen us in him before the foundation of the world, that we should be holy and without blame before him in love: having predestinated us unto the adoption of children by Jesus Christ to himself, according to the good pleasure of his will, to the praise of the glory of his grace, wherein he hath made us accepted in the beloved" (Ephesians 1:4–6).

- *He redeemed us for His glory:* "[Christ] gave himself for our sins, that he might deliver us from this present evil world, according to the will of God and our Father: to whom be glory for ever and ever" (Galatians 1:4-5).

- *He pardons us for His own sake*: "I, even I, am he that blotteth out thy transgressions for mine own sake, and will not remember thy sins" (Isaiah 43:25).

- *He sanctifies and secures us for His own glory*: "The Lord shall deliver me from every evil work, and will preserve me unto his heavenly kingdom: to whom be glory for ever and ever" (2 Timothy 4:18).

The entire scheme of salvation is supremely for the glory of God: Witness the ceaseless praise of the glorified in heaven. Can our praying be acceptable if it has any other governing ambition than to promote God's glory?

The "for ever" with which Christ concluded the doxology of the Lord's Prayer shows us the eternity and immutability of our God. In doing so it teaches us first the invaluable lesson that our praying must bear the stamp of eternity on it. We must always pray in the light of that "for ever."

"For Ever" Sets Us and Our Praying on an Immovable Foundation

The second lesson the phrase "for ever" teaches us is that amid all the upheavals and changes of life we and our praying are firmly grounded on an immovably stable foundation. The Lord Jesus teaches us that we call on our Father in heaven for the things we do because His "is the kingdom, and the power, and the glory, for ever." In other words, whatever else changes around us, we may be assured that our God is eternal and does not change.

God's Unchangeable Person

He declares, "I am the Lord, I change not; therefore ye sons of Jacob are not consumed" (Malachi 3:6). The creature is subject to change, but not the creator. He is always true to and consistent with Himself. Thus, Paul calls on us to remember that "the end" of the faith of the elders of the New Testament church is "Jesus Christ the same yesterday, and to day, and for ever" (Hebrews 13:7–8). The terminus of the faith of the saints of God—the place where it comes to rest—is the immutability of God's Son and our Saviour, Jesus Christ.

We are in a changing world, but we have an immovable stability that is rooted in the eternity and the immutability of our God. He is our rock, the strength of our life, and our sure foundation. Our stability rests on Him—not on our character, intellect, ability, success, or anything that we may perform, but on Him alone. It is what He is that guarantees our salvation and security now and for ever. We can be sure that we will never be consumed, because our God says, "I am the Lord, I change not."

God's Unchangeable Purpose

God's purpose toward us is an eternal purpose and will never change. We are "called according to his purpose" (Romans 8:28) and nothing can alter that purpose "for the gifts and calling of God are without repentance" (Romans 11: 29)—that is, God will never repent or change His mind about calling us and giving us His saving grace. No passage states this more clearly or beautifully than

Romans chapter eight: "We know that all things work together for good to them that love God, to them who are the called according to his purpose. For whom he did foreknow, he also did predestinate to be conformed to the image of his Son, that he might be the firstborn among many brethren. Moreover whom he did predestinate, them he also called: and whom he called, them he also justified: and whom he justified, them he also glorified" (verses 28–30). Here Paul enumerates the links in the unbreakable chain of sovereign grace. It is this chain of gracious acts that leads to the glorious climax of the chapter: "Who shall separate us from the love of Christ? shall tribulation, or distress, or persecution, or famine, or nakedness, or peril, or sword? As it is written, For thy sake we are killed all the day long; we are accounted as sheep for the slaughter. Nay, in all these things we are more than conquerors through him that loved us. For I am persuaded, that neither death, nor life, nor angels, nor principalities, nor powers, nor things present, nor things to come, nor height, nor depth, nor any other creature, shall be able to separate us from the love of God, which is in Christ Jesus our Lord" (Romans 8:35–39). What stability this truth brings to our hearts in the midst of the change and decay of earth!

God's Unchangeable Promise

God's covenant of grace is an everlasting covenant and will not change. He says, "My covenant will I not break, nor alter the thing that is gone out of my lips" (Psalm 89:34). He will not fail in fulfilling His promise; He cannot. When David says, "Thou hast magnified thy word above all thy name" (Psalm 138:2), he means that the Lord's faithfulness to His word is the divine attribute that is most discernible in His dealings with His people. Nothing in time can alter His covenant promise. Nothing in eternity can change it: "The grass withereth, the flower fadeth: but the word of our God shall stand for ever" (Isaiah 40:8).

God's unchangeable promise brings a wonderful sense of security to the heart of a believer. According to an old saying, "It is the blood of Christ that atones, but it is the word of God that assures." As believers in Christ, we know we are saved because we have God's unshakable promise that we are saved. He cannot lie or be unfaithful to His promise. John emphasizes the role of the word of God in assuring us both that we are saved and that we will be heard in prayer: "These things have I written unto you that believe on the name of the Son of God; that ye may know that ye have eternal life, and that ye may believe on the name of the Son of God" (here is the assurance of salvation); "And this is the confidence that we have in him, that, if we ask any thing according to his will, he heareth us: and if we know that he hear us, whatsoever we ask, we know that we have the petitions that we desired of him" (here is the assurance of answered prayer) (1 John 5:13–15).

God's Unchangeable Presence

The presence of God with His people cannot be altered for two obvious reasons. First, God's presence with us is supremely realized in the incarnation of His Son, and the incarnation is an irreversible act. Our Immanuel is "God with us," and only if He were to cease being Immanuel would God's presence with us fail. Second, God has given us His sworn word that He will never remove His presence from us: "He hath said, I will never leave thee, nor forsake thee" (Hebrews 13:5).

What stability these truths bring! Around us blow the winds of change. The world is reeling like a drunkard and finds no stable peace or assured certainty in its politics, religion, or business pursuits. But God's people have a sure foundation for the present and a secure hope for the future. David expressed his sense of stability on account of the Lord's immutability: "I will love thee, O Lord, my strength. The Lord is my rock, and my fortress, and my deliverer; my God, my strength, in whom I will trust; my buckler, and the horn of my salvation, and my high tower" (Psalm 18:1–2). Again he testified, "He only is my rock and my salvation; he is my defence; I shall not be greatly moved" (Psalm 62: 2). The English hymnwriter Augustus Toplady captured the believer's sense of stability and security in his immutable God in his hymn of testimony "A Debtor to Mercy Alone." Drawing his inspiration from Isaiah the prophet, he penned these striking lines:

> My name from the palms of His hands
> Eternity cannot erase;
> Impressed on His heart it remains
> In marks of indelible grace.
> And I to the end shall endure,
> As sure as the earnest is given;
> More happy but not more secure,
> When glorified with Him in heaven.

This is the stability that God's people enjoy and that sets their praying on the immovable foundation of the eternal immutability of their God.

"For Ever" Settles the Tendency and Outcome of History

The third lesson we learn from the phrase "for ever" is that the eternity and immutability of God settle the tendency and outcome of all history. The doxology of the Lord's Prayer establishes God's sovereignty; it exhibits His power; it expresses His glory: "Thine is the kingdom, and the power, and the glory for ever." This teaches us that God rules and will rule for ever, whether or not men like it. He is glorified whether men consent or not. "Surely the wrath of man shall praise thee; and the remainder of wrath shalt thou restrain" (Psalm 76:10).

Nothing that occurs in history can derail or defeat the plan and purpose of God. The counsels of eternity govern the circumstances of time. When evil men, both Jews and Gentiles, conspired to put Christ to death, they were indulging their own evil passions. They acted according to their nature and choice. Yet God had foreordained their action: "Of a truth against thy holy child Jesus, whom thou hast anointed, both Herod, and Pontius Pilate, with the Gentiles, and the people of Israel, were gathered together, for to do whatsoever thy hand and thy counsel determined before to be done" (Acts 4:27–28).

How God foreordains whatever comes to pass and settles the tendency and results of all the events of history is a mystery beyond human comprehension. It is enough for us to know that He does it. He will be eternally glorified by what occurs in time. His is the glory for ever. He will have the preeminence in both heaven and hell as the saved will manifest the glory of His justice satisfied by Christ's atonement, and the damned will manifest the glory of His justice untempered by Christ's merits. Those in heaven will sing eternally, willingly, and joyfully to the glory of God's everlasting grace, while those in hell will wail in the misery of their sin, suffering the punishment of His righteous wrath. "As I live, saith the Lord, every knee shall bow to me, and every tongue shall confess to God" (Romans 14:11). That is the point to which everyone and everything in history is moving, even those people and events that are intentionally anti-God and anti-Christ. History's ordained end is the eternal glory of God.

In the light of this truth, we can pray with complete confidence. We need not be overawed by the power or apparent success of those who rise up against God and His Son. Everything will proceed to its ordained climax of glorifying God eternally. Rather than worrying about the power of man's rebellion, we should pray in the assurance that we are on the winning side. Paul felt strengthened by this truth: "Now thanks be unto God, which always causeth us to triumph in Christ, and maketh manifest the savour of his knowledge by us in every place. For we are unto God a sweet savour of Christ, in them that are saved, and in them that perish: to the one we are the savour of death unto death; and to the other the savour of life unto life" (2 Corinthians 1:14–16).

We are in a similar position to the Israelites during the years before God's promise to Abraham was fulfilled. The Lord had assured Abraham that his children would become a great nation and inherit the land of Canaan, but that for four hundred years they would be held in bondage in Egypt. All that happened in the lands of Egypt and Canaan during those years moved inexorably toward the fulfillment of the promise to Abraham. Feeling the pain of their affliction in Egypt, the Israelites were unaware of this movement, but their ignorance did nothing to alter the reality of it. Despite appearances to the contrary, the Lord was weaving the events of history according to the pattern of His eternal purpose. Indeed, they were all essential steps in working out that purpose.

Our position is very like that of the Israelites. At times, God's promise to us seems far from fulfillment, and Satan would cause us to doubt and fear. But our God will just as surely appear for us as He did for Israel. Therefore we can pray with confidence. The tendency of all history is settled by the fact that it is in reality *His story,* which unfolds entirely according to the script He wrote.

"For Ever" Recalls God's Past Acts to Encourage Us

The fourth lesson that the phrase "for ever" teaches us is that the past work of our eternal and immutable God among His people encourages us that He will bless us in a similar way. He is the great *I Am*, the unchangeable God of the everlasting covenant. Throughout history He has done marvelous things for His people: "The Lord hath done great things for us; whereof we are glad" (Psalm 126:3). C. H. Spurgeon titled his sermon on Psalm 44:1 "The Story of God's Mighty Acts." The text reads, "We have heard with our ears, O God, our fathers have told us, what work thou didst in their days, in the times of old." The Lord has done great things for his people. He has not changed or lost His authority. He still accomplishes all He wills. In His sovereignty He is still able to bless and revive His people.

We should recall the Lord's past exploits for His people when we pray. The Bible commands us, "Seek the Lord, and his strength: seek his face evermore. Remember his marvellous works that he hath done; his wonders, and the judgments of his mouth" (Psalm 105:4–5). If we obey this instruction we will be encouraged to pray with fervency and faith. Isaiah provides us with a good example of using the history of God's acts as an incentive to prayer. He cried, "Awake, awake, put on strength, O arm of the Lord; awake, as in the ancient days, in the generations of old. Art thou not it that hath cut Rahab [Egypt], and wounded the dragon?" (Isaiah 51:9). On another occasion the prophet again looked back into history to contemplate God's mighty acts and soared to the heights of holy eloquence with one of the most passionate prayers for revival in Scripture: "Oh that thou wouldest rend the heavens, that thou wouldest come down, that the mountains might flow down at thy presence, as when the melting fire burneth, the fire causeth the waters to boil, to make thy name known to thine adversaries, that the nations may tremble at thy presence! When thou didst terrible things which we looked not for, thou camest down, the mountains flowed down at thy presence" (Isaiah 64:1–3).

These are appropriate prayers for today. They are inspired by a conviction of the eternal immutability of God. Why is there such weakness in prayer in the modern church? Is it mere coincidence that this weakness in prayer comes at a time when there is a general disinterest in what is called "theology proper," that is, the study of the person, nature, decrees, and acts of God? Is it mere coincidence that this weakness in prayer comes at a time when there is generally an abysmal ignorance of the biblical and post-biblical history of God's dealings with His church? If ever we are to pray with power and lead our children to do the same, we must learn well the lesson the phrase "for ever" teaches us about recalling the Lord's past acts. When we see what He did in the past, we will be stirred to ask Him to work with equal grace and power in our day.

One of the great historical narratives of the book of Psalms is found in Psalm 78. It clearly establishes the truth that it is by constantly recalling the Lord's past actions that we not only stir our own souls to pray but instruct our children so that they too may trust Him: "I will open my mouth in a parable: I will utter dark sayings of old: which we have heard and known, and our fathers have told us. We will not hide them from their children, shewing to the generation to come the praises of the Lord, and his strength, and his wonderful works that he hath done. For he established a testimony in Jacob, and appointed a law in Israel, which he commanded our fathers, that they should make them known to their children: that the generation to come might know them, even the children which should be born; who should arise and declare them to their children: that they might set their hope in God, and not forget the works of God, but keep his commandments" (Psalm 78:2–7).

One of the most pressing concerns of Christian parents today is insuring that their children embrace Christ and fully follow Him. Psalm 78 supplies a vital lesson in attaining this goal. Parents, especially fathers, should take the time to engage their children's interest in the word of God, particularly the story of His mighty acts—including the story of Christ's life, death, and resurrection, the mightiest of all God's acts. This is how our children will come to know Him and set their hope and trust in Him.

Gimmicks will never succeed in stirring God's people to effective prayer or encourage them to become faithful prayer warriors. Books that reduce Christian devotion to a mechanical series of how-to instructions will never fill the believer's heart with the joy of faith and assurance in prayer. These blessings come from immersing our souls in the revelation of the Lord's glorious person and works. The importance of saturating our souls with the knowledge of what God did in the past for His people cannot be overstated. It is essential to our happiness in the present and our hope for the future.

"For Ever" Teaches Us that Heavenly Worship Will Soon Replace Earthly Prayer and Praise

The final lesson the phrase "for ever" teaches us is that our earthly prayer and praise will soon give place to the everlasting worship of heaven. "Thine is the kingdom, and the power, and the glory, for ever." The Lord will be praised for ever. In various places the psalmist says he will praise the Lord for ever (for example, Psalm 30:12). This is a statement of his intention, but it is more. It is a prophecy. We are going to praise God for ever. We praise Him now, but how imperfectly! Soon we will start praising Him perfectly and will continue for all eternity: "This God is our God for ever and ever: he will be our guide even unto [or, over] death" (Psalm 48:14). Paul assures us that he is "confident of this very thing, that he which hath begun a good work in you will perform it until the day of Jesus Christ" (Philippians 1:6). Part of the good work that He has begun is to create in us a worshipping heart despite our sins. He will not fail to bring this work to perfection and to make us sinless worshippers in heaven.

The words *for ever* in the Lord's Prayer emphasize our assurance of heaven. They point us to the truth that the Lord gave through Malachi: "They that feared the Lord spake often one to another: and the Lord hearkened, and heard it, and a book of remembrance was written before him for them that feared the Lord, and that thought upon his name. And they shall be mine, saith the Lord of hosts, in that day when I make up my jewels" (Malachi 3:16–17).

This assurance concerning our eternal destiny brings rock-like stability to our lives in the midst of an unstable world. All around us nations, economies, businesses, churches, belief-systems, and individual lives are disintegrating. We are moving inevitably toward the day of which Hebrews 12:26–27 speaks: "He [God] hath promised, saying, Yet once more I shake not the earth only, but also heaven. And this word, Yet once more, signifieth the removing of those things that are shaken, as of things that are made, that those things which cannot be shaken may remain." There are things that cannot be shaken, such as the security Christ bought for His people with His own blood. His salvation is for ever and He will assuredly bring all in whom He has begun His good work to the perfect joy of eternal glory.

Our God is eternal and immutable. It is our privilege to glorify Him now and for ever. If, as Thomas Manton says (*Works,* 1.243), "Glory is excellence discovered with praise," then prayer and praise are heaven begun. Heaven will be the full enjoyment of the blessings of communion with God that we have only feebly experienced or barely comprehended in the place of prayer. This place of prayer, then, is a foretaste of heaven. In it we catch a glimpse of God's power and glory. David yearned "to see thy power and thy glory, so as I have seen thee in the sanctuary" (Psalm 63:2). What a profound prayer! In effect it says, "Let me experience God in life's desert places as I have seen Him by faith in the secret place. As I travel through this vale of tears, I look forward to seeing Thee, O Lord, in all Thy perfection. I have caught a glimpse of Thee in the sanctuary but I long for the day when feeble faith in the sanctuary will give place to the beatific vision, the full view of Thy glory."

God help us to be people of prayer, to enter the prayer closet expecting a foretaste of heaven, and then to look forward to heaven as the fulfillment of everything that we have glimpsed by faith in the sanctuary.

Faith's Final, Fervent Word in Prayer

"Amen."   *Matthew 6:13*

T he "Amen" at the end of the Lord's Prayer is not merely a convenient way of bringing it to a close. It is an important summation—indeed, the consummation—of the entire worship and waiting upon God that the Lord Jesus Christ has been teaching us throughout this prayer. *Amen* belongs to an illustrious family of Hebrew words. Its root verb, *aman,* means "to support, to bring up, or to nourish." Other forms of the word mean "to be firm, true, faithful, established, or sure." Nouns deriving from the root verb mean "truth, faithfulness, steadiness, stability," or even, in a few places, "covenant."

This range of meaning makes this group of words particularly useful for describing our covenant God. Moses wrote, "Know therefore that the Lord thy God, he is God, the faithful God" (Deuteronomy 7:9). Isaiah calls Him "the God of truth," literally, "the Amen God" (Isaiah 65:16). Thus when God's people say, "Amen," in His presence they are expressing assent to and acceptance of His truth. It is a word of faith, one that states the assurance of trust in God and His word. But it is more, it is a prayer that expresses a fervent desire for God to do all He has said: "The prophet Jeremiah said, Amen: the Lord do so: the Lord perform thy words which thou hast prophesied" (Jeremiah 28:6). This text is an inspired commentary on the meaning of *Amen.* It is a response to the promise of God and it says, "Let it be," or as Jeremiah put it, "The Lord do so."

Putting together the information we gather from the Old Testament we can appreciate that the ideas of truth and faithfulness, together with the note of yearning introduced by Jeremiah, make *Amen* an apt word to use at the end of a prayer. The New Testament gives an additional—and if anything, a better—reason to use it, for it reveals that *Amen* is a descriptive name of the Lord Jesus Christ. "Unto the angel of the church of the Laodiceans write; these things saith the Amen, the faithful and true witness" (Revelation 3:14). Thus the "Amen" at the end of the Lord's Prayer actually invokes the name of Christ. We have noted how Isaiah called God "the Amen God." We may justly speak of the Lord Jesus Christ as "the Amen God" incarnate. That is why He so often prefaced some of His most solemn utterances with "Verily, Verily, I say unto you"—literally, "Amen, Amen, I say unto you." It is true of God and none else that "because he could swear by no greater, he sware by himself" (Hebrew 6:13), which is precisely what Christ does in using the "Amen, Amen" formula to emphasize the solemn truth of what He says.

The Lord Jesus is "the Amen God" incarnate, and when we say, "Amen," it is His name that we invoke. In doing so we employ the very best reason for making the final plea to the Father, "May the Lord do so." To our expressed desire we add the name of His Son. We thus end our prayer on the high note of sincere desire, fervent faith, hearty dependence, and well-grounded assurance, all based on God's incarnate Son, our Saviour Jesus Christ.

By appending "Amen" to the Lord's Prayer, the Lord Jesus surely shows us that our prayers are not to meander meaninglessly or to peter out; rather they must arrive at the final "Amen" with sincere desire and quickened faith. It is as if the words that we have been praying have stirred our hearts and quickened our desire, so that now we reach the pinnacle of trust and assurance. With the "Amen" we rise from our knees confident that we have met with God and that He has heard our cry.

Having taken time to summarize the pedigree and underlying meaning of *Amen,* we must now see what this information means for our praying. We will see that far from being merely a convenient way of bringing a prayer to a close, *Amen* is faith's final, fervent word in prayer. By using it we do four things.

We Assert Our Sincerity

Amen is a word of truth. It is closely related to the Hebrew words for truth and faithfulness. Thus the use of *Amen* is a way of solemnly asserting the truth of what we say. When Jesus said, "Verily I say unto you," He meant, "I solemnly assure you" or "I tell you in all truth." So when we pray, the word *Amen* stresses the solemn truth of what we say to God. It says, "I pray this in all truth and sincerity." Prayer is not just a matter of well chosen words; it must be the honest expression of the heart. *Amen* is therefore a word of wholeheartedness. It is a denial of coldness and formality.

By using it we call God to witness that our praying is not an empty, thoughtless ritual, but something that flows from the depths of our hearts. We mean what we say in prayer and therefore cry, "Amen," as do the living creatures around God's throne: "Every creature which is in heaven, and on the earth, and under the earth, and such as are in the sea, and all that are in them, heard I saying, Blessing, and honour, and glory, and power, be unto him that sitteth upon the throne, and unto the Lamb for ever and ever. And the four beasts said, Amen. And the four and twenty elders fell down and worshipped him that liveth for ever and ever" (Revelation 5:13–14). The intensity and wholehearted love and sincerity of the heavenly worshipers are eloquently expressed by that fervent "Amen."

"Amen" also expresses assent and agreement in prayer. It states our entire commitment to what is said. This is particularly applicable to public prayer, as Paul shows in 1 Corinthians 14:16. He commanded the Corinthians to pray in an understandable language, "else when thou shalt bless with the spirit, how shall he that occupieth the room of the unlearned say Amen at thy giving of thanks, seeing he understandeth not what thou sayest?" Here the "Amen" denotes our agreement with another's words in prayer so as to make them the expression of our own heart to the Lord. It is interesting that Paul used the definite article, "*the* Amen," showing that "Amen" is the well-known, expected response of Christians to the words of their brethren who lead the congregation in public prayer. This is how we are expected to pray. When we lead others in prayer, we must pray intelligibly so as to encourage their participation and fellowship with us in our worship. When others are leading us in prayer we should be actively involved with them in approaching the throne of God and should sincerely add our "Amen" to their words. The place of public prayer is the last place we should play with words or seek to impress men. And as others cry out to God, we must not sit idly in detachment or disinterest and then mumble an unmeant "Amen."

Noting that the "Amen" supports the entire Lord's Prayer, C. H. Waller says that by using it we bind ourselves to live as we pray. That is, the "Amen" is our pledge to the Lord that we will seek to support our prayers by our works. Praying is not an alternative to working; it is a commitment to work. Christians often piously pray, "God bless your work," but do little or nothing to further that work. Such praying is at best ineffectual, and it is probably hypocritical. It puts prayer in the place of personal endeavor instead of making it the basis for it. Dr. Ian Paisley has a vivid way of pressing home the connection between sincere prayer and zealous service. He often exhorts believers to "put legs to their prayers." The ultimate proof of the sincerity that we profess in prayer is our willingness to be the Lord's instruments in answering our petitions.

We Declare Our Faith in Our Faithful God

We have seen that the root meaning of the verb from which *Amen* comes is "to support or nourish." Waller paints a lovely picture of a man who places his arms under a child to bear its weight, support it, and nourish it. That is what the Lord does with His children. Using a different figure of speech, Isaiah makes the same point: "He shall feed his flock like a shepherd: he shall gather the lambs with his arm, and carry them in his bosom, and shall gently lead those that are with young" (Isaiah 40:11). The "Amen" reminds us of the Lord's support of His people.

It also says, "We believe and rely on Him." We place "Amen" at the end of our prayer because we believe in the God whom we address in the beginning of the Lord's Prayer, our Father in heaven who places His arms under us. It states our personal assurance of the truth that Moses taught the people of Israel, "The eternal God is thy refuge, and underneath are the everlasting arms" (Deuteronomy 33:27). "Amen" at the end of our prayer says we believe that our God is faithful. He is the "Amen God," as Isaiah tells us, and His promise is the *Amen promise,* as Paul tells us: "For all the promises of God in him [Christ] are yea, and in him Amen, unto the glory of God by us" (2 Corinthians 1:20). As Paul also says, "Faithful is he that calleth you, who also will do it" (1 Thessalonians 5:24). It is probable that if this were written in Hebrew instead of Greek, it would read, "Amen is he." This is the confidence we express when we say, "Amen," the confidence that Solomon felt when he rejoiced, "Blessed be the Lord God of Israel, who hath with his hands fulfilled that which he spake with his mouth" (2 Chronicles 6:4). Our "Amen" declares our faith in our faithful God.

We Express Our Trust in Christ's Mediation and Merits

As we have seen, the final word of the Lord's Prayer is actually a title of the Lord Jesus Christ. He calls Himself, "The Amen, the faithful and true witness" (Revelation 3:14). Thus when we support our prayer with "Amen" we invoke the name of the Lord Jesus. This is sufficient answer to those who reject the Lord's Prayer as being unfit for the church age, in part because, as they allege, it is not offered in Jesus' name. It is true that prayer may reach the Father only in Jesus' name. However, Amen is His name—and that is what supports the entire Lord's Prayer. It confesses that He is the sole mediator between God and men (1 Timothy 2:5) and declares our complete trust in His mediation.

It is interesting that the Greek *martus,* "witness," is the word that gives us the word *martyr* and is so translated three times in the New Testament. A martyr is a witness who seals his testimony by dying for it: "Antipas was my faithful martyr, who was slain among you" (Revelation 2:13). In calling Himself the "true and faithful *martus,*" does the Lord Jesus make reference to His sealing of His witness with His blood? It is a fascinating possibility that in the very text in which He calls Himself the Amen, the Lord Jesus may at once direct our thoughts to

His sacrificial death. We confess Him as the only mediator and His shed blood as our only merit before God. Thus when we place "Amen" under our prayer, we draw the attention of heaven to the fact that we come to God not in our own name but in the name of Jesus Christ our Lord. We pray not in our own merit but in the merit of the shed blood of our Lord Jesus Christ who lived and died to provide us with saving merit before God. "Amen" recognizes this truth and gladly repudiates every other approach to God as an insult to Him.

Far from being a trite word of convenience with which to bring our praying to a stop, "Amen" is the concentration of all our thinking upon this glorious truth. It is our way of stating our conviction that we have "boldness to enter into the holiest by the blood of Jesus, by a new and living way, which he hath consecrated for us, through the veil, that is to say, his flesh" (Hebrews 10:19–20). We have no mediator but Jesus Christ. We plead no authority but that of His name. We bring before God no merit but that of His blood. This is what "Amen" is meant to express—our trust in the mediation and merits of our Saviour.

We Proclaim Our Expectation of God's Answer to Our Prayer

"Amen" is both a plea and a statement of confidence. It means "May it be" or "Let it be." Usually we explain it as "So be it." We have seen the inspired explanation of the word in Jeremiah 28:6. Jeremiah, a man who lived in close communion with the Lord, gives us a further insight into the significance of "Amen": God said, "I will be your God: that I may perform the oath which I have sworn unto your fathers, to give them a land flowing with milk and honey, as it is this day. Then answered I, and said, So be it, O Lord"—or, "Amen, Lord" (Jeremiah 11:4–5). "Amen" is the opposite of the phrase translated in the Authorized Version, "God forbid," which simply means, "May it not be." "Amen" says, "May it be! Do it, Lord!" It is the strongest affirmation of the fact that we expect God to answer us. It is not simply a statement of desire or hope. It is both, but it is much more. "Amen" expresses our expectation—based upon our "Amen God" and His "Amen promise," which we claim on the merits of our Lord Jesus Christ, who says, "I am the Amen"—that our Father will hear us.

We may consider this assurance from another angle. *Amen* is a word of submission to God's will. "So be it" places everything we desire in God's hands and leaves all to His wise and gracious disposal. Since it is a word of submission to God's will, *Amen* is also a word of assurance of God's answer. John makes this clear: "This is the confidence that we have in him, that, if we ask any thing according to his will, he heareth us: and if we know that he hear us, whatsoever we ask, we know that we have the petitions that we desired of him" (1 John 5:14–15). To put it another way, God cannot ignore our "Amen." It is a statement of the ground of our assurance.

Our expectation will not be disappointed. John writes, "The four and twenty elders and the four beasts fell down and worshipped God that sat on the throne, saying, Amen; Alleluia" (Revelation 19:4). In heaven the "Amen" of asking gives place to the "Amen" of acknowledgment and it leads to the "Alleluia," "Praise ye the Lord." He who can honestly place "Amen" to his prayer will undoubtedly place "Alleluia" to his praise, and that for all eternity.

That is faith's final, fervent word in prayer.